THE KOVELS'
ILLUSTRATED PRICE GUIDE
TO
❧ROYAL❧
DOULTON

BOOKS BY RALPH AND TERRY KOVEL

Dictionary of Marks—Pottery and Porcelain
A Directory of American Silver, Pewter and Silver Plate
American Country Furniture, 1780–1875
Know Your Antiques,® Revised
The Kovels' Antiques Price List
The Kovels' Complete Bottle Price List
The Kovels' Collector's Guide to American Art Pottery
Kovels' Organizer for Collectors
The Kovels' Price Guide for Collector Plates, Figurines, Paperweights, and
    Other Limited Editions
The Kovels' Illustrated Price Guide to Depression Glass

THE KOVELS'
ILLUSTRATED PRICE GUIDE
TO
ROYAL
DOULTON

Ralph and Terry Kovel

CROWN PUBLISHERS, INC. NEW YORK

Library of Congress Catalog Card Number: 80-66666

ISBN: 0-517-540223

10 9 8 7 6 5 4 3

Contents

Authors' Note to Readers

Writing a book on a new subject can be full of hazards, mysteries, and discoveries. It can also be full of information that is not easily found. This is a report of the Royal Doulton market in the United States from September 1979 to February 1980. All prices that are included are for pieces that have actually been offered for sale during that period. The Royal Doulton Company was helpful in offering information and pictures, but no information was given on prices. During the time the prices were reported the Canadian dollar was worth about $.87 in U.S. currency and the English pound was worth from $2.24 to $2.28 in U.S. currency. Prices from these countries are not included, but they should be comparable.

We are researchers and collectors and we have tried to read every book and article available about the Royal Doulton wares (see bibliography for complete list of books). There are several important books with much information, and these books have been credited in their proper chapter. Other books were also helpful and we would be remiss not to thank and credit the authors of all of them.

There are many things still unsolved. The series ware rouge flambé and miscellaneous pieces are included in spite of the obvious omissions. We thought it better to "light one little candle" and show a bit of the path to many collectors. Dealers and collectors from all over the world have helped us to compile the many lists and histories. If you have any information that can be added, please write to us in care of Crown Publishers, Inc., One Park Avenue, New York, New York 10016.

Ralph M. Kovel—American Society of Appraisers, Senior Member

Terry H. Kovel—American Society of Appraisers, Senior Member

Acknowledgments

Many, many people helped us with this book. Thank you to all those listed here. Each bit of information, large or small, added to the jigsaw puzzle that became this book. Thank you also to the authors of the other books on this subject. It is only proper to include both the authors and the titles, with complete information about finding the books. Please see the bibliography for this list.

Doulton and Company, Inc.

David Allen
Paul Atterbury
Karen Casoni
Michael Doulton

Stephanie Hart
Arthur Mills
Elizabeth Rice
David Showalter

Dealers

Mrs. Vance Bartlett
Reynoldsburg, Ohio

Betty and Penny Crandall
Crandall's Antiques
Rocky River, Ohio

Robert M. Fortune
Astabula Antique Import Co., Inc.
Astabula, Ohio

Gossland Collectibles
Muswell Hill, London, England

Gourmet Plates and Antiques
Mansfield, Ohio

Barbara Hoyt
Alen Cove, N.Y.

Jamens Collectibles
Merrick, N.Y.

Pat H. Johnston
Pottery Collectors Newsletter
Asheville, N.C.

V. Jones
University Heights, Ohio

Judy's House of Hope
Atlanta, Ga.

Jeffrey Kahn
Beachwood, Ohio

Joanne M. Kochn
Temples Antiques
Minneapolis, Minn.

Laughing Dog Antiques
Ellicott City, Md.

Pat and Joe Mancuso
Antiqua 4
La Mesa, Calif.

Ed Pascoe
Pascoe and Soloman Antiques
New York, N.Y.

Ed Pry
The Post House
Crestline, Ohio

John Re
Pittsburgh, Penn.

Wilma Saxton
Wilma Saxton, Inc.
Audubon, N.J.

Roger and Ellen Slugg
Windsor Antiques
Mansfield, Ohio

Marie Spagnola
Bedford, Ohio

Trademarks by Olga
Marysville, Ohio

VIP Antiques
Atlanta, Ga.

Princess and Berry Weiss
Yesterdays
New City, N.Y.

Wanda Bowman Wempe
The Trinket Box
Champlin, Minn.

Paul Williams Upholstery
Columbus, Ohio

Ye Olde Shoppe
St. Louis, Mo.

Constance L. Alex
Mrs. C. E. Ambrose
Mary Anderson
Miss R. Arnold

Nancy Barber
Bertha Barker
John J. Barthelme
Ann Quinn Bartley
Daniel Bausch
Dave Bausch
Mrs. Robert M. Baxter
Mrs. David Bell
Mrs. C. A. Brewer
Janet Brewer
Mrs. W. L. Brinegar
Mrs. Homer Brookside
Mrs. R. C. Brown
James Byrd
Mrs. A. A. Carlson
Mrs. J. D. Chaffin
Ashton Chapman
Mrs. T. H. Claussen
Mary N. Coffman
Ella May Collier
Mary Colville
Mary Cooper
Elizabeth A. Coppin
Carol Miller Cosenza
Mrs. James Coy
Jacqueline Cray
Frank Daniel
Ruth E. Davis
Viola Dixon
Eileen Doremus
Mr. and Mrs. Edwin J. Douglas
Helen L. Dudak
Radonna Edmison
Mrs. R. A. Ellis
Mrs. Phyllis Eustace
Mrs. Marie Fairlee
Katherine Fishback
Mrs. Donald O. Flahart
Ray Fredman
Joe B. Frey

Cletus Caroland Gems
George Gerow
LaRue and Floyd Gilbert
Beverly Gordon
Carolyn J. Graham
Mrs. Hester M. Graham
F. P. Greene
L. E. and Gwen Grove
June M. Gwin
Mrs. William A. Hall
Allie Handley
Deborah Harpula
Patricia Hayes
Jean Henderson
Mrs. George Hone
Nancy P. Huntley
Mrs. George Hussey
Mary L. Iugraw
Bernard Jacobson
Lorraine K. Jaworski
Anne Ewell Jay
Mrs. Douglas M. Jeannero
Rita Jewell
Mrs. Gerry Johnson
Mrs. Jerry Johnson
Leo Jokel
Esther Jones
Anne and Carl Justis
Mrs. W. Karlyn
Rosemary Kemp
Mrs. R. Kimmins
Mrs. Wayne King
Florence T. Krauss
C. K. Langfitt
Madeline M. Larsen
Avis Leamon
Mary L. Lee
Mrs. Paul Leidy
Grayce Lupton
Mrs. Harry Luton

Jessica S. McDonongh
Mrs. R. B. McFarland
Mr. and Mrs. Frank McGrothers
Lorie McIntosh
Helen MacIntyre
Mrs. William W. McKenna
Mrs. Angus McLeod
Mrs. Thomas McMillan
Sam D. Mansfield
Mrs. Frank P. Marsico
Mason Color and Chemical Works, Inc.
Virginia Miller
Mrs. F. Mitchell
Mrs. Paul H. Monroe
Virginia H. Morin
Mrs. C. Mosher
Mrs. Mary Nangle
Mrs. Erving Nelson
Ken Neubeiser
Illeen Nommay
Mrs. G. O'Brien
Dr. and Mrs. George M. O'Brien
Mrs. L. M. O'Brien
Ms. Anne O'Grady
Lena M. O'Neill
Mrs. Leon D. Ostrander
Vera Outtrim
Mrs. Stewart Payne
Una Phillips
Mary Pickarts
Mary Frances Pirkey
Elizabeth M. Powell
Hazel Proctor
Mrs. William Reece
Joan Rice
Betty Riley
Ines Rosser
Mrs. Arthur Russell
Alise Scott
Theodore Searl

Betty Shough
Ethel Snyder
Lorna L. Snyder
Mrs. Charles Spangler
Rosannah Steinhoff
Mrs. Gwen Starr
C. Strayton
Mrs. Norma Swanson
Marvin J. Thomas
Mrs. C. Tiedemann
Dottie Trier
Robert Tuttle
Mrs. Forest Van Vleck
Rita Voss

Mrs. Ralph E. Wadleigh
David Westcott
Mrs. Jean W. Willes
Mrs. Fred L. Williams, Jr.
Mrs. F. M. Williams
Mildred Winner
Mrs. Warren Wistendahl
Mrs. J. E. Worthing
Ethel M. Wright
Marion Young
W. H. Young
Mrs. Fern Zancanaro
Elizabeth Zimmerman
Mrs. Louise Zivirello

Introduction

The Royal Doulton porcelains that are so popular with today's collectors are made by a company with a long history of ceramic production.

John Doulton was born at Fulham, England, on November 17, 1793. He apprenticed at the Fulham Pottery of London, England, from 1805 to 1812. He was a "thrower" who threw the lump of clay on the wheel and manipulated it until a vessel was shaped. He left in 1815 to become a partner of John Watts and Mrs. John Jones (widow of a potter who owned the house) in a pothouse in Vauxhall Walk, Lambeth, England.

Jones, Watts, and Doulton made stoneware bottles, jugs, figural flasks, whistles, rushlight holders, inkstands, pitchers, candlesticks, money boxes, and other domestic pottery. They also made Toby jugs.

Mrs. Jones left the partnership in 1820 and Doulton and Watts continued the business. The pothouse prospered and by 1826 it moved to High Street, Lambeth, where their location gave room for further expansion. A new kiln was built and over a two-year period the firm gradually moved from the old Vauxhall Walk buildings. By 1827 the company began making stoneware water pipes water filters and continued making domestic wares and tiles. They also began experimenting with special containers for use in the chemical industry. By the 1830s they were making blacking bottles, jam jars, and ink bottles.

Henry Doulton, John's second son, was born in 1820. He was only fifteen when he chose to become a potter. The factory continued expanding and made a variety of chemical and domestic wares. Henry Doulton, who was trained as a potter, took some chemistry courses, worked with engineers, and learned basics needed to develop new products. He experimented to produce a cream-colored opaque-glazed ware. He also developed an airtight covered jar for food storage and a screw-stoppered bottle, and he received many patents for improvements to kilns, jars, vases, and tanks. The company developed improvements in sewer pipes, including an important special self-adjusting joint that was popular with the industry.

In 1846 Henry Doulton founded a sewer pipeworks, called "Henry Doulton and Company," with his father John Doulton and his younger brother Frederick Doulton. John Doulton, Jr., started his own factory in 1847 and continued with his business until 1853. John Watts decided to retire in 1853, and the three companies, Doulton and Watts, Henry Doulton and Company, and John Doulton, Junior, all dissolved and the new firm of Doulton and Company was formed. Henry Doulton's pipe business had been the most valuable, so when the new company was formed he became the largest shareholder. A series of Doulton brothers and sons entered and left the company, shares changed hands, and the firm grew and prospered. John Doulton, Sr., died in 1873.

Doulton and Company continued the family tradition of innovation, research, and successful management. The last half of the 1800s produced many new types of pottery and porcelain with varied glazes and designs. The company worked with John Sparkes and the Lambeth School of Art after 1863. This association led to the hiring of several artists, including George Tinsworth and Hannah Barlow, and to the eventual development of salt-glazed stonewares. The company developed many other new ceramic bodies and glazes, including Lambeth faïence, Crown Lambeth, impasto ware, silicon ware, carrara ware, marqueterie ware, ciné ware, natural foliage ware, cipper ware, majolica, Persian ware, velluma ware, and others. The factory also made many commemorative pieces, jugs, and Toby jugs.

In 1877 the firm bought an interest in a Burslem pottery factory that was called Pinder, Bourne and Company. The entire company became part of Doulton and Company in 1882. They only made earthenwares at first but chinaware was soon made. They made earthenware and porcelain tablewares, art wares, and lamps, as well as sanitary wares. Henry Doulton died in 1897. His son Lewis became head of the company. It became Doulton and Company, Limited, in 1899. The words "Royal Doulton" were used after 1902.

Charles John Noke joined Doulton in 1889. He modeled vases and by 1893 was making Parian figures up to 20 inches in height. He developed Lactolian ware, Holbein ware, Rembrandt ware, and Titanian ware. In 1914 he became the art director, and he was succeeded by his son Cecil J. Noke in 1936. With the help of other artists and chemists, the factory continued producing new products and glazes, including Sung, chang, sang de boeuf, and rouge flambé.

The factory continued making sanitary wares, pipes, and other money-making but unglamorous products; however, the part of the history of the Doulton Company that is important to this book is the development of the art wares and tablewares made after 1900. The figurines, Toby jugs, character jugs, animals, limited editions, commemorative wares, and series wares produced during this time are all part of that story.

Users of this book should note that a single asterisk (*) following a descriptive entry indicates that the piece is illustrated in black and white, and that double asterisks (**) indicate that the piece is illustrated in the color insert found after page 128.

Marks

The Doulton factory used a series of backstamps, which included a lion, crown, the words "Doulton" or "Royal Doulton," and other symbols (see chart below).

The company was first called Doulton and Company, and in 1899 it became Doulton and Company, Limited. The Royal Warrant of Appointment was given to the factory in 1901. They were permitted to add the word "Royal" to their products. The mark with the words "Royal Doulton" was first used in 1902. Another company name that has been used since 1972 is Royal Doulton Tableware Limited.

Many pieces include a copyright date, written "Copr.," and the numeral representing the year. These dates represent the year the design was listed, but the piece was usually not offered for sale until at least one year later. A copyright date of 1957 on a piece in current production merely means that the first time that particular piece was made was in 1957. It may have been made anytime from 1957 to the present time.

The HN mark was first used in 1913. The initials HN were for Harry Nixon, the artist in charge of painting the figures. The numbers were more or less in chronological order until about 1940. After that time, groups of numbers have been held to be used by a single modeler over a period of time. Some numbers have never been used for production figures. Some numbers were given to a figurine that was not produced for several years after being numbered.

The style of type used as part of the backstamp on Royal Doulton figurines, character jugs, and other pieces changed slightly through the years. The name of the figurine, such as "Boy with Turban," was handwritten from 1902 to 1932. The name of the figurine was handwritten on M figures from 1932 to 1949. These names were enclosed in quotation marks. The marks from the 1960s used a type style that resembled ⌐Darling.⌐ The marks from the 1970s were modernized to a type style that resembled ⌐DARLING.⌐

The M numbers were given to miniature figures starting in 1932. The M numbers were stopped in 1949, although some of the miniature Dickens figures are still being made without the number. More recent figurines of this group were made with slight color changes. Early figures were marked "Doulton" or "Doulton England," and they usually had an impressed number. Later ones had the full Royal Doulton mark.

The words "Potted by Doulton and Co." or "Potted by Royal Doulton" were sometimes handwritten on figurines before 1939. Impressed dates are sometimes found on figures, but these are often the date that the mold was made and not the date of production of the figure. These dates were not used after the 1930s. Occasionally, after 1927, a printed number can be found to the right of the crown on the base of a figurine. Add 1927 to the number and that will give the year of manufacture. Thus, if you see "12" on a figurine, add 1927 and find that it was made in the year 1939. The words "Bone China" were added to some marks about 1932. Registration dates appear about 1945.

Doulton and Company, Limited
Burslem, England, 1882–

Impressed or printed mark on decorated stoneware, 1879–1902; china after 1884.
The word "England" was added after 1891.

Impressed or printed mark, 1885–1902.
The word "England" was added after 1891.

Royal Doulton Marks
Burslem, England, 1902–
Lambeth, England, 1902–1956

First "Royal" Doulton mark. Printed or impressed mark, 1902–1922, 1927–1932.
The words "Made in England" added after 1930.

Printed or impressed on Lambeth pieces, 1922–1956.

Printed on Burslem pieces,
1922–1927.

Printed on Burslem earthenware pieces, 1932–present.
The words "Bone China" are
added underneath, 1932–
1959.
The words "English Fine Bone
China" are added underneath,
1959–present.
The words "English Translucent China" are added underneath, 1960–present.

"Potted" mark, before 1939.

Michael Doulton signature,
1978–.

Registered mark; "Registered
in Australia" mark.

Rd Nº 821285.
REGᵈ IN AUSTRALIA

"A" mark
(full explanation in Character
Jug chapter), internal factory
mark in 1950

Current mark
(notice shortened lines between the words "Royal Doulton" and "England"), since
1960s.

The number 14 indicates the
year. Add 1927 to determine
actual year of dating. This jug
was made in 1941.

D mark

Rd. Registered mark in type
style used before 1970s.

FIGURINES

FIGURINES

Charles John Noke joined the Doulton Company in 1889 as the chief modeler for the firm. It was customary for companies that exhibited at the large national and international exhibitions to make exceptional, often unique, large works as special display pieces. Noke made several pieces for the Chicago Exhibition in 1893. Several large vases, one of which was almost 6 feet high, were shown. A few figures were also made, but there was apparently no mention of them in the newspaper accounts of the time. He made "Jack Point," "Moorish Minstrel," "Lady Jester," "A Jester" (seated), "Mirth and Melancholy," and an unnamed figure of a double-sided jester. From 1893 to 1897 he made a few figures, including "A Jester" (standing), "Pierrot," "Shylock," "A Geisha," "Ellen Terry as Queen Catherine," "Henry Irving as Cardinal Wolsey," the double figure "Mephistopeheles and Marguerite," and the double figure "Oh Law!" These figures, ranging from 8 to 20 inches high, were larger than the later ones made with the HN markings. They were made of a Parian porcelain, tinted ivory and mainly decorated in pink and green. Very few of these pastel figures appear to have been sold.

It was not until 1909 that Charles Noke decided to try again to make a commercial line of figurines. He invited several sculptors to design small figures. In 1913, twenty models were introduced and modeled by Charles Noke, George Lambert, Phoebe Stabler, F. C. Stone, Charles Vyse, or William White. The figurines were eventually given HN numbers, but the first group had not been numbered when Queen Mary visited the factory in 1913. She commented on a figure that was called "Bedtime." She called it "a darling." The name was changed and "Darling" became HN 1. Several figures modeled in earlier years by Noke were included in the series of figurines after 1913 and given numbers that might suggest a later date. Some figurines were slightly modified or changed in color or decoration and given new HN numbers. The figurines did not seem to sell well, and the records show that only 680 were made from 1913 to September of 1917.

Many other artists and decorators worked on the figurines. The production appeared to be small into the 1920s. Many of the earlier figures were discontinued from 1941 to 1949. Desmond Eyles, in his book *Royal Doulton Figures Produced at Burslem,* says that "of those figures which had been withdrawn by 1949, it is unlikely that as many as 2,000 of any one had been made—probably far fewer of many of them." After the war the figurine line was expanded and the numbers grew. Over 2,000 models have been made and less than 200 are in current production.

It was in the early 1970s that the collectors began to seriously research for the out-of-production and rarer figurines. Many people had purchased a few figurines for home display and enjoyment, but the thought of a Royal Doulton figurine collection was new.

Some problems remain in the discussion of figurines. We have seen a figurine that appeared to have the HN number 1 although it was a figurine that should have been marked 1354. The Doulton factory has assured us that there might have been an error of some sort at the factory and the number decal was probably torn or damaged before the firing.

A series of black-and-white figurines may cause a problem. Four black and four white figures were made and called "Tranquility," "Peace," "Family," and "Lovers." They were first made in 1978. They will be available for sale in 1980 in either black or white. Three other similar figures are also to be offered in 1980: "Mother and Daughter," "Awakening," and "Sympathy."

"Princess Badoura" is listed but no price has been published. The company has said that if you order the figure today it will be delivered in a year or two at a price established on the day of order.

A "prototype" figure occasionally appears on the market. These were usually made for consumer-testing panels and were never put into general production. We have seen some of these prototypes offered for sale, so we have included their prices and titles. We understand that they were not commercially produced figurines and were probably removed from exhibitions and still might legally be property of the Doulton factory; consequently they should never be offered for sale.

A few Royal Doulton figurines have been made as limited editions. These are included in this list.

LIMITED EDITION FIGURINES

Figurine	HN number	Date	Edition Limit
Indian Brave	2376	1967	500
The Palio	2428	1971	500
Dancers of the World (still available)			
Flamenco Dancer	2831	1977	750
Indian Temple Dancer	2830	1977	750
Philippine Dancer	2439	1978	750
Scottish Dancer	2436	1978	750
Lady Musicians (sold out by 1979)			
Cello	2331	1971	750
Chitarrone	2700	1974	750
Cymbals	2699	1974	750
Dulcimer	2798	1975	750
Flute	2483	1973	750
French Horn	2795	1976	750
Harp	2482	1973	750
Hurdy Gurdy	2796	1975	750
Lute	2431	1972	750
Viola D'Amore	2797	1976	750
Violin	2427	1972	750
Virginals	2427	1971	750
Soldiers of the Revolution (still available)			
Captain, 2nd New York Regt., 1775	2755	1976	350
Corporal, 1st New Hampshire Regt., 1778	2780	1975	350

Major, 3rd New Jersey Regt., 1776	2752	1975	350
Private, Colonel Crafts' Massachusetts Regt., 1778	2760	1977	350
Private, Haslet's Delaware Regt., 1776	2761	1977	350
Private, Pennsylvania Rifle Battalion, 1775	2846	1978	350
Private, Rhode Island Regt., 1781	2759	1977	350
Private, 1st Georgia Regt., 1777	2779	1975	350
Private, 2nd South Carolina Regt., 1781	2717	1975	350
Private, 3rd North Carolina Regt., 1778	2754	1977	350
Private, 4th Connecticut Regt., 1777	2845	1978	350
Sergeant, 1st Continental Light Dragoons, Virginia, 1777	2844	1978	350

Garbe Figurines (out of production by 1939).

TITLE	HN Number	EDITION
Beethoven	HN1778	25
Cloud, The		25
Lady of the Snows	HN1780	25
Macaw	HN1779	25
Salome	HN1775	100
Spirit of the Wind	HN1777	50
Spring	HN1774	100
West Wind	HN1776	25

Figurine	HN Number	Date	Price
A La Mode, Haute Ensemble Series	HN 2544	1974-1978	129.00 to 160.00
A'Courting	HN 2004	1947-1953	420.00 to 490.00
Abdullah*	HN 2104	1953-1962	475.00 to 510.00

Abdullah Hn2104

Adrienne, Blue	HN 2304	1964-Present	65.00 to 115.00
Afternoon Tea	HN 1747	1935-Present	122.00 to 235.00
Alchemist	HN 1259	1927-1938	120.00 to 135.00
Alexandra	HN 2398	1970-1976	110.00 to 145.00

Alfred Jingle, see Dickens, Alfred Jingle

Alison	HN 2336	1966-Present	67.00 to 115.00
Angela, Potted	HN 1204	1926-1938	425.00
Anna, Kate Greenaway Series	HN 2802	1976-Present	34.00 to 60.00
Annabella	HN 1872	1938-1949	395.00 to 425.00
Annette	HN 1550	1933-1949	275.00 to 350.00
Antoinette	HN 2326	1967-1978	79.00 to 105.00

Artful Dodger, see Dickens, Artful Dodger

At Ease	HN 2473	1973-1978	100.00 to 140.00
Autumn	HN 2087	1952-1959	325.00 to 450.00
Autumn Breezes, Green	HN 1913	1939-1971	96.00 to 175.00
Autumn Breezes, Pink	HN 1911	1939-1976	100.00 to 125.00
Autumn Breezes, Red	HN 1934	1940-Present	72.00 to 115.00
Babie*	HN 1679	1935-Present	40.00 to 50.00
Baby Bunting	HN 2108	1953-1959	130.00 to 185.00
Bachelor*	HN 2319	1964-1975	95.00 to 198.00
Ballad Seller	HN 2266	1968-1973	165.00 to 275.00
Ballerina	HN 2116	1953-1973	165.00 to 250.00
Balloon Man*	HN 1954	1940-Present	65.00 to 125.00
Balloon Seller	HN 583	1923-1949	295.00 to 375.00

Balloon Seller With Child, see Balloon Seller
Balloon Woman, see Balloon Seller

Balloon Man Hn1954

Babie Hn1679

Bachelor Hn2319

Barba	N 1421	1930-1938	475.00
Barba	1432	1930-1938	500.00
Basket	2245	1959-1962	400.00
Bather,	687	1924-1949	395.00 to 550.00
Bather,	1708	1935-1938	900.00
Beacho	2487	1973-1976	95.00 to 175.00
Bedtime	1978	1945-Present	20.00 to 40.00
Bedtime	2059	1950-Present	90.00 to 160.00
Beggar	26	1921-1949	450.00 to 500.00
Beggar	175	1956-1962	415.00 to 500.00
Belle	340	1968-Present	28.00 to 50.00
Belle O' 1	HN 1997	1947-1978	100.00 to 175.00
Bernice	HN 2071	1951-1953	300.00 to 600.00
Bess, Red	HN 2002	1947-1969	150.00 to 250.00
Betsy	HN 2111	1953-1959	225.00 to 375.00
Biddy	HN 1445	1931-1938	155.00 to 250.00
Biddy	HN 1513	1932-1951	150.00
Biddy, Potted	HN 1513	1932-1951	190.00 to 195.00
Biddy-Penny-Farthing	HN 1843	1938-Present	125.00

Bill Sykes, see Dickens, Bill Sykes

Blacksmith Of Williamsburg	HN 2240	1960-Present	75.00 to 115.00
Blithe Morning, Red	HN 2065	1950-1973	115.00 to 165.00
Bluebeard, Green	HN 2105	1953-Present	158.00 to 275.00
Bluebeard, Red	HN 1528	1932-1949	550.00
Bo Peep	HN 1811	1937-Present	42.00 to 75.00
Boatman	HN 2417	1971-Present	53.00 to 115.00
Bon Appetit	HN 2444	1972-1976	100.00 to 150.00
Bonnie Lassie	HN 1626	1934-1953	195.00 to 325.00
Boudoir, Haute Ensemble Series	HN 2542	1974-1978	200.00
Bouquet	HN 428	1921-1938	350.00
Boy From Williamsburg	HN 2183	1969-Present	60.00
Boy With Turban	HN 1212	1926-1938	265.00 to 365.00
Bride	HN 1600	1933-1949	200.00 to 475.00
Bride	HN 1762	1936-1949	300.00 to 425.00
Bride	HN 2166	1956-1976	100.00 to 185.00
Bridesmaid	M 12	1932-1945	235.00
Bridesmaid	M 30	1932-1945	235.00
Bridesmaid*	HN 2148	1955-1959	210.00 to 250.00
Buddies	HN 2546	1973-1976	80.00 to 125.00

Bumble, see Dickens, Bumble

Bunny	HN 2141	1954-1975	60.00 to 75.00
Buttercup	HN 2309	1964-Present	65.00 to 115.00
Butterfly	HN 719	1925-1938	500.00 to 550.00

Butterfly*	HN 720	1925-1938	595.00 to 625.00

Butterfly Woman, see Butterfly
Buz Fuz, see Dickens, Buz Fuz

Called Love, A Little Boy	HN 1545	1933-1949	225.00
Calumet*	HN 1428	1930-1949	650.00
Calumet	HN 1689	1935-1949	350.00 to 750.00
Calumet	HN 2068	1950-1953	350.00 to 675.00
Camille, Potted	HN 1586	1933-1949	475.00
Camille	HN 1648	1934-1949	190.00 to 420.00
Captain	HN 2260	1965-Present	175.00

Captain Cuttle, see Dickens, Captain Cuttle

Captain MacHeath	HN 464	1921-1949	550.00
Captain, 2nd New York Regt., 1775*			
	HN 2755	1976	750.00
Carmen	HN 1267	1928-1938	450.00
Carmen, Haute Ensemble Series	HN 2545	1974-1978	149.00 to 185.00
Carolyn	HN 2112	1953-1965	195.00 to 285.00
Carpet Seller*	HN 1464	1931-1969	175.00 to 250.00
Carrie, Kate Greenaway Series	HN 2800	1976-Present	55.00
Cavalier*	HN 2716	1976-Present	83.00 to 115.00

Cavallini, see Doris Keene As Cavallini

Celeste*	HN 2237	1959-1971	135.00 to 165.00

Butterfly Hn 720

Calumet Hn1428

Captain, 2nd New York Regt., 1775 Hn2755

Carpet Seller Hn1464

Cavalier Hn2716

Celeste Hn2237

Celia, Green	HN 1727	1935-1949	675.00
Cellist	HN 2226	1960-1967	350.00 to 465.00
Cello, Lady Musicians Series	HN 2331	1970	300.00
Cerise	HN 1607	1933-1949	200.00 to 215.00
Charley's Aunt	HN 35	1914-1938	400.00
Charlotte	HN 2421	1972-Present	75.00 to 140.00
Chelsea Pair, Female	HN 577	1923-1938	475.00
Chelsea Pensioner	HN 689	1924-1938	850.00
Cherie	HN 2341	1966-Present	45.00 to 75.00
Chief	HN 2892	1979	116.00 to 150.00
Child Of Williamsburg	HN 2154	1964-Present	45.00 to 60.00
Child Study	HN 603	1924-1938	235.00 to 275.00

Chitarrone, Lady Musicians Series*	HN 2700	1974	350.00
Chloe	M 29	1932-1945	245.00
Chloe	HN 1470	1931-1949	235.00 to 275.00
Chloe, Potted	HN 1470	1931-1949	325.00
Chloe	HN 1479	1931-1949	225.00
Chloe	HN 1765	1936-1950	165.00 to 275.00
Choir Boy	HN 2141	1954-1975	45.00 to 95.00
Christine*	HN 2792	1978-Present	99.00 to 185.00
Christmas Morn	HN 1992	1947-Present	65.00 to 115.00
Christmas Parcels**	HN 2851	1978-Present	75.00 to 115.00
Christmas Time	HN 2110	1953-1967	275.00 to 385.00
Cissie	HN 1809	1937-Present	45.00 to 75.00
Claribel	HN 1951	1940-1949	210.00 to 265.00
Clarinda*	HN 2724	1975-Present	98.00 to 185.00

Cymbals, Lady Musicians Series Hn2699

Clarinda Hn2724

Christine Hn2792

Clarissa	HN 1525	1932-1938	525.00 to 650.00
Clarissa	HN 2345	1968-Present	140.00
Clemency	HN 1633	1935-1938	360.00 to 425.00
Cleopatra And Slave	HN 2868	1979	750.00
Clockmaker	HN 2279	1961-1975	150.00 to 200.00
Clothilde	HN 1598	1933-1949	435.00
Clown	HN 2890	1979-Present	116.25 to 200.00
Coachman*	HN 2282	1963-1971	325.00 to 450.00
Cobbler	HN 1706	1935-1969	175.00 to 325.00
Collinette	HN 1999	1947-1949	300.00 to 395.00
Columbine	HN 1296	1928-1938	500.00
Columbine	HN 1297	1928-1938	500.00

Coachman Hn2282   *Cookie Hn2218*

Columbine	HN 2185	1957-1969	125.00 to 150.00
Cookie*	HN 2218	1958-1975	75.00
Coppelia	HN 2115	1953-1959	250.00 to 500.00
Coralie	HN 2307	1964-Present	65.00 to 115.00
Corinthian	HN 1973	1941-1949	800.00
Corporal, 1st New Hampshire Regt., 1778			
	HN 2780	1975	750.00
Country Lass*	HN 1991	1975-Present	52.50 to 100.00
Cradle Song	HN 2246	1959-1962	275.00 to 400.00
Craftsman	HN 2284	1961-1965	465.00 to 500.00
Cup Of Tea	HN 2322	1964-Present	55.00 to 100.00
Curly Knob	HN 1627	1934-1949	350.00 to 450.00
Curly Locks	HN 2049	1949-1953	175.00 to 265.00
Curtsey	HN 66A	1916-1938	795.00 to 900.00
Cymbals, Lady Musicians Series*	HN 2699	1974	325.00
Cynthia	HN 1685	1935-1949	550.00

Country Lass Hn1991   *Chitarrone, Lady Musicians Series Hn2700*

Daffy Down Dilly*	HN 1712	1935-1975	155.00 to 240.00
Daffy Down Dilly	HN 1713	1935-1949	155.00 to 275.00
Dainty May	HN 1639	1934-1949	175.00 to 235.00
Daisy	HN 1575	1933-1949	175.00
Daisy	HN 1961	1941-1949	195.00
Damaris	HN 2079	1951-1952	800.00

Dancers of the World Series, see individual figurines

Dancing Eyes & Sunny Hair	HN 1543	1933-1949	150.00
Dancing Years*	HN 2235	1965-1971	255.00 to 300.00
Daphne	HN 2268	1963-1975	135.00 to 175.00
Darby	HN 1427	1930-1949	195.00
Darby	HN 2024	1949-1959	250.00
Darling	HN 1319	1929-1959	26.50 to 125.00
Darling	HN 1985	1946-Present	40.00

Daffy Down Dilly Hn1712

Dancing Years Hn2235

David Copperfield, see Dickens, David Copperfield

Dawn	HN 1858	1938-1949	600.00
Daydreams	HN 1731	1935-Present	65.00 to 115.00
Daydreams	HN 1944	1940-1949	270.00
Debbie*	HN 2385	1969-Present	45.00 to 75.00
Debutante	HN 2210	1963-1967	220.00 to 285.00
Deidre	HN 2020	1949-1955	275.00 to 350.00
Delight	HN 1772	1936-1967	110.00 to 200.00
Delphine	HN 2136	1954-1967	195.00 to 275.00
Denise*	HN 2273	1964-1971	150.00 to 275.00
Derrick	HN 1398	1930-1938	250.00 to 600.00
Detective*	HN 2359	1977-Present	54.00 to 115.00
Diana*	HN 1986	1946-1975	75.00

Debbie Hn2385

Denise Hn2273

Detective Hn2359

Diana Hn1986

Dick Swiveller, see Dickens, Dick Swiveller

Dickens, Alfred Jingle, 3 3/4 In.	M 52	1932-Present	21.95
Dickens, Artful Dodger, 3 3/4 In.	M 55	1932-Present	21.95
Dickens, Bill Sykes, 3 3/4 In.	M 54	1932-Present	21.95
Dickens, Bumble, 4 1/2 In.	M 76	1939-Present	21.95
Dickens, Buz Fuz, 3 3/4 In.	M 53	1932-Present	21.95
Dickens, Captain Cuttle, 4 1/2 In.	M 77	1939-Present	21.95
Dickens, David Copperfield, 4 1/2 In.			
	M 88	1949-Present	21.95
Dickens, Dick Swiveller, 4 1/2 In.	M 90	1949-Present	21.95
Dickens, Fagin, 7 In.	M 49	1932-Present	21.95
Dickens, Fat Boy, 3 1/2 In.	M 44	1932-Present	21.95
Dickens, Little Nell, 4 In.	M 51	1932-Present	21.95
Dickens, Mr. Micawber, 3 1/2 In.	M 42	1932-Present	21.95
Dickens, Mr. Pecksniff, 3 3/4 In.	M 43	1932-Present	21.95
Dickens, Mr. Pickwick, 3 3/4 In.	M 41	1932-Present	21.95
Dickens, Mrs. Bardell, 4 1/2 In.	M 86	1949-Present	21.95
Dickens, Oliver Twist, 4 1/2 In.	M 89	1949-Present	21.95
Dickens, Sairey Gamp, 4 In.	M 46	1932-Present	21.95
Dickens, Sam Weller, 4 In.	M 47	1932-Present	21.95
Dickens, Scrooge, 4 1/2 In.	M 87	1949-Present	21.95

Dickens, Stiggins, 3 3/4 In.	M 50	1932-Present	21.95
Dickens, Tiny Tim, 3 1/2 In.	M 56	1932-Present	21.95
Dickens, Tony Weller, 3 1/2 In.	M 47	1932-Present	21.95
Dickens, Trotty Veck, 4 1/2 In.	M 91	1949-Present	21.95
Dickens, Uriah Heep, 4 In.	M 45	1932-Present	21.95
Dimity	HN 2169	1956-1959	310.00 to 325.00
Dinky Do	HN 1678	1934-Present	29.50 to 50.00
Doctor	HN 2858	1979	84.00 to 150.00
Dolly Vardon	HN 1514	1932-1938	450.00
Dorcas	HN 1490	1932-1938	225.00
Dorcas	HN 1491	1932-1938	350.00
Dorcas, Potted	HN 1491	1932-1938	250.00
Dorcas	HN 1558	1933-1952	175.00 to 270.00
Doris Keene As Cavallini	HN 90	1918-1936	800.00
Dreamweaver	HN 2283	1972-1976	115.00 to 130.00
Drummer Boy	HN 2679	1976-Present	122.00 to 275.00
Dulcimer, Lady Musicians Series*	HN 2798	1975	375.00
Dunce	HN 6	1913-1938	850.00 to 1000.00
Easter Day	HN 1976	1945-1951	205.00 to 325.00
Easter Day	HN 2039	1949-1969	185.00 to 295.00
Eleanor Of Provence	HN 2009	1948-1953	450.00
Eleanore	HN 1754	1936-1949	225.00
Elegance	HN 2264	1961-Present	67.00 to 115.00
Elfreda	HN 2078	1951-1955	425.00 to 600.00
Eliza, Haute Ensemble Series	HN 2543	1974-1978	150.00 to 180.00
Elsie Maynard	HN 639	1924-1949	600.00
Elyse	HN 2429	1972-Present	75.00 to 140.00
Emma, Kate Greenaway Series	HN 2834	1977-Present	42.00 to 60.00
Enchantment	HN 2178	1957-Present	67.00 to 115.00
Ermine	M 40	1933-1945	300.00
Ermine Coat	HN 1981	1945-1967	150.00 to 250.00

Ermine Muff, see Lady Ermine

Esmeralda	HN 2168	1956-1959	275.00 to 325.00
Estelle	HN 1566	1933-1938	500.00
Eventide	HN 2814	1977-Present	54.00 to 115.00

Fagin, see Dickens, Fagin

Fair Lady, Coral Pink	HN 2835	1977-Present	75.00 to 115.00
Fair Lady, Green	HN 2193	1963-Present	115.00
Fair Lady, Red	HN 2832	1977-Present	115.00
Fair Maiden	HN 2211	1967-Present	45.00 to 75.00
Falstaff	HN 571	1923-1938	600.00
Falstaff	HN 575	1923-1938	550.00 to 600.00
Falstaff	HN 608	1924-1938	600.00
Falstaff	HN 609	1924-1938	600.00

Falstaff	HN 619	1924-1938	600.00
Falstaff	HN 638	1924-1938	600.00
Falstaff	HN 1216	1926-1949	600.00
Falstaff**	HN 1606	1933-1949	600.00
Falstaff	HN 2054	1950-Present	57.00 to 100.00
Family Album*	HN 2321	1966-1973	120.00 to 225.00
Family, Black	HN 2721	1978	95.00
Family, White	HN 2720	1978	95.00

Fanny, see Angela

Faraway	HN 2133	1958-1962	133.25 to 195.00
Farmer's Boy	HN 2520	1938-1960	695.00 to 825.00
Farmer's Wife	HN 2069	1951-1955	400.00 to 500.00

Fat Boy, see also Dickens, Fat Boy

Fat Boy	HN 1893	1938-1952	400.00
Fat Boy	HN 2096	1952-1967	300.00
Favourite	HN 2249	1960-Present	85.00 to 115.00
Fiddler	HN 2171	1956-1962	600.00 to 800.00
Fiona	HN 1925	1940-1949	500.00
Fiona	HN 1933	1940-1949	645.00
Fiona	HN 2694	1974-Present	140.00
First Dance*	HN 2803	1977-Present	75.00 to 140.00
First Steps	HN 2242	1959-1965	400.00 to 450.00
First Waltz	HN 2862	1979	116.25 to 155.00
Fleur	HN 2368	1968-Present	70.00 to 140.00
Fleurette	HN 1587	1933-1949	290.00 to 395.00
Flora*	HN 2349	1966-1973	155.00 to 225.00

Family Album Hn2321

Flora Hn2349

First Dance Hn2803

Flower Seller	HN 789	1926-1938	425.00
Flower Seller's Children**	HN 1206	1926-1949	365.00 to 450.00
Flower Seller's Children	HN 1342	1929-Present	200.00 to 300.00
Flute, Lady Musicians Series*	HN 2483	1973	450.00
Foaming Quart	HN 2162	1955-Present	75.00 to 115.00
Folly	HN 1750	1936-1949	845.00 to 1050.00
Fortune Teller	HN 2159	1955-1967	375.00 to 425.00
Forty Thieves	HN 667	1924-1938	425.00

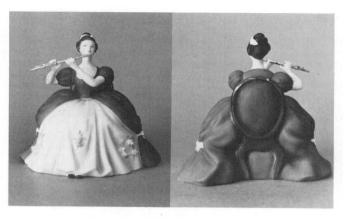

Flute, Lady Musicians Series Hn2483

Forty Winks*	HN 1974	1945-1973	135.00 to 250.00
Four O'Clock	HN 1760	1936-1949	550.00
Fragrance*	HN 2334	1966-Present	63.00 to 140.00
Francine	HN 2422	1972-Present	38.50 to 75.00
French Horn, Lady Musicians Series*			
	HN 2795	1976	400.00
French Peasant	HN 2075	1951-1955	425.00 to 500.00
Friar Tuck	HN 2143	1954-Present	300.00 to 525.00
Gaffer	HN 2053	1950-1959	325.00 to 425.00
Gainsborough Hat	HN 705	1925-1938	795.00
Gay Morning	HN 2135	1954-1967	185.00 to 350.00
Geisha	HN 779	1919-1938	550.00
Geisha, Potted	HN 779	1919-1938	550.00 to 1000.00
Genevieve*	HN 1962	1941-1975	135.00 to 225.00
Gentleman From Williamsburg	HN 2227	1960-Present	75.00 to 115.00
Gentlewoman	HN 1632	1934-1949	385.00
George Washington At Prayer	HN 2861	1977	875.00
Georgiana	HN 2093	1952-1955	250.00

Forty Winks Hn1974

*French Horn,
Lady Musicians Series Hn2795*

Genevieve Hn1962

Fragrance Hn2334

Geraldine	HN 2348	1972-1976	95.00 to 145.00
Giselle**	HN 2139	1954-1969	275.00 to 350.00
Giselle, Forest Glade**	HN 2140	1954-1965	315.00 to 350.00
Gloria	HN 1488	1932-1938	425.00
Golden Days	HN 2274	1964-1973	115.00 to 145.00
Gollywog	HN 1979	1945-1959	150.00 to 185.00
Gollywog	HN 2040	1949-1959	200.00
Good Catch	HN 2258	1966-Present	60.00 to 115.00
Good King Wenceslas	HN 2118	1953-1976	150.00 to 195.00
Good Morning	HN 2671	1974-1976	110.00 to 135.00
Goody Two Shoes	HN 2037	1949-Present	45.00 to 70.00
Goosegirl	HN 425	1921-1938	1000.00
Gossips	HN 1429	1930-1949	170.00
Gossips	HN 2025	1949-1967	235.00 to 325.00
Grace	HN 2318	1966-Present	67.00 to 115.00
Grand Manner	HN 2723	1975-Present	80.00 to 185.00
Grandma	HN 2052	1950-1959	265.00 to 325.00

Granny's Heritage	HN 2031	1949-1969	325.00 to 450.00
Granny's Shawl	HN 1647	1934-1949	250.00 to 290.00
Greta	HN 1485	1931-1953	150.00 to 165.00
Gretchen	HN 1397	1933-1938	500.00
Griselda	HN 1993	1947-1953	395.00
Guy Fawkes*	HN 98	1918-1949	650.00 to 950.00
Gwynneth	HN 1980	1945-1952	245.00 to 370.00
Gypsy Dance	HN 2157	1955-1957	250.00 to 400.00
Gypsy Dance	HN 2230	1959-1971	195.00 to 335.00
Harlequin	HN 2186	1957-1969	125.00 to 195.00
Harlequinade, Black, Green, Yellow	HN 585	1923-1938	500.00
Harlequinade, Black, Green, Yellow, Potted			
	HN 585	1923-1938	550.00
Harlequinade, Gold	HN 635	1924-1938	550.00 to 650.00
Harlequinade, Pink, Blue, Black, Orange			
	HN 780	1926-1938	575.00
Harmony**	HN 2824	1978-Present	75.00 to 140.00
Harp, Lady Musicians Series*	HN 2482	1973	300.00
Hazel	HN 1796	1936-1949	300.00
Hazel	HN 1797	1936-1949	225.00
He Loves Me	HN 2046	1949-1962	110.00

Guy Fawkes Hn 98

Harp, Lady Musicians Series Hn2482

Heart To Heart*	HN 2276	1961-1971	340.00 to 369.00
Helen	HN 1508	1932-1938	600.00
Helmsman	HN 2499	1974-Present	150.00
Henrietta Maria	HN 2005	1948-1953	450.00 to 550.00
Henry Lytton As Jack Point	HN 610	1924-1949	700.00
Her Ladyship	HN 1977	1945-1959	195.00 to 275.00
Here A Little Child I Stand	HN 1546	1933-1949	225.00
Hermione	HN 2058	1950-1952	700.00
Highwayman	HN 527	1921-1949	350.00

Highwayman, Potted	HN 527	1921-1949	475.00
Hilary*	HN 2335	1967-Present	140.00
Hinged Parasol	HN 1578	1933-1949	300.00
Hinged Parasol	HN 1579	1933-1949	450.00
Home Again	HN 2167	1956-Present	60.00 to 90.00
Honey	HN 1909	1939-1949	295.00 to 360.00
Honey	HN 1910	1939-1949	375.00
Hornpipe	HN 2161	1955-1962	575.00
Hostess Of Williamsburg	HN 2209	1960-Present	75.00 to 115.00
Huntsman	HN 2492	1974-1978	125.00 to 225.00
Hurdy-Gurdy, Lady Musicians Series*			
	HN 2796	1975	375.00

Heart To Heart Hn2276

Hilary Hn2335

Hurdy-Gurdy, Lady Musicians Series Hn2796

Dulcimer, Lady Musicians Series Hn2798

Indian Brave, Prestige Figure*	HN 2376	1975	2500.00 to 3000.00
Indian Temple, Dancers Of The World**			
	HN 2830	1978	550.00
Innocence	HN 2842	1979	71.25 to 115.00
Invitation	HN 2170	1956-1975	60.00 to 125.00
Irene	HN 1621	1934-1951	195.00 to 275.00
Irish Colleen	HN 767	1925-1938	800.00
Ivy	HN 1768	1936-1978	35.00 to 50.00
Jack*	HN 2060	1950-1971	80.00 to 120.00
Jack Point, Prestige Figure	HN 2080	1952-Present	1200.00

Indian Brave, Prestige Figure Hn2376

Indian Temple, Dancers Of The World Hn2830

Jacqueline	HN 2001	1947-1951	395.00
Jane*	HN 2014	1948-1951	350.00
Janet	M 75	1936-1949	235.00
Janet	HN 1537	1932-Present	90.00 to 185.00
Janet	HN 1538	1932-1949	295.00
Janet	HN 1916	1939-1949	125.00
Janice	HN 2022	1949-1955	295.00 to 395.00
Janine	HN 2461	1971-Present	140.00
Jasmine	HN 1862	1938-1949	500.00
Jean	HN 2032	1949-1959	195.00 to 275.00

Jersey Milkmaid, see also Milkmaid

Jersey Milkmaid, Blue	HN 2057	1950-1959	150.00 to 195.00
Jester**	HN 71	1917-1938	500.00
Jester	HN 1295	1928-1949	500.00
Jester	HN 2016	1949-Present	82.00 to 150.00
Jill*	HN 2061	1950-1971	60.00 to 100.00
Joan	HN 1422	1930-1949	195.00
Joan	HN 2023	1949-1959	195.00 to 250.00

Jack Hn2060

Jill Hn2061

Jane Hn2014

Jolly Sailor	HN 2172	1956-1965	500.00 to 550.00
Jovial Monk*	HN 2144	1954-1976	105.00 to 155.00
Judge	HN 2443	1972-Present	71.25 to 125.00
Judith	HN 2089	1952-1959	200.00 to 350.00
Julia	HN 2705	1975-Present	60.00 to 115.00
June	HN 1690	1935-1949	285.00
June	HN 1691	1935-1949	275.00 to 350.00
Karen	HN 1994	1947-1955	275.00 to 375.00
Kate*	HN 2789	1978-Present	65.00 to 115.00
Kate Hardcastle	HN 1719	1935-1949	375.00 to 475.00
Kate Hardcastle	HN 1919	1939-1949	550.00
Kate Hardcastle	HN 2028	1949-1952	450.00 to 495.00
Katharine	HN 341	1919-1938	300.00 to 600.00
Kathleen	HN 1252	1927-1938	475.00
Kathleen	HN 1279	1928-1938	395.00
Kathleen	HN 1357	1929-1938	550.00
Katrina	HN 2327	1965-1969	225.00 to 350.00

Kate Hn2789

Jovial Monk Hn2144

King Charles	**HN 404**	**1920-1951**	**525.00 to 575.00**
King Charles, Prestige Figure	**HN 2084**	**1952-Present**	**750.00**

King Wenceslas, see Good King Wenceslas

Kirsty	**HN 2381**	**1971-Present**	**86.25 to 140.00**
Kurdish, Dancers Of The World	**HN 2867**	**1979**	**550.00**
La Sylphide**	**HN 2138**	**1956-1965**	**395.00**
Lady Anne Nevill	**HN 2006**	**1948-1953**	**1000.00**
Lady April	**HN 1958**	**1940-1959**	**225.00 to 350.00**
Lady Betty	**HN 1967**	**1941-1951**	**275.00 to 425.00**
Lady Charmian	**HN 1948**	**1940-1973**	**150.00 to 200.00**
Lady Charmian*	**HN 1949**	**1940-1973**	**150.00 to 225.00**
Lady Clare	**HN 1465**	**1931-1938**	**400.00 to 500.00**
Lady Ermine	**HN 54**	**1916-1938**	**850.00**
Lady Fayre	**HN 1265**	**1928-1938**	**450.00 to 500.00**
Lady From Williamsburg	**HN 2228**	**1960-Present**	**79.50 to 115.00**

Lady Musicians Series, see individual figurines

Lady Pamela	**HN 2718**	**1974-Present**	**86.00 to 140.00**

Lady With Parasol, see Miss Demure

Laird*	**HN 2361**	**1969-Present**	**60.00 to 125.00**
Lambeth Walk	**HN 1880**	**1938-1949**	**800.00 to 900.00**
Lambing Time	**HN 1890**	**1938-Present**	**75.00 to 100.00**
Last Waltz	**HN 2315**	**1967-Present**	**75.00 to 140.00**
Laurianne	**HN 2719**	**1974-1978**	**80.00 to 125.00**
Lavinia	**HN 1955**	**1940-1978**	**45.00 to 85.00**
Leading Lady	**HN 2269**	**1965-1976**	**100.00 to 115.00**
Leisure Hour	**HN 2055**	**1950-1965**	**345.00 to 400.00**
Lido Lady	**HN 1220**	**1927-1938**	**500.00**
Lights Out	**HN 2262**	**1965-1969**	**200.00**

Lady Charmian Hn1949

Laird Hn2361

Lily Hn1798

Lisa Hn2310

Little Boy Blue Hn2062

Lilac Shawl	HN 44	1915-1938	800.00
Lilac Shawl, Potted	HN 44	1915-1938	940.00
Lilac Time	HN 2137	1954-1969	185.00 to 325.00
Lily*	HN 1798	1936-1949	75.00 to 130.00
Linda	HN 2106	1953-1976	60.00 to 85.00
Lisa*	HN 2310	1969-Present	70.00 to 140.00
Little Boy Blue*	HN 2062	1950-1973	80.00 to 100.00
Little Bridesmaid	HN 1433	1930-1951	115.00 to 195.00
Little Bridesmaid	HN 1434	1930-1949	110.00
Little Child So Rare And Sweet	HN 1542	1933-1949	260.00
Little Jack Horner	HN 2063	1950-1953	220.00
Little Mistress	HN 1449	1931-1949	285.00 to 325.00

Little Nell, see Dickens, Little Nell

Lizana	HN 1756	1936-1949	500.00
Lobster Man	HN 2317	1964-Present	53.00 to 85.00
London Cry, Strawberries	HN 749	1925-1938	600.00
London Cry, Strawberries	HN 772	1925-1938	600.00
London Cry, Turnips & Carrots	HN 752	1925-1938	600.00
London Cry, Turnips & Carrots	HN 771	1925-1938	600.00
Long John Silver	HN 2204	1957-1965	325.00 to 435.00
Loretta	HN 2337	1966-Present	65.00 to 115.00

Lorna*	**HN 2311**	**1965-Present**	**50.00 to 90.00**
Love Letter*	**HN 2149**	**1958-1976**	**145.00 to 195.00**
Lovers, Black	**HN 2763**	**1978**	**95.00**
Lovers, White	**HN 2762**	**1978**	**95.00**
Lucy Ann	**HN 1502**	**1932-1951**	**190.00 to 250.00**
Lucy Lockett	**HN 524**	**1921-1949**	**495.00**
Lucy Lockett	**HN 695**	**1925-1949**	**550.00**
Lunchtime	**HN 2485**	**1973-Present**	**80.00 to 150.00**
Lute, Lady Musicians Series*	**HN 2431**	**1972**	**600.00**
Lydia	**HN 1907**	**1939-1949**	**245.00**
Lydia	**HN 1908**	**1939-Present**	**48.00 to 80.00**
Lynne	**HN 2329**	**1971-Present**	**77.00 to 140.00**
Maisie	**HN 1619**	**1934-1939**	**275.00 to 395.00**
Major, 3rd New Jersey Regt., 1776*	**HN 2752**	**1975**	**750.00**

Love Letter Hn2149

Lorna Hn2311

Lute, Lady Musicians Series Hn2431

Major, 3rd New Jersey Regt.,
1776 Hn2752

Make Believe	HN 2225	1962-Present	65.00 to 80.00
Mam'Selle	HN 724	1925-1938	300.00 to 600.00
Mantilla, Haute Ensemble Series	HN 2712	1974-1978	240.00
Margaret	HN 1989	1947-1959	200.00 to 275.00
Margery	HN 1413	1930-1949	280.00 to 400.00
Margot	HN 1628	1934-1938	425.00
Marguerite	HN 1928	1940-1959	200.00 to 325.00
Marguerite	HN 1946	1940-1949	225.00 to 265.00
Marianne	HN 2074	1951-1953	385.00
Marie	HN 1370	1930-Present	35.00 to 50.00
Marietta	HN 1341	1929-1949	450.00 to 550.00
Marietta, Potted	HN 1341	1929-1949	450.00 to 550.00
Marietta, Potted	HN 1446	1931-1949	575.00
Market Day	HN 1991	1947-1955	300.00 to 365.00
Mary Had A Little Lamb	HN 2048	1949-Present	55.00 to 75.00
Mary Jane	HN 1990	1947-1959	200.00 to 400.00
Mary Mary*	HN 2044	1949-1973	110.00 to 150.00
Mask Seller	HN 2103	1953-Present	78.00 to 125.00
Mask, Black With Blue, Yellow Dots**			
	HN 1271	1928-1938	650.00
Mask, Blue With Pink Stripes	HN 785	1926-1938	650.00
Mask, Red With Black Squares**	HN 729	1925-1938	650.00
Mask, White With Black Squares	HN 733	1925-1938	650.00
Mask, White With Black Trim**	HN 657	1924-1938	650.00
Masque	HN 2554	1973-Present	115.00 to 140.00
Masquerade, Female, Grey	HN 2251	1960-1965	225.00 to 265.00
Masquerade, Female, Red	HN 600	1924-1949	550.00
Masquerade, Female, Red	HN 2259	1960-1965	225.00 to 265.00
Masquerade, Male	HN 599	1924-1949	550.00
Master*	HN 2325	1967-Present	85.00 to 115.00
Master Sweep	HN 2205	1957-1962	495.00 to 525.00
Matador And Bull, Prestige Figure	HN 2324	1964-Present	9500.00

Mary Mary Hn2044

Master Hn2325

Matilda	HN 2011	1948-1953	475.00 to 695.00
Maureen, Pink	HN 1770	1936-1959	175.00 to 250.00
Mayor	HN 2280	1963-1971	275.00 to 325.00
Maytime	HN 2113	1953-1967	195.00 to 325.00
Meditation	HN 2330	1971-Present	115.00 to 185.00
Melanie	HN 2271	1965-Present	85.00 to 140.00
Melody	HN 2202	1957-1962	145.00 to 325.00
Memories	HN 1855	1938-1949	270.00 to 350.00
Memories	HN 2030	1949-1959	285.00 to 400.00
Mendicant	HN 1365	1929-1969	195.00 to 225.00
Mephistopheles & Marguerite	HN 755	1925-1949	1200.00 to 1400.00
Mermaid	HN 97	1918-1936	425.00 to 700.00
Meryll, Also Called Toinetie	HN 1917	1939-1940	700.00
Mexican, Dancers Of The World	HN 2866	1979	550.00
Michelle*	HN 2234	1967-Present	70.00 to 95.00
Midinette	HN 2090	1952-1965	195.00 to 325.00
Midsummer Noon	HN 1900	1939-1949	425.00
Midsummer Noon	HN 2033	1949-1955	395.00
Milking Time, Potted	HN 3	1913-1938	1200.00

Milkmaid, see also Jersey Milkmaid

Milkmaid, Green*	HN 2057	1975-Present	100.00
Minuet, Red	HN 2066	1950-1955	375.00 to 385.00
Minuet, White	HN 2019	1949-1971	225.00 to 290.00
Mirable	M 74	1936-1949	200.00
Miss Demure, Potted*	HN 1402	1930-1975	175.00 to 225.00
Miss Muffet, Green	HN 1937	1940-1952	95.00 to 225.00
Miss Muffet, Red	HN 1936	1940-1967	125.00 to 175.00

Michelle Hn2234

Miss Demure, Potted
Hn1402

Milkmaid, Green Hn2057

Nicola Hn2839

My Pet Hn2238

Nina Hn2347

Miss Winsome	HN 1665	1934-1949	395.00 to 425.00
Monica	HN 1467	1931-Present	50.00 to 75.00
Moor, Prestige Figure	HN 2082	1952-Present	1200.00
Mother's Helper	HN 2151	1962-1969	100.00 to 200.00

Mr. Micawber, see also Dickens, Mr. Micawber

| Mr. Micawber | HN 557 | 1923-1939 | 325.00 to 350.00 |
| Mr. Micawber | HN 2097 | 1952-1967 | 235.00 to 325.00 |

Mr. Pecksniff, see Dickens, Mr. Pecksniff
Mr. Pickwick, see also Dickens, Mr. Pickwick

| Mr. Pickwick | HN 556 | 1923-1939 | 275.00 to 300.00 |
| Mr. Pickwick | HN 2099 | 1952-1967 | 235.00 to 325.00 |

Mrs. Bardell, see Dickens, Mrs. Bardell

Mrs. Fitzherbert	HN 2007	1948-1953	1000.00
My Love	HN 2339	1969-Present	90.00 to 140.00
My Pet*	HN 2238	1962-1975	95.00 to 175.00
My Teddy	HN 2177	1962-1967	195.00 to 250.00
Nadine, Green	HN 1885	1938-1949	350.00
Nadine, Purple	HN 1886	1938-1949	425.00
Nanny	HN 2221	1958-Present	71.50 to 125.00
Nell Gwynn	HN 1882	1938-1949	500.00
New Bonnet	HN 1957	1940-1949	350.00 to 450.00
Newsboy	HN 2244	1959-1965	395.00 to 550.00
Nicola*	HN 2839	1978-Present	105.00 to 185.00
Nina*	HN 2347	1969-1976	90.00 to 115.00
Ninette	HN 2379	1971-Present	79.00 to 140.00
Noelle	HN 2179	1957-1967	200.00 to 400.00
Norma	M 37	1933-1945	300.00

Old Balloon Seller Hn1315

Old Mother Hubbard
Hn2314

Omar Khayyam
Hn2247

Odds & Ends	HN 1844	1938-1949	600.00
Old Balloon Seller*	HN 1315	1929-Present	95.00 to 125.00
Old King	HN 2134	1954-Present	350.00
Old King Cole	HN 2217	1963-1967	625.00 to 900.00
Old Meg	HN 2494	1974-1976	625.00 to 900.00
Old Mother Hubbard*	HN 2314	1964-1975	135.00 to 190.00
Olga	HN 2463	1972-1975	145.00 to 175.00

Oliver Twist, see Dickens, Oliver Twist

Olivia	HN 1995	1947-1951	350.00 to 425.00
Omar Khayyam*	HN 2247	1965-Present	65.00 to 115.00
Once Upon A Time	HN 2047	1949-1955	130.00 to 230.00
One That Got Away	HN 2153	1955-1959	265.00
Orange Lady, Green	HN 1953	1940-1975	150.00 to 225.00
Orange Lady, Pink*	HN 1759	1936-1975	115.00 to 225.00
Orange Vendor	HN 72	1917-1938	600.00 to 950.00
Organ Grinder	HN 2173	1956-1965	550.00
Owd Willum*	HN 2042	1949-1973	150.00 to 200.00
Paisley Shawl, Potted	HN 1392	1930-1949	325.00
Paisley Shawl, 6 In.	HN 1392	1930-1949	275.00
Paisley Shawl, 9 In.	HN 1392	1930-1949	275.00
Paisley Shawl	HN 1987	1946-1959	175.00 to 225.00
Paisley Shawl*	HN 1988	1946-1975	95.00 to 200.00

Orange Lady, Pink Hn1759

Owd Willum Hn2042

Paisley Shawl Hn1988

Palio*	HN 2428	1971	2500.00
Pantalettes, Green Skirt	HN 1362	1929-1938	190.00 to 325.00
Pantalettes, Green Skirt, Potted	HN 1362	1929-1938	365.00
Pantalettes, Pink Skirt	HN 1412	1930-1949	350.00
Pantalettes, Yellow Dress	HN 1507	1932-1949	390.00
Parisian	HN 2445	1972-1975	125.00 to 150.00
Parson's Daughter	HN 564	1923-1949	225.00 to 300.00
Past Glory	HN 2484	1973-1978	165.00 to 235.00

Palio Hn2428

Patchwork Quilt	HN 1984	1945-1959	250.00 to 365.00
Patricia	M 28	1932-1945	250.00
Patricia, Green	HN 1462	1931-1938	225.00
Patricia, Red	HN 1567	1933-1949	425.00 to 450.00
Patricia, Yellow	HN 1414	1930-1949	395.00
Pauline	HN 1444	1931-1938	290.00 to 350.00
Peace, Black	HN 2433	1978	95.00
Peace, White	HN 2470	1978	95.00
Pearly Boy	HN 1482	1931-1949	275.00
Pearly Boy	HN 1547	1933-1949	210.00
Pearly Boy	HN 2035	1949-1959	125.00 to 265.00
Pearly Girl	HN 1483	1931-1949	150.00 to 175.00
Pecksniff	HN 2098	1952-1967	275.00 to 365.00
Peggy	HN 1941	1940-1949	98.00
Peggy	HN 2038	1949-1978	45.00 to 55.00
Penelope	HN 1901	1939-1975	250.00 to 325.00
Penny	HN 2338	1968-Present	25.00 to 50.00
Pensive Moments*	HN 2704	1975-Present	115.00 to 140.00
Perfect Pair	HN 581	1923-1938	650.00 to 700.00
Philippa Of Hainault	HN 2008	1948-1953	550.00
Philippine, Dancers Of The World	HN 2439	1978	550.00
Phyllis	HN 1420	1930-1949	325.00 to 395.00
Picnic	HN 2308	1965-Present	49.00 to 80.00
Pied Piper	HN 2102	1953-1976	140.00 to 195.00
Pierrette	HN 644	1924-1938	525.00 to 600.00
Pirouette	HN 2216	1959-1967	190.00 to 200.00
Poacher	HN 2043	1949-1959	250.00 to 295.00
Poke Bonnet	HN 612	1924-1938	750.00 to 800.00
Polka	HN 2156	1955-1969	195.00 to 250.00
Polly Peachum, Pink, Curtsey	HN 549	1922-1949	195.00 to 410.00
Polly Peachum, Standing On Base	HN 550	1922-1949	265.00 to 375.00
Potter	HN 1493	1932-Present	175.00 to 275.00
Premiere*	HN 2343	1969-1978	175.00 to 200.00

Pensive Moments Hn2704

Premiere Hn2343

Princess Badoura**	**HN 2081**	**1952-Present**	**xxxx**
Prinknash Nun, Our Lady Of Lourdes		1936-1945	750.00
Priscilla	HN 1337	1929-1938	350.00
Priscilla	HN 1340	1929-1949	240.00 to 325.00
Priscilla, Potted	HN 1340	1929-1949	265.00 to 375.00
Priscilla	HN 1495	1932-1949	350.00
Private, Haslet's Delaware Regt., 1776			
	HN 2761	1977	750.00
Private, Massachusetts Regt., 1778*			
	HN 2760	1977	750.00
Private, Penn. Rifle Battalion, 1776	HN 2846	1978	750.00
Private, Rhode Island Regt., 1781	HN 2759	1977	750.00
Private, 1st Georgia Regt., 1777	HN 2779	1975	750.00
Private, 2nd S. Carolina Regt., 1781*			
	HN 2717	1975	750.00
Private, 3rd N. Carolina Regt., 1778*			
	HN 2754	1976	750.00
Private, 4th Connecticut Regt., 1777			
	HN 2845	1978	750.00

Private, Massachusetts Regt., 1778 Hn2760

Private, 2nd S. Carolina Regt., 1781 Hn2717

Private, 3nd N. Carolina Regt., 1778 Hn2754

Professor	HN 2281	1965-Present	95.00 to 125.00
Proposal, Lady, Pink Dress	HN 788	1926-1938	60.00
Proposal, Lady, Red Dress**	HN 715	1925-1938	60.00
Proposal, Lady, White Dress	HN 716	1925-1938	60.00
Proposal, Male, Blue Coat	HN 1209	1926-1938	60.00
Proposal, Male, Red Coat**	HN 725	1925-1938	60.00
Prue	HN 1996	1947-1955	200.00 to 345.00
Puppetmaker	HN 2253	1962-1973	295.00 to 375.00
Pyjams	HN 1942	1940-1949	325.00
Queen Elizabeth II	HN 2502	1973-1978	600.00

Queen Elizabeth II, see miscellaneous chapter, busts

Rag Doll	HN 2142	1952-Present	60.00
Regal Lady	HN 2709	1975-Present	115.00 to 140.00
Regency Beau	HN 1972	1941-1949	800.00
Rendezvous*	HN 2212	1962-1971	310.00
Repose	HN 2272	1972-1978	120.00 to 175.00
Reverie	HN 2306	1964-Present	155.00 to 185.00
Rhapsody	HN 2267	1961-1973	175.00 to 220.00
Rhoda	HN 1573	1933-1949	575.00
Rhythm	HN 1903	1939-1949	600.00
River Boy*	HN 2128	1962-1975	70.00 to 95.00
Rocking Horse	HN 2072	1951-1953	950.00 to 1400.00
Romance	HN 2430	1972-Present	75.00 to 100.00
Rosabell	HN 1620	1934-1938	550.00
Rosalind	HN 2393	1970-1975	125.00 to 145.00
Rosamund	M 32	1932-1945	195.00
Rosamund	M 33	1932-1945	300.00

Rendezvous Hn2212

River Boy Hn2128

Royal Governor's Cook Hn2233

Sandra Hn2275

Rosamund	HN 1320	1929-1938	900.00 to 3000.00
Rose	HN 1368	1930-Present	35.00 to 70.00
Roseanna	HN 1926	1940-1959	250.00 to 350.00
Rosebud	HN 1983	1945-1952	285.00 to 395.00
Rosemary	HN 2091	1952-1959	325.00 to 400.00
Rosina	HN 1358	1929-1938	425.00 to 450.00
Rosina	HN 1364	1929-1938	395.00
Rosina	HN 1556	1933-1938	425.00
Rowena	HN 2077	1951-1955	250.00 to 525.00
Royal Governor's Cook, Williamsburg*			
	HN 2233	1960-Present	115.00
Ruby	HN 1724	1935-1949	195.00
Sabbath Morn	HN 1982	1945-1959	195.00 to 250.00
Sailor's Holiday	HN 2442	1972-1978	95.00 to 125.00

Sairey Gamp, see also Dickens, Sairey Gamp

Sairey Gamp	HN 2100	1952-1967	265.00 to 300.00

Sam Weller, see Dickens, Sam Weller

Sandra*	HN 2275	1969-Present	115.00
Saucy Nymph	HN 1539	1933-1949	195.00 to 215.00
Schoolmarm	HN 2223	1958-Present	72.50 to 95.00
Scotties, Potted	HN 1281	1928-1938	575.00
Scotties	HN 1349	1929-1949	315.00

Scottish Highland, Dancers Of The World

	HN 2436	1978	550.00
Scribe	HN 305	1918-1936	800.00

Scrooge, see Dickens, Scrooge

Sea	HN 2191	1958-1962	170.00 to 235.00
Sea Harvest*	HN 2257	1969-1976	75.00 to 120.00
Seafarer	HN 2455	1972-1976	110.00 to 135.00
Seashore	HN 2263	1961-1965	190.00 to 240.00
Secret Thoughts	HN 2382	1971-Present	160.00
Serena	HN 1868	1938-1949	1200.00
Sergeant, 1st Continental Dragoons, Va.			
	HN 2844	1978	750.00
Sergeant, 6th Maryland Regt., 1777	HN 2815	1976	750.00
She Loves Me Not	HN 2045	1949-1962	95.00 to 125.00
Shepherd**	HN 751	1925-1938	700.00
Shepherd*	HN 1975	1945-1975	110.00 to 210.00
Shepherdess, Pink Bodice, Yellow Skirt			
	HN 750	1925-1938	700.00
Shepherdess, Purple Bodice, Blue Skirt**			
	HN 735	1925-1938	700.00
Shore Leave*	HN 2254	1965-1978	95.00 to 165.00
Shy Anne	HN 64	1916-1938	250.00
Sibell	HN 1668	1934-1949	375.00 to 400.00
Siesta	HN 1305	1928-1938	850.00
Silks And Ribbons	HN 2017	1949-Present	75.00 to 100.00
Silversmith Of Williamsburg	HN 2208	1960-Present	90.00 to 115.00
Simone	HN 2378	1971-Present	115.00 to 140.00
Sir Walter Raleigh	HN 1751	1936-1949	550.00 to 575.00

Shepherd Hn1975

Sea Harvest Hn2257

Shore Leave Hn2254

Sir Walter Raleigh Hn2015

Solitude Hn2810

Sir Walter Raleigh*	HN 2015	1948-1955	475.00 to 595.00
Skater	HN 2117	1953-1971	240.00 to 350.00
Sleepyhead	HN 2114	1953-1955	800.00 to 850.00
Snake Charmer	HN 1317	1929-1938	800.00
Soiree	HN 2312	1967-Present	115.00 to 140.00

Soldiers of the Revolution, see individual figurines

Solitude*	HN 2810	1977-Present	135.00 to 160.00
Sophie, Kate Greenaway Series	HN 2833	1977-Present	60.00
Southern Belle**	HN 2229	1958-Present	86.25 to 140.00
Spanish Lady	HN 1262	1927-1938	250.00
Spanish Lady	HN 1294	1928-1938	500.00 to 550.00
Spanish, Dancers Of The World**	HN 2831	1977	550.00

Spanish, Dancers Of The World Hn2831

Spring	HN 2085	1952-1959	285.00 to 450.00
Spring Flowers	HN 1807	1937-1959	195.00 to 325.00
Spring Morning, Green*	HN 1922	1940-1973	135.00 to 220.00
Spring Morning, Pink	HN 1923	1940-1949	165.00 to 225.00
St. George**	HN 2051	1950-Present	225.00
St. George**	HN 2067	1950-1976	185.00 to 210.00
St. George, Prestige Figure	HN 2856	1978-Present	6000.00
Stayed At Home	HN 2207	1958-1969	70.00 to 145.00
Stephanie*	HN 2807	1977-Present	85.00 to 140.00

Stiggins, see Dickens, Stiggins

Stitch In Time	HN 2352	1966-Present	75.00 to 100.00
Stop Press*	HN 2683	1977-Present	95.00 to 125.00
Suitor	HN 2132	1962-1971	295.00 to 375.00
Summer	HN 2086	1952-1959	285.00 to 450.00
Summer's Day	HN 2181	1957-1962	200.00 to 450.00

Spring Morning Hn1922

Stephanie Hn2807

Stop Press Hn2683

Sunday Best	HN 2206	1979-Present	195.00 to 235.00
Sunday Morning	HN 2184	1963-1969	250.00 to 400.00
Susan	HN 2056	1950-1959	265.00 to 310.00
Susanna	HN 1233	1927-1938	375.00 to 450.00
Suzette	HN 1487	1931-1950	250.00 to 325.00
Suzette	HN 2026	1949-1959	250.00 to 275.00
Sweet & Twenty**	HN 1298	1928-1969	165.00 to 250.00
Sweet & Twenty**	HN 1360	1929-1938	245.00 to 275.00
Sweet & Twenty**	HN 1589	1933-1949	250.00
Sweet & Twenty, Potted	HN 1610	1933-1938	195.00
Sweet Anne	M 5	1932-1945	235.00
Sweet Anne	M 6	1932-1945	235.00
Sweet Anne	HN 1318	1929-1949	145.00 to 200.00
Sweet Anne	HN 1330	1929-1949	150.00 to 250.00
Sweet Anne, Potted	HN 1330	1929-1930	250.00 to 295.00
Sweet Anne	HN 1331	1929-1949	210.00
Sweet Anne	HN 1496	1932-1967	130.00 to 190.00
Sweet April	HN 2215	1965-1967	275.00 to 400.00
Sweet Dreams	HN 2380	1971-Present	75.00 to 100.00
Sweet Lavender	HN 1373	1930-1949	375.00 to 400.00
Sweet Maid	HN 1505	1932-1938	340.00
Sweet Maid	HN 2092	1952-1955	200.00 to 400.00
Sweet Seventeen*	HN 2734	1975-Present	140.00
Sweet Sixteen	HN 2231	1958-1965	175.00 to 275.00
Sweeting*	HN 1935	1940-1973	75.00 to 99.00
Swimmer	HN 1270	1928-1938	600.00
Symphony	HN 2287	1961-1965	375.00 to 400.00
Tailor	HN 2174	1956-1959	450.00 to 750.00
Taking Things Easy*	HN 2677	1975-Present	150.00

Sweeting Hn1935

Sweet Seventeen Hn2734

Taking Things Easy Hn2677

Thanks Doc Hn2731

Tall Story	HN 2248	1968-1975	80.00 to 125.00
Tea Time	HN 2255	1972-Present	115.00
Teenager	HN 2203	1957-1962	200.00 to 275.00
Teresa, Red	HN 1682	1935-1949	550.00 to 600.00
Tess, Kate Greenaway Series	HN 2865	1978-Present	36.00
Tete-A-Tete	HN 799	1926-1938	475.00 to 550.00
Thanks Doc*	HN 2731	1975-Present	150.00
Thanksgiving	HN 2446	1972-1976	110.00 to 145.00
This Little Pig	HN 1793	1936-Present	37.50 to 60.00
Tildy	HN 1576	1933-1938	425.00 to 500.00
Tinkle Bell	HN 1677	1935-Present	40.00 to 50.00
Tinsmith	HN 2146	1962-1967	200.00 to 400.00

Tiny Tim, see Dickens, Tiny Tim

To Bed	HN 1805	1937-1959	90.00 to 125.00

Toinette, see Meryll
Tony Weller, see also Dickens, Tony Weller

Tony Weller	HN 684	1924-1938	495.00 to 800.00
Tootles*	HN 1680	1935-1975	50.00 to 115.00
Top O' The Hill	HN 1833	1937-1971	125.00 to 150.00
Top O' The Hill, Pink	HN 1849	1938-1975	110.00 to 140.00
Top O' The Hill, Red	HN 1834	1937-Present	95.00 to 115.00
Town Crier	HN 2119	1953-1976	140.00 to 175.00
Toymaker*	HN 2250	1959-1973	225.00 to 350.00
Tranquility, Black	HN 2426	1978	95.00
Tranquility, White	HN 2469	1978	95.00
Treasure Island*	HN 2243	1962-1975	75.00 to 110.00

Tootles Hn1680

Treasure Island Hn2243

Toymaker Hn2250

Trotty Veck, see Dickens, Trotty Veck

Tuppence A Bag	HN 2320	1968-Present	85.00 to 115.00
Twilight	HN 2256	1971-1976	90.00 to 180.00
Two-A-Penny	HN 1359	1929-1938	600.00 to 840.00
Uncle Ned	HN 2094	1952-1965	225.00

Uriah Heep, see also Dickens, Uriah Heep

Uriah Heep	HN 554	1923-1939	275.00 to 335.00
Uriah Heep	HN 2101	1952-1967	275.00 to 350.00
Valerie	HN 2107	1953-Present	60.00 to 75.00
Vanessa	HN 1836	1938-1949	375.00 to 400.00
Vanity	HN 2475	1973-Present	60.00 to 75.00
Veneta	HN 2722	1974-Present	140.00
Vera	HN 1729	1935-1938	335.00
Veronica	HN 1517	1932-1951	200.00 to 210.00
Veronica, Potted	HN 1517	1932-1951	210.00 to 275.00
Victoria	HN 2471	1973-Present	140.00
Victorian Lady	HN 727	1925-1938	175.00
Victorian Lady, Potted	HN 727	1925-1938	285.00
Victorian Lady	HN 728	1925-1952	170.00
Victorian Lady, Potted	HN 728	1925-1952	175.00 to 230.00
Victorian Lady	HN 1345	1929-1949	275.00
Viking	HN 2375	1973-1976	135.00 to 165.00

Viola D'Amore, Lady Musicians Series*

	HN 2797	1976	400.00
Violin, Lady Musicians Series*	HN 2432	1972	450.00 to 600.00
Virginals, Lady Musicians Series	HN 2427	1971	250.00
Vivienne	HN 2073	1951-1967	165.00 to 260.00
Votes For Women**	HN 2816	1978 Present	185.00
Wandering Minstrel	HN 1224	1927-1938	450.00 to 600.00
Wardrobe Mistress	HN 2145	1954-1967	350.00 to 425.00
Wayfarer	HN 2362	1970-1976	110.00 to 125.00
Wedding Morn	HN 1866	1938-1949	850.00
Wee Willie Winkie	HN 2050	1949-1953	190.00 to 200.00
Wendy	HN 2109	1953-Present	50.00 to 60.00
Wigmaker Of Williamsburg	HN 2239	1960-Present	115.00
Willy-Won't He, Potted	HN 1561	1933-1949	350.00 to 375.00
Willy-Won't He	HN 2150	1955-1959	275.00 to 325.00
Windflower	HN 2029	1949-1952	290.00 to 300.00
Windmill Lady	HN 1400	1930-1938	800.00
Winsome	HN 2220	1960-Present	115.00
Winter	HN 2088	1952-1959	285.00 to 450.00
Wistful	HN 2396	1979-Present	146.25 to 155.00
Wizard	HN 2877	1979-Present	115.00 to 155.00
Wood Nymph	HN 2192	1958-1962	170.00 to 235.00
Woodsman, Prototype		1978	675.00
Yardley's Old English Lavender		1925	450.00 to 650.00
Yeoman Of The Guard	HN 688	1924-1938	600.00
Young Love*	HN 2735	1975-Present	540.00
Young Miss Nightingale	HN 2010	1948-1953	500.00 to 600.00
Young Widow	HN 1399	1930-1930	650.00 to 700.00

Viola D'Amore, Lady Musicians Series Hn2797

Violin, Lady Musicians Series Hn2432

Young Love Hn2735

FIGURINES LISTED BY HN NUMBER

HN 3	Milking Time, Potted	1913-1938	1200.00
HN 6	Dunce	1913-1938	850.00 to 1000.00
HN 35	Charley's Aunt	1914-1938	400.00
HN 44	Lilac Shawl	1915-1938	800.00
HN 44	Lilac Shawl, Potted	1915-1938	940.00
HN 54	Lady Ermine	1916-1938	850.00
HN 64	Shy Anne	1916-1938	250.00
HN 71	Jester**	1917-1938	500.00
HN 72	Orange Vendor	1917-1938	600.00 to 950.00
HN 90	Doris Keene As Cavallini	1918-1936	800.00
HN 97	Mermaid	1918-1936	425.00 to 700.00
HN 98	Guy Fawkes*	1918-1949	650.00 to 950.00
HN 305	Scribe	1918-1936	800.00
HN 341	Katharine	1919-1938	300.00 to 600.00
HN 404	King Charles	1920-1951	525.00 to 575.00
HN 425	Goosegirl	1921-1938	1000.00
HN 428	Bouquet	1921-1938	350.00
HN 464	Captain MacHeath	1921-1949	550.00
HN 524	Lucy Lockett	1921-1949	495.00
HN 526	Beggar	1921-1949	450.00 to 500.00
HN 527	Highwayman	1921-1949	350.00
HN 527	Highwayman, Potted	1921-1949	475.00
HN 549	Polly Peachum, Pink, Curtsey	1922-1949	195.00 to 410.00
HN 550	Polly Peachum, Standing On Base	1922-1949	265.00 to 375.00
HN 554	Uriah Heep	1923-1939	275.00 to 335.00
HN 556	Mr. Pickwick	1923-1939	275.00 to 300.00
HN 557	Mr. Micawber	1923-1939	325.00 to 350.00

HN 564	Parson's Daughter	1923-1949	225.00 to 300.00
HN 571	Falstaff	1923-1938	600.00
HN 575	Falstaff	1923-1938	550.00 to 600.00
HN 577	Chelsea Pair, Female	1923-1938	475.00
HN 581	Perfect Pair	1923-1938	650.00 to 700.00
HN 583	Balloon Seller	1923-1949	295.00 to 375.00
HN 585	Harlequinade, Black, Green, Yellow	1923-1938	500.00
HN 585	Harlequinade, Black, Green, Yellow, Potted	1923-1938	550.00
HN 599	Masquerade, Male	1924-1949	550.00
HN 600	Masquerade, Female, Red	1924-1949	550.00
HN 603	Child Study	1924-1938	235.00 to 275.00
HN 608	Falstaff	1924-1938	600.00
HN 609	Falstaff	1924-1938	600.00
HN 610	Henry Lytton As Jack Point	1924-1949	700.00
HN 612	Poke Bonnet	1924-1938	750.00 to 800.00
HN 619	Falstaff	1924-1938	600.00
HN 635	Harlequinade, Gold	1924-1938	550.00 to 650.00
HN 638	Falstaff	1924-1938	600.00
HN 639	Elsie Maynard	1924-1949	600.00
HN 644	Pierrette	1924-1938	525.00 to 600.00
HN 657	Mask, White With Black Trim**	1924-1938	650.00
HN 66A	Curtsey	1916-1938	795.00 to 900.00
HN 667	Forty Thieves	1924-1938	425.00
HN 684	Tony Weller	1924-1938	495.00 to 800.00
HN 687	Bather, Naked	1924-1949	395.00 to 550.00
HN 688	Yeoman Of The Guard	1924-1938	600.00
HN 689	Chelsea Pensioner	1924-1938	850.00
HN 695	Lucy Lockett	1925-1949	550.00
HN 705	Gainsborough Hat	1925-1938	795.00
HN 715	Proposal, Lady, Red Dress**	1925-1938	60.00
HN 716	Proposal, Lady, White Dress	1925-1938	60.00
HN 719	Butterfly	1925-1938	500.00 to 550.00
HN 720	Butterfly*	1925-1938	595.00 to 625.00
HN 724	Mam'Selle	1925-1938	300.00 to 600.00
HN 725	Proposal, Male, Red Coat**	1925-1938	60.00
HN 727	Victorian Lady	1925-1938	175.00
HN 727	Victorian Lady, Potted	1925-1938	285.00
HN 728	Victorian Lady	1925-1952	170.00
HN 728	Victorian Lady, Potted	1925-1952	175.00 to 230.00
HN 729	Mask, Red With Black Squares**	1925-1938	650.00
HN 733	Mask, White With Black Squares	1925-1938	650.00
HN 735	Shepherdess, Purple Bodice, Blue Skirt**	1925-1938	700.00
HN 749	London Cry, Strawberries	1925-1938	600.00
HN 750	Shepherdess, Pink Bodice, Yellow Skirt	1925-1938	700.00
HN 751	Shepherd**	1925-1938	700.00

HN 752	London Cry, Turnips & Carrots	1925-1938	600.00
HN 755	Mephistopheles & Marguerite	1925-1949	1200.00 to 1400.00
HN 767	Irish Colleen	1925-1938	800.00
HN 771	London Cry, Turnips & Carrots	1925-1938	600.00
HN 772	London Cry, Strawberries	1925-1938	600.00
HN 779	Geisha	1919-1938	550.00
HN 779	Geisha, Potted	1919-1938	550.00 to 1000.00
HN 780	Harlequinade, Pink, Blue, Black, Orange		
		1926-1938	575.00
HN 785	Mask, Blue With Pink Stripes	1926-1938	650.00
HN 788	Proposal, Lady, Pink Dress	1926-1938	60.00
HN 789	Flower Seller	1926-1938	425.00
HN 799	Tete-A-Tete	1926-1938	475.00 to 550.00
HN 1204	Angela, Potted	1926-1938	425.00
HN 1206	Flower Seller's Children**	1926-1949	365.00 to 450.00
HN 1209	Proposal, Male, Blue Coat	1926-1938	60.00
HN 1212	Boy With Turban	1926-1938	265.00 to 365.00
HN 1216	Falstaff	1926-1949	600.00
HN 1220	Lido Lady	1927-1938	500.00
HN 1224	Wandering Minstrel	1927-1938	450.00 to 600.00
HN 1233	Susanna	1927-1938	375.00 to 450.00
HN 1252	Kathleen	1927-1938	475.00
HN 1259	Alchemist	1927-1938	120.00 to 135.00
HN 1262	Spanish Lady	1927-1938	250.00
HN 1265	Lady Fayre	1928-1938	450.00 to 500.00
HN 1267	Carmen	1928-1938	450.00
HN 1270	Swimmer	1928-1938	600.00
HN 1271	Mask, Black With Blue, Yellow Dots**	1928-1938	650.00
HN 1279	Kathleen	1928-1938	395.00
HN 1281	Scotties, Potted	1928-1938	575.00
HN 1294	Spanish Lady	1928-1938	500.00 to 550.00
HN 1295	Jester	1928-1949	500.00
HN 1296	Columbine	1928-1938	500.00
HN 1297	Columbine	1928-1938	500.00
HN 1298	Sweet & Twenty**	1928-1969	165.00 to 250.00
HN 1305	Siesta	1928-1938	850.00
HN 1315	Old Balloon Seller*	1929-Present	95.00 to 125.00
HN 1317	Snake Charmer	1929-1938	800.00
HN 1318	Sweet Anne	1929-1949	145.00 to 200.00
HN 1319	Darling	1929-1959	26.50 to 125.00
HN 1320	Rosamund	1929-1938	900.00 to 3000.00
HN 1330	Sweet Anne	1929-1949	150.00 to 250.00
HN 1330	Sweet Anne, Potted	1929-1930	250.00 to 295.00
HN 1331	Sweet Anne	1929-1949	210.00
HN 1337	Priscilla	1929-1938	350.00
HN 1340	Priscilla	1929-1949	240.00 to 325.00
HN 1340	Priscilla, Potted	1929-1949	265.00 to 375.00
HN 1341	Marietta	1929-1949	450.00 to 550.00

HN 1341	Marietta, Potted	1929-1949	450.00 to 550.00
HN 1342	Flower Seller's Children	1929-Present	200.00 to 300.00
HN 1345	Victorian Lady	1929-1949	275.00
HN 1349	Scotties	1929-1949	315.00
HN 1357	Kathleen	1929-1938	550.00
HN 1358	Rosina	1929-1938	425.00 to 450.00
HN 1359	Two-A-Penny	1929-1938	600.00 to 840.00
HN 1360	Sweet & Twenty**	1929-1938	245.00 to 275.00
HN 1362	Pantalettes, Green Skirt	1929-1938	190.00 to 325.00
HN 1362	Pantalettes, Green Skirt, Potted	1929-1938	365.00
HN 1364	Rosina	1929-1938	395.00
HN 1365	Mendicant	1929-1969	195.00 to 225.00
HN 1368	Rose	1930-Present	35.00 to 70.00
HN 1370	Marie	1930-Present	35.00 to 50.00
HN 1373	Sweet Lavender	1930-1949	375.00 to 400.00
HN 1392	Paisley Shawl, Potted	1930-1949	325.00
HN 1392	Paisley Shawl, 6 In.	1930-1949	275.00
HN 1392	Paisley Shawl, 9 In.	1930-1949	275.00
HN 1397	Gretchen	1933-1938	500.00
HN 1398	Derrick	1930-1938	250.00 to 600.00
HN 1399	Young Widow	1930-1930	650.00 to 700.00
HN 1400	Windmill Lady	1930-1938	800.00
HN 1402	Miss Demure, Potted*	1930-1975	175.00 to 225.00
HN 1412	Pantalettes, Pink Skirt	1930-1949	350.00
HN 1413	Margery	1930-1949	280.00 to 400.00
HN 1414	Patricia, Yellow	1930-1949	395.00
HN 1420	Phyllis	1930-1949	325.00 to 395.00
HN 1421	Barbara	1930-1938	475.00
HN 1422	Joan	1930-1949	195.00
HN 1427	Darby	1930-1949	195.00
HN 1428	Calumet*	1930-1949	650.00
HN 1429	Gossips	1930-1949	170.00
HN 1432	Barbara	1930-1938	500.00
HN 1433	Little Bridesmaid	1930-1951	115.00 to 195.00
HN 1434	Little Bridesmaid	1930-1949	110.00
HN 1444	Pauline	1931-1938	290.00 to 350.00
HN 1445	Biddy	1931-1938	155.00 to 250.00
HN 1446	Marietta, Potted	1931-1949	575.00
HN 1449	Little Mistress	1931-1949	285.00 to 325.00
HN 1462	Patricia, Green	1931-1938	225.00
HN 1464	Carpet Seller*	1931-1969	175.00 to 250.00
HN 1465	Lady Clare	1931-1938	400.00 to 500.00
HN 1467	Monica	1931-Present	50.00 to 75.00
HN 1470	Chloe	1931-1949	235.00 to 275.00
HN 1470	Chloe, Potted	1931-1949	325.00
HN 1479	Chloe	1931-1949	225.00
HN 1482	Pearly Boy	1931-1949	275.00
HN 1483	Pearly Girl	1931-1949	150.00 to 175.00

HN 1485	Greta	1931-1953	150.00 to 165.00
HN 1487	Suzette	1931-1950	250.00 to 325.00
HN 1488	Gloria	1932-1938	425.00
HN 1490	Dorcas	1932-1938	225.00
HN 1491	Dorcas	1932-1938	350.00
HN 1491	Dorcas, Potted	1932-1938	250.00
HN 1493	Potter	1932-Present	175.00 to 275.00
HN 1495	Priscilla	1932-1949	350.00
HN 1496	Sweet Anne	1932-1967	130.00 to 190.00
HN 1502	Lucy Ann	1932-1951	190.00 to 250.00
HN 1505	Sweet Maid	1932-1938	340.00
HN 1507	Pantalettes, Yellow Dress	1932-1949	390.00
HN 1508	Helen	1932-1938	600.00
HN 1513	Biddy	1932-1951	150.00
HN 1513	Biddy, Potted	1932-1951	190.00 to 195.00
HN 1514	Dolly Vardon	1932-1938	450.00
HN 1517	Veronica	1932-1951	200.00 to 210.00
HN 1517	Veronica, Potted	1932-1951	210.00 to 275.00
HN 1525	Clarissa	1932-1938	525.00 to 650.00
HN 1528	Bluebeard, Red	1932-1949	550.00
HN 1537	Janet	1932-Present	90.00 to 185.00
HN 1538	Janet	1932-1949	295.00
HN 1539	Saucy Nymph	1933-1949	195.00 to 215.00
HN 1542	Little Child So Rare And Sweet	1933-1949	260.00
HN 1543	Dancing Eyes & Sunny Hair	1933-1949	150.00
HN 1545	Called Love, A Little Boy	1933-1949	225.00
HN 1546	Here A Little Child I Stand	1933-1949	225.00
HN 1547	Pearly Boy	1933-1949	210.00
HN 1550	Annette	1933-1949	275.00 to 350.00
HN 1556	Rosina	1933-1938	425.00
HN 1558	Dorcas	1933-1952	175.00 to 270.00
HN 1561	Willy-Won't He, Potted	1933-1949	350.00 to 375.00
HN 1566	Estelle	1933-1938	500.00
HN 1567	Patricia, Red	1933-1949	425.00 to 450.00
HN 1573	Rhoda	1933-1949	575.00
HN 1575	Daisy	1933-1949	175.00
HN 1576	Tildy	1933-1938	425.00 to 500.00
HN 1578	Hinged Parasol	1933-1949	300.00
HN 1579	Hinged Parasol	1933-1949	450.00
HN 1586	Camille, Potted	1933-1949	475.00
HN 1587	Fleurette	1933-1949	290.00 to 395.00
HN 1589	Sweet & Twenty**	1933-1949	250.00
HN 1598	Clothilde	1933-1949	435.00
HN 1600	Bride	1933-1949	200.00 to 475.00
HN 1606	Falstaff**	1933-1949	600.00
HN 1607	Cerise	1933-1949	200.00 to 215.00
HN 1610	Sweet & Twenty, Potted	1933-1938	195.00
HN 1619	Maisie	1934-1939	275.00 to 395.00

HN 1620	Rosabell	1934-1938	550.00
HN 1621	Irene	1934-1951	195.00 to 275.00
HN 1626	Bonnie Lassie	1934-1953	195.00 to 325.00
HN 1627	Curly Knob	1934-1949	350.00 to 450.00
HN 1628	Margot	1934-1938	425.00
HN 1632	Gentlewoman	1934-1949	385.00
HN 1633	Clemency	1935-1938	360.00 to 425.00
HN 1639	Dainty May	1934-1949	175.00 to 235.00
HN 1647	Granny's Shawl	1934-1949	250.00 to 290.00
HN 1648	Camille	1934-1949	190.00 to 420.00
HN 1665	Miss Winsome	1934-1949	395.00 to 425.00
HN 1668	Sibell	1934-1949	375.00 to 400.00
HN 1677	Tinkle Bell	1935-Present	40.00 to 50.00
HN 1678	Dinky Do	1934-Present	29.50 to 50.00
HN 1679	Babie*	1935-Present	40.00 to 50.00
HN 1680	Tootles*	1935-1975	50.00 to 115.00
HN 1682	Teresa, Red	1935-1949	550.00 to 600.00
HN 1685	Cynthia	1935-1949	550.00
HN 1689	Calumet	1935-1949	350.00 to 750.00
HN 1690	June	1935-1949	285.00
HN 1691	June	1935-1949	275.00 to 350.00
HN 1706	Cobbler	1935-1969	175.00 to 325.00
HN 1708	Bather, Painted Bathing Suit**	1935-1938	900.00
HN 1712	Daffy Down Dilly*	1935-1975	155.00 to 240.00
HN 1713	Daffy Down Dilly	1935-1949	155.00 to 275.00
HN 1719	Kate Hardcastle	1935-1949	375.00 to 475.00
HN 1724	Ruby	1935-1949	195.00
HN 1727	Celia, Green	1935-1949	675.00
HN 1729	Vera	1935-1938	335.00
HN 1731	Daydreams	1935-Present	65.00 to 115.00
HN 1747	Afternoon Tea	1935-Present	122.00 to 235.00
HN 1750	Folly	1936-1949	845.00 to 1050.00
HN 1751	Sir Walter Raleigh	1936-1949	550.00 to 575.00
HN 1754	Eleanore	1936-1949	225.00
HN 1756	Lizana	1936-1949	500.00
HN 1759	Orange Lady, Pink*	1936-1975	115.00 to 225.00
HN 1760	Four O'Clock	1936-1949	550.00
HN 1762	Bride	1936-1949	300.00 to 425.00
HN 1765	Chloe	1936-1950	165.00 to 275.00
HN 1768	Ivy	1936-1978	35.00 to 50.00
HN 1770	Maureen, Pink	1936-1959	175.00 to 250.00
HN 1772	Delight	1936-1967	110.00 to 200.00
HN 1793	This Little Pig	1936-Present	37.50 to 60.00
HN 1796	Hazel	1936-1949	300.00
HN 1797	Hazel	1936-1949	225.00
HN 1798	Lily*	1936-1949	75.00 to 130.00
HN 1805	To Bed	1937-1959	90.00 to 125.00
HN 1807	Spring Flowers	1937-1959	195.00 to 325.00

HN 1809	Cissie	1937-Present	45.00 to 75.00
HN 1811	Bo Peep	1937-Present	42.00 to 75.00
HN 1833	Top O' The Hill	1937-1971	125.00 to 150.00
HN 1834	Top O' The Hill, Red	1937-Present	95.00 to 115.00
HN 1836	Vanessa	1938-1949	375.00 to 400.00
HN 1843	Biddy-Penny-Farthing	1938-Present	125.00
HN 1844	Odds & Ends	1938-1949	600.00
HN 1849	Top O' The Hill, Pink	1938-1975	110.00 to 140.00
HN 1855	Memories	1938-1949	270.00 to 350.00
HN 1858	Dawn	1938-1949	600.00
HN 1862	Jasmine	1938-1949	500.00
HN 1866	Wedding Morn	1938-1949	850.00
HN 1868	Serena	1938-1949	1200.00
HN 1872	Annabella	1938-1949	395.00 to 425.00
HN 1880	Lambeth Walk	1938-1949	800.00 to 900.00
HN 1882	Nell Gwynn	1938-1949	500.00
HN 1885	Nadine, Green	1938-1949	350.00
HN 1886	Nadine, Purple	1938-1949	425.00
HN 1890	Lambing Time	1938-Present	75.00 to 100.00
HN 1893	Fat Boy	1938-1952	400.00
HN 1900	Midsummer Noon	1939-1949	425.00
HN 1901	Penelope	1939-1975	250.00 to 325.00
HN 1903	Rhythm	1939-1949	600.00
HN 1907	Lydia	1939-1949	245.00
HN 1908	Lydia	1939-Present	48.00 to 80.00
HN 1909	Honey	1939-1949	295.00 to 360.00
HN 1910	Honey	1939-1949	375.00
HN 1911	Autumn Breezes, Pink	1939-1976	100.00 to 125.00
HN 1913	Autumn Breezes, Green	1939-1971	96.00 to 175.00
HN 1916	Janet	1939-1949	125.00
HN 1917	Meryll, Also Called Toinetie	1939-1940	700.00
HN 1919	Kate Hardcastle	1939-1949	550.00
HN 1922	Spring Morning, Green*	1940-1973	135.00 to 220.00
HN 1923	Spring Morning, Pink	1940-1949	165.00 to 225.00
HN 1925	Fiona	1940-1949	500.00
HN 1926	Roseanna	1940-1959	250.00 to 350.00
HN 1928	Marguerite	1940-1959	200.00 to 325.00
HN 1933	Fiona	1940-1949	645.00
HN 1934	Autumn Breezes, Red	1940-Present	72.00 to 115.00
HN 1935	Sweeting*	1940-1973	75.00 to 99.00
HN 1936	Miss Muffet, Red	1940-1967	125.00 to 175.00
HN 1937	Miss Muffet, Green	1940-1952	95.00 to 225.00
HN 1941	Peggy	1940-1949	98.00
HN 1942	Pyjams	1940-1949	325.00
HN 1944	Daydreams	1940-1949	270.00
HN 1946	Marguerite	1940-1949	225.00 to 265.00
HN 1948	Lady Charmian	1940-1973	150.00 to 200.00
HN 1949	Lady Charmian*	1940-1973	150.00 to 225.00

HN 1951	Claribel .	1940-1949	210.00 to 265.00
HN 1953	Orange Lady, Green	1940-1975	150.00 to 225.00
HN 1954	Balloon Man*	1940-Present	65.00 to 125.00
HN 1955	Lavinia	1940-1978	45.00 to 85.00
HN 1957	New Bonnet	1940-1949	350.00 to 450.00
HN 1958	Lady April	1940-1959	225.00 to 350.00
HN 1961	Daisy	1941-1949	195.00
HN 1962	Genevieve*	1941-1975	135.00 to 225.00
HN 1967	Lady Betty	1941-1951	275.00 to 425.00
HN 1972	Regency Beau	1941-1949	800.00
HN 1973	Corinthian	1941-1949	800.00
HN 1974	Forty Winks*	1945-1973	135.00 to 250.00
HN 1975	Shepherd*	1945-1975	110.00 to 210.00
HN 1976	Easter Day	1945-1951	205.00 to 325.00
HN 1977	Her Ladyship	1945-1959	195.00 to 275.00
HN 1978	Bedtime	1945-Present	20.00 to 40.00
HN 1979	Gollywog	1945-1959	150.00 to 185.00
HN 1980	Gwynneth	1945-1952	245.00 to 370.00
HN 1981	Ermine Coat	1945-1967	150.00 to 250.00
HN 1982	Sabbath Morn	1945-1959	195.00 to 250.00
HN 1983	Rosebud	1945-1952	285.00 to 395.00
HN 1984	Patchwork Quilt	1945-1959	250.00 to 365.00
HN 1985	Darling	1946-Present	40.00
HN 1986	Diana	1946-1975	75.00
HN 1987	Paisley Shawl	1946-1959	175.00 to 225.00
HN 1988	Paisley Shawl*	1946-1975	95.00 to 200.00
HN 1989	Margaret	1947-1959	200.00 to 275.00
HN 1990	Mary Jane	1947-1959	200.00 to 400.00
HN 1991	Country Lass*	1975-Present	52.50 to 100.00
HN 1991	Market Day	1947-1955	300.00 to 365.00
HN 1992	Christmas Morn	1947-Present	65.00 to 115.00
HN 1993	Griselda	1947-1953	395.00
HN 1994	Karen	1947-1955	275.00 to 375.00
HN 1995	Olivia	1947-1951	350.00 to 425.00
HN 1996	Prue	1947-1955	200.00 to 345.00
HN 1997	Belle O' The Ball	1947-1978	100.00 to 175.00
HN 1999	Collinette	1947-1949	300.00 to 395.00
HN 2001	Jacqueline	1947-1951	395.00
HN 2002	Bess, Red	1947-1969	150.00 to 250.00
HN 2004	A'Courting	1947-1953	420.00 to 490.00
HN 2005	Henrietta Maria	1948-1953	450.00 to 550.00
HN 2006	Lady Anne Nevill	1948-1953	1000.00
HN 2007	Mrs. Fitzherbert	1948-1953	1000.00
HN 2008	Philippa Of Hainault	1948-1953	550.00
HN 2009	Eleanor Of Provence	1948-1953	450.00
HN 2010	Young Miss Nightingale	1948-1953	500.00 to 600.00
HN 2011	Matilda	1948-1953	475.00 to 695.00
HN 2014	Jane*	1948-1951	350.00

HN 2015	Sir Walter Raleigh*	1948-1955	475.00 to 595.00
HN 2016	Jester	1949-Present	82.00 to 150.00
HN 2017	Silks And Ribbons	1949-Present	75.00 to 100.00
HN 2019	Minuet, White	1949-1971	225.00 to 290.00
HN 2020	Deidre	1949-1955	275.00 to 350.00
HN 2022	Janice	1949-1955	295.00 to 395.00
HN 2023	Joan	1949-1959	195.00 to 250.00
HN 2024	Darby	1949-1959	250.00
HN 2025	Gossips	1949-1967	235.00 to 325.00
HN 2026	Suzette	1949-1959	250.00 to 275.00
HN 2028	Kate Hardcastle	1949-1952	450.00 to 495.00
HN 2029	Windflower	1949-1952	290.00 to 300.00
HN 2030	Memories	1949-1959	285.00 to 400.00
HN 2031	Granny's Heritage	1949-1969	325.00 to 450.00
HN 2032	Jean	1949-1959	195.00 to 275.00
HN 2033	Midsummer Noon	1949-1955	395.00
HN 2035	Pearly Boy	1949-1959	125.00 to 265.00
HN 2037	Goody Two Shoes	1949-Present	45.00 to 70.00
HN 2038	Peggy	1949-1978	45.00 to 55.00
HN 2039	Easter Day	1949-1969	185.00 to 295.00
HN 2040	Gollywog	1949-1959	200.00
HN 2042	Owd Willum*	1949-1973	150.00 to 200.00
HN 2043	Poacher	1949-1959	250.00 to 295.00
HN 2044	Mary Mary*	1949-1973	110.00 to 150.00
HN 2045	She Loves Me Not	1949-1962	95.00 to 125.00
HN 2046	He Loves Me	1949-1962	110.00
HN 2047	Once Upon A Time	1949-1955	130.00 to 230.00
HN 2048	Mary Had A Little Lamb	1949-Present	55.00 to 75.00
HN 2049	Curly Locks	1949-1953	175.00 to 265.00
HN 2050	Wee Willie Winkie	1949-1953	190.00 to 200.00
HN 2051	St. George**	1950-Present	225.00
HN 2052	Grandma	1950-1959	265.00 to 325.00
HN 2053	Gaffer	1950-1959	325.00 to 425.00
HN 2054	Falstaff	1950-Present	57.00 to 100.00
HN 2055	Leisure Hour	1950-1965	345.00 to 400.00
HN 2056	Susan	1950-1959	265.00 to 310.00
HN 2057	Jersey Milkmaid, Blue	1950-1959	150.00 to 195.00
HN 2057	Milkmaid, Green*	1975-Present	100.00
HN 2058	Hermione	1950-1952	700.00
HN 2059	Bedtime Story	1950-Present	90.00 to 160.00
HN 2060	Jack*	1950-1971	80.00 to 120.00
HN 2061	Jill*	1950-1971	60.00 to 100.00
HN 2062	Little Boy Blue*	1950-1973	80.00 to 100.00
HN 2063	Little Jack Horner	1950-1953	220.00
HN 2065	Blithe Morning, Red	1950-1973	115.00 to 165.00
HN 2066	Minuet, Red	1950-1955	375.00 to 385.00
HN 2067	St. George**	1950-1976	185.00 to 210.00
HN 2068	Calumet	1950-1953	350.00 to 675.00

HN 2069	Farmer's Wife	1951-1955	400.00 to 500.00
HN 2071	Bernice	1951-1953	300.00 to 600.00
HN 2072	Rocking Horse	1951-1953	950.00 to 1400.00
HN 2073	Vivienne	1951-1967	165.00 to 260.00
HN 2074	Marianne	1951-1953	385.00
HN 2075	French Peasant	1951-1955	425.00 to 500.00
HN 2077	Rowena	1951-1955	250.00 to 525.00
HN 2078	Elfreda	1951-1955	425.00 to 600.00
HN 2079	Damaris	1951-1952	800.00
HN 2080	Jack Point, Prestige Figure	1952-Present	1200.00
HN 2081	Princess Badoura**	1952-Present	xxxx
HN 2082	Moor, Prestige Figure	1952-Present	1200.00
HN 2084	King Charles, Prestige Figure	1952-Present	1200.00
HN 2085	Spring	1952-1959	285.00 to 450.00
HN 2086	Summer	1952-1959	285.00 to 450.00
HN 2087	Autumn	1952-1959	325.00 to 450.00
HN 2088	Winter	1952-1959	285.00 to 450.00
HN 2089	Judith	1952-1959	200.00 to 350.00
HN 2090	Midinette	1952-1965	195.00 to 325.00
HN 2091	Rosemary	1952-1959	325.00 to 400.00
HN 2092	Sweet Maid	1952-1955	200.00 to 400.00
HN 2093	Georgiana	1952-1955	250.00
HN 2094	Uncle Ned	1952-1965	225.00
HN 2096	Fat Boy	1952-1967	300.00
HN 2097	Mr. Micawber	1952-1967	235.00 to 325.00
HN 2098	Pecksniff	1952-1967	275.00 to 365.00
HN 2099	Mr. Pickwick	1952-1967	235.00 to 325.00
HN 2100	Sairey Gamp	1952-1967	265.00 to 300.00
HN 2101	Uriah Heep	1952-1967	275.00 to 350.00
HN 2102	Pied Piper	1953-1976	140.00 to 195.00
HN 2103	Mask Seller	1953-Present	78.00 to 125.00
HN 2104	Abdullah*	1953-1962	475.00 to 510.00
HN 2105	Bluebeard, Green	1953-Present	158.00 to 275.00
HN 2106	Linda	1953-1976	60.00 to 85.00
HN 2107	Valerie	1953-Present	60.00 to 75.00
HN 2108	Baby Bunting	1953-1959	130.00 to 185.00
HN 2109	Wendy	1953-Present	50.00 to 60.00
HN 2110	Christmas Time	1953-1967	275.00 to 385.00
HN 2111	Betsy	1953-1959	225.00 to 375.00
HN 2112	Carolyn	1953-1965	195.00 to 285.00
HN 2113	Maytime	1953-1967	195.00 to 325.00
HN 2114	Sleepyhead	1953-1955	800.00 to 850.00
HN 2115	Coppelia	1953-1959	250.00 to 500.00
HN 2116	Ballerina	1953-1973	165.00 to 250.00
HN 2117	Skater	1953-1971	240.00 to 350.00
HN 2118	Good King Wenceslas	1953-1976	150.00 to 195.00
HN 2119	Town Crier	1953-1976	140.00 to 175.00
HN 2128	River Boy*	1962-1975	70.00 to 95.00

HN 2132	Suitor	1962-1971	295.00 to 375.00
HN 2133	Faraway	1958-1962	133.25 to 195.00
HN 2134	Old King	1954-Present	350.00
HN 2135	Gay Morning	1954-1967	185.00 to 350.00
HN 2136	Delphine	1954-1967	195.00 to 275.00
HN 2137	Lilac Time	1954-1969	185.00 to 325.00
HN 2138	La Sylphide**	1956-1965	395.00
HN 2139	Giselle**	1954-1969	275.00 to 350.00
HN 2140	Giselle, Forest Glade**	1954-1965	315.00 to 350.00
HN 2141	Bunny	1954-1975	60.00 to 75.00
HN 2141	Choir Boy	1954-1975	45.00 to 95.00
HN 2142	Rag Doll	1952-Present	60.00
HN 2143	Friar Tuck	1954-Present	300.00 to 525.00
HN 2144	Jovial Monk*	1954-1976	105.00 to 155.00
HN 2145	Wardrobe Mistress	1954-1967	350.00 to 425.00
HN 2146	Tinsmith	1962-1967	200.00 to 400.00
HN 2148	Bridesmaid	1955-1959	210.00 to 250.00
HN 2149	Love Letter*	1958-1976	145.00 to 195.00
HN 2150	Willy-Won't He	1955-1959	275.00 to 325.00
HN 2151	Mother's Helper	1962-1969	100.00 to 200.00
HN 2153	One That Got Away	1955-1959	265.00
HN 2154	Child Of Williamsburg	1964-Present	45.00 to 60.00
HN 2156	Polka	1955-1969	195.00 to 250.00
HN 2157	Gypsy Dance	1955-1957	250.00 to 400.00
HN 2159	Fortune Teller	1955-1967	375.00 to 425.00
HN 2161	Hornpipe	1955-1962	575.00
HN 2162	Foaming Quart	1955-Present	75.00 to 115.00
HN 2166	Bride	1956-1976	100.00 to 185.00
HN 2167	Home Again	1956-Present	60.00 to 90.00
HN 2168	Esmeralda	1956-1959	275.00 to 325.00
HN 2169	Dimity	1956-1959	310.00 to 325.00
HN 2170	Invitation	1956-1975	60.00 to 125.00
HN 2171	Fiddler	1956-1962	600.00 to 800.00
HN 2172	Jolly Sailor	1956-1965	500.00 to 550.00
HN 2173	Organ Grinder	1956-1965	550.00
HN 2174	Tailor	1956-1959	450.00 to 750.00
HN 2175	Beggar	1956-1962	415.00 to 500.00
HN 2177	My Teddy	1962-1967	195.00 to 250.00
HN 2178	Enchantment	1957-Present	67.00 to 115.00
HN 2179	Noelle	1957-1967	200.00 to 400.00
HN 2181	Summer's Day	1957-1962	200.00 to 450.00
HN 2183	Boy From Williamsburg	1969-Present	60.00
HN 2184	Sunday Morning	1963-1969	250.00 to 400.00
HN 2185	Columbine	1957-1969	125.00 to 150.00
HN 2186	Harlequin	1957-1969	125.00 to 195.00
HN 2191	Sea	1958-1962	170.00 to 235.00
HN 2192	Wood Nymph	1958-1962	170.00 to 235.00
HN 2193	Fair Lady, Green	1963-Present	115.00

HN 2202	Melody	1957-1962	145.00 to 325.00
HN 2203	Teenager	1957-1962	200.00 to 275.00
HN 2204	Long John Silver	1957-1965	325.00 to 435.00
HN 2205	Master Sweep	1957-1962	495.00 to 525.00
HN 2206	Sunday Best	1979-Present	195.00 to 235.00
HN 2207	Stayed At Home	1958-1969	70.00 to 145.00
HN 2208	Silversmith Of Williamsburg	1960-Present	90.00 to 115.00
HN 2209	Hostess Of Williamsburg	1960-Present	75.00 to 115.00
HN 2210	Debutante	1963-1967	220.00 to 285.00
HN 2211	Fair Maiden	1967-Present	45.00 to 75.00
HN 2212	Rendezvous*	1962-1971	310.00
HN 2215	Sweet April	1965-1967	275.00 to 400.00
HN 2216	Pirouette	1959-1967	190.00 to 200.00
HN 2217	Old King Cole	1963-1967	625.00 to 900.00
HN 2218	Cookie*	1958-1975	75.00
HN 2220	Winsome	1960-Present	115.00
HN 2221	Nanny	1958-Present	71.50 to 125.00
HN 2223	Schoolmarm	1958-Present	72.50 to 95.00
HN 2225	Make Believe	1962-Present	65.00 to 80.00
HN 2226	Cellist	1960-1967	350.00 to 465.00
HN 2227	Gentleman From Williamsburg	1960-Present	75.00 to 115.00
HN 2228	Lady From Williamsburg	1960-Present	79.50 to 115.00
HN 2229	Southern Belle**	1958-Present	86.25 to 140.00
HN 2230	Gypsy Dance	1959-1971	195.00 to 335.00
HN 2231	Sweet Sixteen	1958-1965	175.00 to 275.00
HN 2233	Royal Governor's Cook, Williamsburg*		
		1960-Present	115.00
HN 2234	Michelle*	1967-Present	70.00 to 95.00
HN 2235	Dancing Years*	1965-1971	255.00 to 300.00
HN 2237	Celeste*	1959-1971	135.00 to 165.00
HN 2238	My Pet*	1962-1975	95.00 to 175.00
HN 2239	Wigmaker Of Williamsburg	1960-Present	115.00
HN 2240	Blacksmith Of Williamsburg	1960-Present	75.00 to 115.00
HN 2242	First Steps	1959-1965	400.00 to 450.00
HN 2243	Treasure Island*	1962-1975	75.00 to 110.00
HN 2244	Newsboy	1959-1965	395.00 to 550.00
HN 2245	Basket Weaver	1959-1962	400.00
HN 2246	Cradle Song	1959-1962	275.00 to 400.00
HN 2247	Omar Khayyam*	1965-Present	65.00 to 115.00
HN 2248	Tall Story	1968-1975	80.00 to 125.00
HN 2249	Favourite	1960-Present	85.00 to 115.00
HN 2250	Toymaker*	1959-1973	225.00 to 350.00
HN 2251	Masquerade, Female, Grey	1960-1965	225.00 to 265.00
HN 2253	Puppetmaker	1962-1973	295.00 to 375.00
HN 2254	Shore Leave*	1965-1978	95.00 to 165.00
HN 2255	Tea Time	1972-Present	115.00
HN 2256	Twilight	1971-1976	90.00 to 180.00
HN 2257	Sea Harvest*	1969-1976	75.00 to 120.00

HN 2258	Good Catch	1966-Present	60.00 to 115.00
HN 2259	Masquerade, Female, Red	1960-1965	225.00 to 265.00
HN 2260	Captain	1965-Present	175.00
HN 2262	Lights Out	1965-1969	200.00
HN 2263	Seashore	1961-1965	190.00 to 240.00
HN 2264	Elegance	1961-Present	67.00 to 115.00
HN 2266	Ballad Seller	1968-1973	165.00 to 275.00
HN 2267	Rhapsody	1961-1973	175.00 to 220.00
HN 2268	Daphne	1963-1975	135.00 to 175.00
HN 2269	Leading Lady	1965-1976	100.00 to 115.00
HN 2271	Melanie	1965-Present	85.00 to 140.00
HN 2272	Repose	1972-1978	120.00 to 175.00
HN 2273	Denise*	1964-1971	150.00 to 275.00
HN 2274	Golden Days	1964-1973	115.00 to 145.00
HN 2275	Sandra*	1969-Present	115.00
HN 2276	Heart To Heart*	1961-1971	340.00 to 369.00
HN 2279	Clockmaker	1961-1975	150.00 to 200.00
HN 2280	Mayor	1963-1971	275.00 to 325.00
HN 2281	Professor	1965-Present	95.00 to 125.00
HN 2282	Coachman*	1963-1971	325.00 to 450.00
HN 2283	Dreamweaver	1972-1976	115.00 to 130.00
HN 2284	Craftsman	1961-1965	465.00 to 500.00
HN 2287	Symphony	1961-1965	375.00 to 400.00
HN 2304	Adrienne, Blue	1964-Present	65.00 to 115.00
HN 2306	Reverie	1964-Present	155.00 to 185.00
HN 2307	Coralie	1964-Present	65.00 to 115.00
HN 2308	Picnic	1965-Present	49.00 to 80.00
HN 2309	Buttercup	1964-Present	65.00 to 115.00
HN 2310	Lisa*	1969-Present	70.00 to 140.00
HN 2311	Lorna*	1965-Present	50.00 to 90.00
HN 2312	Soiree	1967-Present	115.00 to 140.00
HN 2314	Old Mother Hubbard*	1964-1975	135.00 to 190.00
HN 2315	Last Waltz	1967-Present	75.00 to 140.00
HN 2317	Lobster Man	1964-Present	53.00 to 85.00
HN 2318	Grace	1966-Present	67.00 to 115.00
HN 2319	Bachelor*	1964-1975	95.00 to 198.00
HN 2320	Tuppence A Bag	1968-Present	85.00 to 115.00
HN 2321	Family Album*	1966-1973	120.00 to 225.00
HN 2322	Cup Of Tea	1964-Present	55.00 to 100.00
HN 2324	Matador And Bull, Prestige Figure	1964-Present	7000.00
HN 2325	Master*	1967-Present	85.00 to 115.00
HN 2326	Antoinette	1967-1978	79.00 to 105.00
HN 2327	Katrina	1965-1969	225.00 to 350.00
HN 2329	Lynne	1971-Present	77.00 to 140.00
HN 2330	Meditation	1971-Present	115.00 to 185.00
HN 2331	Cello, Lady Musicians Series	1970	300.00
HN 2334	Fragrance*	1966-Present	63.00 to 140.00
HN 2335	Hilary*	1967-Present	140.00

HN 2336	Alison	1966-Present	67.00 to 115.00
HN 2337	Loretta	1966-Present	65.00 to 115.00
HN 2338	Penny	1968-Present	25.00 to 50.00
HN 2339	My Love	1969-Present	90.00 to 140.00
HN 2340	Belle	1968-Present	28.00 to 50.00
HN 2341	Cherie	1966-Present	45.00 to 75.00
HN 2343	Premiere*	1969-1978	175.00 to 200.00
HN 2345	Clarissa	1968-Present	140.00
HN 2347	Nina*	1969-1976	90.00 to 115.00
HN 2348	Geraldine	1972-1976	95.00 to 145.00
HN 2349	Flora*	1966-1973	155.00 to 225.00
HN 2352	Stitch In Time	1966-Present	75.00 to 100.00
HN 2359	Detective*	1977-Present	54.00 to 115.00
HN 2361	Laird*	1969-Present	60.00 to 125.00
HN 2362	Wayfarer	1970-1976	110.00 to 125.00
HN 2368	Fleur	1968-Present	70.00 to 140.00
HN 2375	Viking	1973-1976	135.00 to 165.00
HN 2376	Indian Brave, Prestige Figure*	1975	2500.00 to 3000.00
HN 2378	Simone	1971-Present	115.00 to 140.00
HN 2379	Ninette	1971-Present	79.00 to 140.00
HN 2380	Sweet Dreams	1971-Present	75.00 to 100.00
HN 2381	Kirsty	1971-Present	86.25 to 140.00
HN 2382	Secret Thoughts	1971-Present	160.00
HN 2385	Debbie*	1969-Present	45.00 to 75.00
HN 2393	Rosalind	1970-1975	125.00 to 145.00
HN 2396	Wistful	1979-Present	146.25 to 155.00
HN 2398	Alexandra	1970-1976	110.00 to 145.00
HN 2417	Boatman	1971-Present	53.00 to 115.00
HN 2421	Charlotte	1972-Present	75.00 to 140.00
HN 2422	Francine	1972-Present	38.50 to 75.00
HN 2426	Tranquility, Black	1978	95.00
HN 2427	Virginals, Lady Musicians Series	1971	250.00
HN 2428	Palio*	1971	2500.00
HN 2429	Elyse	1972-Present	75.00 to 140.00
HN 2430	Romance	1972-Present	75.00 to 100.00
HN 2431	Lute, Lady Musicians Series*	1972	600.00
HN 2432	Violin, Lady Musicians Series*	1972	450.00 to 600.00
HN 2433	Peace, Black	1978	95.00
HN 2436	Scottish Highland, Dancers Of The World		
		1978	550.00
HN 2439	Philippine, Dancers Of The World	1978	550.00
HN 2442	Sailor's Holiday	1972-1978	95.00 to 125.00
HN 2443	Judge	1972-1978	71.25 to 125.00
HN 2444	Bon Appetit	1972-1976	100.00 to 150.00
HN 2445	Parisian	1972-1975	125.00 to 150.00
HN 2446	Thanksgiving	1972-1976	110.00 to 145.00
HN 2455	Seafarer	1972-1976	110.00 to 135.00
HN 2461	Janine	1971-Present	140.00

HN 2463	Olga	1972-1975	145.00 to 175.00
HN 2469	Tranquility, White	1978	95.00
HN 2470	Peace, White	1978	95.00
HN 2471	Victoria	1973-Present	140.00
HN 2473	At Ease	1973-1978	100.00 to 140.00
HN 2475	Vanity	1973-Present	60.00 to 75.00
HN 2482	Harp, Lady Musicians Series*	1973	300.00
HN 2483	Flute, Lady Musicians Series*	1973	450.00
HN 2484	Past Glory	1973-1978	165.00 to 235.00
HN 2485	Lunchtime	1973-Present	80.00 to 150.00
HN 2487	Beachcomber	1973-1976	95.00 to 175.00
HN 2492	Huntsman	1974-1978	125.00 to 225.00
HN 2494	Old Meg	1974-1976	625.00 to 900.00
HN 2499	Helmsman	1974-Present	150.00
HN 2502	Queen Elizabeth II	1973-Present	325.00
HN 2520	Farmer's Boy	1938-1960	695.00 to 825.00
HN 2542	Boudoir, Haute Ensemble Series	1974-Present	200.00
HN 2543	Eliza, Haute Ensemble Series	1974-1978	150.00 to 180.00
HN 2544	A La Mode, Haute Ensemble Series	1974-1978	129.00 to 160.00
HN 2545	Carmen, Haute Ensemble Series	1974-1978	149.00 to 185.00
HN 2546	Buddies	1973-1976	80.00 to 125.00
HN 2554	Masque	1973-Present	115.00 to 140.00
HN 2671	Good Morning	1974-1976	110.00 to 135.00
HN 2677	Taking Things Easy*	1975-Present	150.00
HN 2679	Drummer Boy	1976-Present	122.00 to 275.00
HN 2683	Stop Press*	1977-Present	95.00 to 125.00
HN 2694	Fiona	1974-Present	140.00
HN 2699	Cymbals, Lady Musicians Series*	1974	325.00
HN 2700	Chitarrone, Lady Musicians Series*	1974	350.00
HN 2704	Pensive Moments*	1975-Present	115.00 to 140.00
HN 2705	Julia	1975-Present	60.00 to 115.00
HN 2709	Regal Lady	1975-Present	115.00 to 140.00
HN 2712	Mantilla, Haute Ensemble Series	1974-1978	240.00
HN 2716	Cavalier*	1976-Present	83.00 to 115.00
HN 2717	Private, 2nd S. Carolina Regt., 1781*	1975	750.00
HN 2718	Lady Pamela	1974-Present	86.00 to 140.00
HN 2719	Laurianne	1974-1978	80.00 to 125.00
HN 2720	Family, White	1978	95.00
HN 2721	Family, Black	1978	95.00
HN 2722	Veneta	1974-Present	140.00
HN 2723	Grand Manner	1975-Present	80.00 to 185.00
HN 2724	Clarinda*	1975-Present	98.00 to 185.00
HN 2731	Thanks Doc*	1975-Present	150.00
HN 2734	Sweet Seventeen*	1975-Present	140.00
HN 2735	Young Love*	1975-Present	540.00
HN 2752	Major, 3rd New Jersey Regt., 1776*	1975	750.00
HN 2754	Private, 3rd N., Carolina Regt., 1778*	1976	750.00
HN 2755	Captain, 2nd New York Regt., 1775*	1976	750.00

HN 2759	Private, Rhode Island Regt., 1781	1977	750.00
HN 2760	Private, Massachusetts Regt., 1778*	1977	750.00
HN 2761	Private, Haslet's Delaware Regt., 1776	1977	750.00
HN 2762	Lovers, White	1978	95.00
HN 2763	Lovers, Black	1978	95.00
HN 2779	Private, 1st Georgia Regt., 1777	1975	750.00
HN 2780	Corporal, 1st New Hampshire Regt., 1778		
		1975	750.00
HN 2789	Kate*	1978-Present	65.00 to 115.00
HN 2792	Christine*	1978-Present	99.00 to 185.00
HN 2795	French Horn, Lady Musicians Series*	1976	400.00
HN 2796	Hurdy-Gurdy, Lady Musicians Series*	1975	375.00
HN 2797	Viola D'Amore, Lady Musicians Series*		
		1976	400.00
HN 2798	Dulcimer, Lady Musicians Series*	1975	375.00
HN 2800	Carrie, Kate Greenaway Series	1976-Present	55.00
HN 2802	Anna, Kate Greenaway Series	1976-Present	34.00 to 60.00
HN 2803	First Dance*	1977-Present	75.00 to 140.00
HN 2807	Stephanie*	1977-Present	85.00 to 140.00
HN 2810	Solitude*	1977-Present	135.00 to 160.00
HN 2814	Eventide	1977-Present	54.00 to 115.00
HN 2815	Sergeant, 6th Maryland Regt., 1777	1976	750.00
HN 2816	Votes For Women**	1978-Present	185.00
HN 2824	Harmony**	1978-Present	75.00 to 140.00
HN 2830	Indian Temple, Dancers Of The World**		
		1978	550.00
HN 2831	Spanish, Dancers Of The World**	1977	550.00
HN 2832	Fair Lady, Red	1977-Present	115.00
HN 2833	Sophie, Kate Greenaway Series	1977-Present	60.00
HN 2834	Emma, Kate Greenaway Series	1977-Present	42.00 to 60.00
HN 2835	Fair Lady, Coral Pink	1977-Present	75.00 to 115.00
HN 2839	Nicola*	1978-Present	105.00 to 185.00
HN 2842	Innocence	1979	71.25 to 115.00
HN 2844	Sergeant, 1st Continental Dragoons, Va.		
		1978	750.00
HN 2845	Private, 4th Connecticut Regt., 1777	1978	750.00
HN 2846	Private, Penn. Rifle Battalion, 1776	1978	750.00
HN 2851	Christmas Parcels**	1978-Present	75.00 to 115.00
HN 2856	St.George, Prestige Figure	1978-Present	6000.00
HN 2858	Doctor	1979	84.00 to 150.00
HN 2861	George Washington At Prayer	1977	875.00
HN 2862	First Waltz	1979	116.25 to 155.00
HN 2865	Tess, Kate Greenaway Series	1978-Present	36.00
HN 2866	Mexican, Dancers Of The World	1979	550.00
HN 2867	Kurdish, Dancers Of The World	1979	550.00
HN 2868	Cleopatra And Slave	1979	750.00
HN 2877	Wizard	1979-Present	115.00 to 155.00
HN 2890	Clown	1979-Present	116.25 to 200.00
HN 2892	Chief	1979	116.00 to 150.00

CHARACTER JUGS

CHARACTER JUGS

The tradition of pitchers or jugs shaped like human figures dates back to the eighteenth century in England. The Staffordshire potters made pitchers shaped like seated men or women. Jugs shaped like humans were made by various medieval potters.

These drinking vessels became popular and were referred to as Toby jugs. It has been said that they were probably named for a character in a 1761 song named "Toby Philpot."

This tradition was well-known to Charles Noke in 1933 when he developed a new type of figural jug, the Royal Doulton character jug. The pitcher or jug was shaped like the bust of a person, and only the head and shoulders were shown. The name "Toby jug" continued to mean a full-figure representation even to Doulton, and they have continued to make character jugs and Toby jugs.

Noke designed a series of jugs picturing famous English characters of history, literature, and song. The first jugs were John Barleycorn, who represented the personification of whiskey, and Old Charley, a night watchman.

A series of the character jugs was developed based on designs by Charles Noke, Leslie Harradine, Harry Fenton, Max Henk, David Brian Biggs, and others. The jugs were made in various sizes, some large—5¼ to 7 inches—some small—3¼ to 4 inches—some miniature—2¼ to 2½ inches—and some tiny—1¼ inch or less. The tiny size was discontinued in 1960.

The character jug is modeled, a mold is made, and the clay is poured into the mold. A molded jug is made, dried, fired, then decorated and fired several times. From 1968 to 1971 the character jugs were made of fine china instead of earthenware. These jugs have a slightly different appearance because of a translucent body. Each character jug has a name that is molded into the back of the jug and printed on the bottom. Each jug has a D number that usually is found on the bottom. Some jugs are marked with the so-called A mark. There have been many stories throughout the years about the meaning of the A mark. There have even been suggestions by the Royal Doulton firm. A 1975 letter to us from the factory says, "By a strange coincidence, we have recently made contact with one of our ex-employees who has been able to confirm that the mark was a factory identification symbol which was used approximately 25 years ago. Apparently, at that time we were compelled to print the words "Made in England" on the base of pieces sent out of the country, particularly to Australia and the U.S.A. Apparently, our warehouse staff experienced difficulty in identifying the pieces destined for overseas markets as the wording was extremely small. Our work's director at the time then came up with the idea to print a large 'A' alongside the trademark which helped identification."

The final decision seems to be that the A mark was a factory-control mark used during production to indicate wares to go to a certain kiln. It is found on some character jugs and also on some tablewares and series wares. It seems likely that the A mark was used between 1939 and 1955.

The words "Reg. applied for" or a single registered design number appear on the early jugs. Later jugs were marked with the printed name of the jug inside quotation marks. About 1950 the factory began using several registered design numbers with the lion and crown trademark and the D number. These registration numbers are different in different countries. Some small jugs, because of the limited space available on the bottom, are marked with only the words "Royal Doulton, Made in England." The words "Reg. in Australia" can be found on some jugs. (See the discussion of marks at the beginning of this book for further information about the Royal Doulton crown and lion mark and its changes.)

DESIGN CHANGES

A few jugs have been made with slight changes through the years. The design was occasionally changed enough for a new D number. Dick Turpin was made from 1934 to 1960, large size, D 5485. The jug had a pistol-shaped handle and an unmasked man. From 1960 a new version of Dick Turpin was made, large size, D 6528. This version shows a masked man and a horse-shaped handle. Robin Hood had plain handles, large size, D 6205, made 1947–1960. A new version D 6527, made 1960–present, has a quiver on the handles and oak leaves on his hat.

A few variations appear in character jugs that have not been renumbered. 'Arriet and 'Arry were first made in 1947, the color was changed in 1951, and in 1960 the jugs were withdrawn. A few jugs were made in either blue or brown with pearl buttons as part of the decorations. Auld Mac has the words "auld mac bang went sixpence" on the back of the hat. The printed name on the bottom was "Owd Mac" from 1938 to 1945. It was marked with the printed mark "Auld Mac" from 1946. Beefeater was made from 1947. The handle has the Royal Cypher GR for George Rex on the handle from 1947 to 1953. After 1953 the handle had the initials ER for Elizabeth Regina. Cavalier, which was introduced in 1940, had a color change in 1950. The style of the collar was altered and the Cavalier lost his goatee. Drake was introduced in 1940 and had a color change in 1950. A few jugs showing Drake with no hat and with earrings were evidently made in an early version. Granny was first made in 1935 with no teeth showing in her mouth. Later versions show a single front tooth. The first John Barleycorn jug that was made in 1933 had a handle ending inside the lip. Later versions had the handle joined to the outside of the lip. A limited edition reissue of the jug was made in 1978. It is clearly marked. Monty was issued in 1946, and in 1954 there was a color change. Old King Cole was first made in 1939. An early version, possibly never made in a production model, shows the figure with a yellow crown and slightly different details. The usual version has an orange brown crown. Three jugs, Lumberjack, North American Indian, and the Trapper, were originally issued in 1967 only in Canada, with the backstamp "Canadian Centennial Series 1867–1967." In 1968 the backstamp was removed and the jugs were sold in all countries. Six jugs picturing Dickens characters, Buz Fuz, Cap'n Cuttle, Fat Boy, Mr. Micawber, Mr. Pickwick, and Sam Weller, were made in a special size, 4½ inches, that was changed to a more typical small size in 1949. Although the size changed, the D number did not. An extra-large version of Tony Weller was made. One jug, McCallum was made for a liquor company to distribute and was not sold through stores.

A few prototype jugs were made that have by some means become available to the public. These jugs were made as samples and were never in production. Buffalo Bill was found in the United States a few years ago. Others that are pictured in the book *Royal Doulton Character and Toby Jugs,* by Desmond Eyles, include the Maori and the Baseball Player. .

Some discrepancies have appeared in the literature while we were gathering our information. The spelling of the name Old Charley (Charlie), of Izaac (Isaac) Walton, and of Sancho Panza (Panca) have caused us continual trouble. We have no explanation for this other than the difference between the United States and the English spellings. (The names impressed on the jugs are those given above that are not in parentheses.)

The dates given for some of the jugs may vary by a year in some listings. The copyright date is printed on the bottom of the jug, but the date that it was actually offered for sale could be as much as twelve months later. Either date seems to be acceptable in the various lists put out by Royal Doulton and others.

Miscellaneous articles that resemble the character jugs were also made and are listed in the Miscellaneous chapter.

'Ard of 'earing represents a man who is partially deaf.

'Ard Of 'Earing, Large	**D.6588**	**1963-1967**	**575.00 to 650.00**
'Ard Of 'Earing, Miniature	**D.6594**	**1963-1967**	**425.00**

'Arriet is a London Cockney costermonger or street trader.

'Arriet, see also Pearly Girl

'Arriet, Large, Marked A*	**D.6208**	**1946-1960**	**95.00**
'Arriet, Miniature	**D.6250**	**1946-1960**	**85.00**
'Arriet, Miniature, Marked A	**D.6250**	**1946-1960**	**37.50**
'Arriet, Small	**D.6236**	**1946-1960**	**15.00 to 70.00**
'Arriet, Small, Marked A	**D.6236**	**1946-1960**	**52.00 to 72.50**
'Arriet, Tiny	**D.6256**	**1946-1960**	**125.00 to 165.00**

'Arry is a London Cockney costermonger or street trader.

'Arriet, Large, Marked A D.6208

'Arry, see also Pearly Boy

'Arry, Miniature	D.6249	1946-1960	45.00 to 54.00
'Arry, Small*	D.6235	1946-1960	45.00 to 65.00
'Arry, Small, Marked A	D.6235	1946-1960	65.00
'Arry, Tiny	D.6255	1946-1960	115.00 to 150.00

Anne Boleyn was the second wife of King Henry VIII in 1533. She had a daughter who became Queen Elizabeth I. Anne Boleyn was beheaded in 1536 and Henry VIII remarried four more times.

Anne Boleyn, Large*	D.6644	1974-Present	27.00 to 44.95

Apothecary is a character from the Williamsburg series depicting the eighteenth-century town inhabitants. The apothecary sold drugs as medicine and sometimes treated patients.

Apothecary, Large*	D.6567	1962-Present	30.00 TO 35.00
Apothecary, Miniature	D.6581	1962-Present	16.95
Apothecary, Small	D.6574	1962-Present	22.50

'Arry, Small D.6235

Apothecary, Large D.6567

Anne Boleyn, Large D.6644

Aramis, Large D.6441

Auld Mac, Large D.5823

Aramis is one of the characters from the book "The Three Musketeers" by Alexandre Dumas.

Aramis, Large*	**D.6441**	**1955-Present**	**35.00 to 44.95**
Aramis, Miniature	**D.6508**	**1955-Present**	**16.95 to 21.95**
Aramis, Small	**D.6454**	**1955-Present**	**22.50 to 29.95**

Athos is one of the characters from the book "The Three Musketeers" by Alexandre Dumas.

Athos, Large*	**D.6439**	**1955-Present**	**35.00 to 44.95**
Athos, Miniature	**D.6509**	**1955-Present**	**16.95 to 21.95**
Athos, Small	**D.6452**	**1955-Present**	**18.00 to 29.95**

Auld Mac represents a thrifty Scot.

Auld Mac, see also Owd Mac

Auld Mac, Large*	**D.5823**	**1937-Present**	**35.00 to 95.00**
Auld Mac, Miniature	**D.6253**	**1946-Present**	**16.95 to 25.00**
Auld Mac, Miniature, Marked A	**D.6253**	**1946-Present**	**25.00 to 65.00**
Auld Mac, Small	**D.5824**	**1937-Present**	**22.50 to 29.95**
Auld Mac, Small, Marked A	**D.5824**	**1937-Present**	**40.00 to 65.00**
Auld Mac, Tiny	**D.6257**	**1946-1960**	**135.00 to 175.00**

Bacchus, Large D.6499

Beefeater, Large, Marked A D.6206

Bacchus is the ancient Greek god of wine and the grape harvest.

Bacchus, Large*	D.6499	1958-Present	35.00 to 44.95
Bacchus, Miniature	D.6521	1958-Present	16.95 to 21.95
Bacchus, Small	D.6505	1958-Present	22.50 to 29.95

Beefeater is the name for a Yeoman of the Guard, a bodyguard for the Queen.

Beefeater, Large, Marked A*	D.6206	1946-Present	45.00
Beefeater, Miniature	D.6251	1946-Present	16.95 to 21.95
Beefeater, Miniature, Marked A	D.6251	1946-Present	25.00 to 31.00
Beefeater, Small	D.6233	1946-Present	20.00 to 50.00
Beefeater, Small, Marked A	D.6233	1946-Present	35.00 to 65.00

Blacksmith is a character from the Williamsburg series depicting the eighteenth-century town inhabitants. The blacksmith was an ironworker.

Blacksmith, Large*	D.6571	1962-Present	30.00 to 35.00
Blacksmith, Miniature	D.6585	1962-Present	16.95
Blacksmith, Small	D.6578	1962-Present	22.50

Bootmaker is a character from the Williamsburg series depicting the eighteenth-century town inhabitants. The bootmaker produced shoes and boots.

Bootmaker, Large*	D.6572	1962-Present	30.00 to 35.00
Bootmaker, Miniature	D.6586	1962-Present	16.95

Cap'n Cuttle, Small D.5842

Blacksmith, Large D.6571

Buffalo Bill was the Wild West show star William Cody.

Buffalo Bill, Experiment   **xxxx**

Buz Fuz, see Sergeant Buz Fuz

Cap'n Cuttle or Captain Edward Cuttle is a character in the book "Dombey and Son" by Charles Dickens.

Cap'n Cuttle, Small*	D.5842	1948-1960	**75.00 to 120.00**

Captain Ahab is a character in the book "Moby Dick" by Herman Melville.

Captain Ahab, Large*	D.6500	1958-Present	**35.00 to 44.95**
Captain Ahab, Miniature	D.6522	1958-Present	**16.00 to 21.95**
Captain Ahab, Small	D.6506	1958-Present	**15.00 to 29.95**

Captain Henry Morgan was a British buccaneer who lived from 1635 to 1688.

Captain Henry Morgan, Large*	D.6467	1957-Present	**35.00 to 44.95**

Captain Ahab, Large D.6500

Captain Henry Morgan, Large D.6467

Captain Henry Morgan, Large, Marked A

	D.6467	1957-Present	28.00
Captain Henry Morgan, Miniature	D.6510	1959-Present	16.95 to 21.95
Captain Henry Morgan, Small	D.6469	1957-Present	15.00 to 29.95

Captain Hook is a pirate captain in the book "Peter Pan" by James M. Barrie.

Captain Hook, Large	D.6497	1964-1971	165.00 to 275.00
Captain Hook, Small	D.6601	1964-1971	150.00 to 200.00

Cardinal represents a dignitary of the Catholic clergy. This mug may depict an actor playing the part of Cardinal Wolsey in the play "Henry VIII" by Shakespeare.

Cardinal, Large*	D.5614	1935-1960	70.00 to 100.00
Cardinal, Large, Marked A	D.5614	1935-1960	79.00 to 115.00
Cardinal, Miniature	D.6129	1939-1960	28.00 to 55.00
Cardinal, Miniature, Marked A	D.6129	1939-1960	30.00 to 40.00
Cardinal, Small	D.6033	1938-1960	35.00 to 60.00
Cardinal, Tiny	D.6258	1946-1960	125.00 to 200.00

Cardinal, Large D.5614

Catherine Howard was the fifth wife of King Henry VIII. She was beheaded.

Catherine Howard, Large*	D.6645	1978-Present	35.00 to 44.95

Catherine of Aragon was the first wife of King Henry VIII. The marriage was annulled.

Catherine Of Aragon, Large*	D.6643	1975-Present	27.00 to 44.95

Cavalier represents an Englishman who fought for Charles I during the Civil War of 1642 to 1649.

Cavalier, Large*	D.6114	1939-1960	69.00 to 145.00
Cavalier, Large, Marked A	D.6114	1939-1960	70.00 to 85.00
Cavalier, Small	D.6173	1940-1960	38.00 to 65.00
Cavalier, Small, Marked A	D.6173	1940-1960	47.00 to 65.00

Catherine Howard, Large D.6645

Catherine Of Aragon, Large D.6643

*Dick Turpin, Horse Handle, Masked,
Large D.6528*

Cavalier, Large D.6114

Clown represents a comic from traditional Italian comedy or the circus of today.

Clown, Red Hair, Large	D.5610	1937-1942	2500.00
Clown, White Hair, Large	D.6322	1950-1955	500.00 to 800.00

Devil, see Mephistopheles

Dick Turpin was an English highwayman in the eighteenth century who was convicted and hanged for his crimes.

Dick Turpin, Gun Handle, Mask Up, Large			
	D.5484	1934-1960	63.00 to 100.00
Dick Turpin, Gun Handle, Mask Up, Small			
	D.5618	1935-1960	55.00
Dick Turpin, Gun, Mask Up, Miniature	D.6128	1934-1960	35.00 to 40.00
Dick Turpin, Gun, Mask, Small, Marked A			
	D.5618	1935-1960	45.00 to 49.50
Dick Turpin, Horse Handle, Masked, Large*			
	D.6528	1959-Present	44.95

Dick Whittington, Large D.6375

Drake, Large D.6115

Dick Turpin, Horse Handle, Masked, Small

	D.6535	1959-Present	22.50 to 70.00
Dick Turpin, Horse, Masked, Miniature	D.6542	1959-Present	21.95 to 25.00

Dick Whittington was the Lord Mayor of London in the fifteenth century. Legend says he became mayor because of his pet cat.

Dick Whittington, Large*	D.6375	1952-1960	250.00 to 350.00

Don Quixote was a character in the book "Don Quixote" by Miguel de Cervantes.

Don Quixote, Large	D.6455	1956-Present	35.00 to 44.95
Don Quixote, Miniature	D.6511	1956-Present	16.95 to 21.95
Don Quixote, Small	D.6460	1956-Present	22.50 to 29.95

Drake or Sir Francis Drake was a famous British seaman. He sailed around the world in 1580.

Drake, Hatless Version			2000.00
Drake, Large*	D.6115	1939-1960	90.00 to 100.00
Drake, Large, Marked A	D.6115	1939-1960	85.00 to 110.00
Drake, Small	D.6174	1939-1960	39.00 to 65.00
Drake, Small, Marked A	D.6174	1939-1960	45.00 to 65.00

Falconer represents the trainer of birds including falcons for hunting.

Falconer, Large*	D.6533	1959-Present	35.00 to 44.95
Falconer, Miniature	D.6547	1959-Present	16.95 to 21.95
Falconer, Small	D.6540	1959-Present	22.50 to 29.95

Falstaff or Sir John Falstaff is a character in the plays "Henry IV" and "The Merry Wives of Windsor" by Shakepeare.

Falstaff, Large*	D.6287	1949-Present	30.00 to 50.00
Falstaff, Miniature	D.6519	1960-Present	16.95 to 21.95
Falstaff, Small	D.6385	1949-Present	17.50 to 35.00

Farmer John represents the English farmer.

Farmer John, Large*	**D.5788**	**1937-1960**	**85.00 to 110.00**
Farmer John, Large, Marked A	**D.5788**	**1937-1960**	**95.00 to 125.00**
Farmer John, Small	**D.5789**	**1937-1960**	**45.00 to 75.00**
Farmer John, Small, Marked A	**D.5789**	**1937-1960**	**50.00 to 75.00**

Fat Boy is a character in the book "Pickwick Papers" by Charles Dickens.

Fat Boy, Miniature*	**D.6139**	**1939-1960**	**40.00 to 55.00**
Fat Boy, Miniature, Marked A	**D.6139**	**1939-1960**	**40.00 to 45.00**
Fat Boy, Small	**D.5840**	**1937-1960**	**44.00 to 100.00**
Fat Boy, Small, Marked A	**D.5840**	**1937-1960**	**45.00 to 65.00**
Fat Boy, Tiny	**D.6142**	**1939-1960**	**69.00 to 110.00**
Fat Boy, 4 1/2 In.	**D.5840**	**1938-1948**	**110.00 to 120.00**

Smuts or Jan Christian Smuts was a famous South African statesman who died in 1950.

Field Marshal Smuts, Large	**D.6198**	**1945-1948**	**1500.00 to 1975.00**
Field Marshal Smuts, Large, Marked A	**D.6198**	**1945-1948**	**1750.00**

Falstaff, Large
D.6287

Farmer John, Large
D.5788

Fat Boy, Miniature   *D.6139*

Fortune Teller represents a gypsy.

Fortune Teller, Large	D.6497	1958-1967	228.00
Fortune Teller, Miniature	D.6523	1960-1967	200.00 to 250.00
Fortune Teller, Small	D.6503	1958-1967	175.00 to 250.00

Friar Tuck was the chaplain who was a member of Robin Hood's band. He is also a character in the book "Ivanhoe" by Sir Walter Scott.

Friar Tuck, Large*	D.6321	1950-1960	250.00 to 300.00
Friar Tuck, Large, Marked A	D.6321	1950-1960	250.00

Gaoler is a character from the Williamsburg series depicting the eighteenth-century town inhabitants. The gaoler was the jailer.

Gaoler, Large*	D.6570	1962-Present	30.00 to 35.00
Gaoler, Miniature	D.6584	1962-Present	16.00 to 16.95
Gaoler, Small	D.6577	1962-Present	22.50

Gardener represents the man who likes to work in the garden.

Gardener, Large*	D.6630	1973-Present	35.00 to 44.95
Gardener, Miniature	D.6638	1973-Present	16.95 to 21.95
Gardener, Small	D.6634	1973-Present	20.00 to 29.95

Gladiator represents the fighters of the Roman days.

Gladiator, Large	D.6550	1960-1967	285.00 to 325.00
Gladiator, Miniature	D.6556	1960-1967	185.00
Gladiator, Small	D.6553	1960-1967	165.00 to 300.00

Golfer represents an Englishman dressed for his favorite game of golf.

Golfer, Large*	D.6623	1973-Present	27.00 to 44.95
Golfer, Large, Marked A	D.6623	1973-Present	28.00

Friar Tuck, Large D.6321

Gardener, Large D.6630

Gone Away, Large D.6531

Guardsman, Large D.6568

Granny, Large D.5521

Gondolier represents the singing boatman who propels his gondola in Venice, Italy.

Gondolier, Large	D.6623	1963-1969	250.00 to 295.00
Gondolier, Miniature	D.6595	1963-1969	275.00 to 290.00
Gondolier, Small	D.6592	1963-1969	250.00 to 300.00

Gone Away represents the huntsman dressed for a fox hunt.

Gone Away, Large*	D.6531	1959-Present	35.00 to 44.95
Gone Away, Large, Marked A	D.6531	1959-Present	28.00
Gone Away, Miniature	D.6545	1959-Present	16.95 to 21.95
Gone Away, Small	D.6538	1959-Present	18.00 to 29.95

Granny represents the grandmother of everyone's childhood.

Granny, Large*	D.5521	1934-Present	35.00 to 74.00
Granny, Large, Marked A	D.5521	1934-Present	50.00 to 75.00
Granny, Miniature	D.6520	1959-Present	16.95 to 21.95
Granny, Small	D.6384	1952-Present	22.50 to 29.95

Guardsman is a character from the Williamsburg series depicting the eighteenth-century town inhabitants.

Guardsman, Large*	D.6568	1962-Present	35.00

Guardsman, Miniature	**D.6582**	**1962-Present**	**16.00 to 16.95**
Guardsman, Small	**D.6575**	**1962-Present**	**22.50**

Gulliver is a character in the book "Gulliver's Travels" by Jonathan Swift.

Gulliver, Large	**D.6560**	**1961-1967**	**269.00 to 325.00**
Gulliver, Large, Marked A	**D.6560**	**1961-1967**	**325.00**
Gulliver, Miniature	**D.6566**	**1961-1967**	**150.00 to 250.00**
Gulliver, Small	**D.6563**	**1961-1967**	**315.00 to 330.00**

Gunsmith is a character from the Williamsburg series depicting the eighteenth-century town inhabitants.

Gunsmith, Large*	**D.6573**	**1962-Present**	**30.00 to 35.00**
Gunsmith, Miniature	**D.6587**	**1962-Present**	**16.95**
Gunsmith, Small	**D.6580**	**1962-Present**	**22.50**

Henry VIII was the ruler of England from 1509 to 1547.

Henry VIII, Large*	**D.6642**	**1975-Present**	**35.00 to 44.95**
Henry VIII, Small	**D.6647**	**1979-Present**	**22.50 to 29.95**

Isaac Walton was the author of many books. He first published "The Compleat Angler" in 1653.

Isaac Walton, Large*	**D.6404**	**1953-Present**	**35.00 to 44.95**

Jane Seymour was the third wife of Henry VIII. She died in 1537.

Jane Seymour, Large*	**D.6646**	**1979-Present**	**35.00 to 44.95**

Gunsmith, Large D.6573

Henry VIII, Large D.6642

Isaac Walton, Large D.6404

Jane Seymour, Large D.6646

Jarge represents the typical country bumpkin.

Jarge, Large*	D.6288	1949-1960	169.00 to 220.00
Jarge, Small	D.6295	1949-1960	95.00 to 150.00

Jester represents the minstrel of the courts in medieval days.

Jester, Small*	D.5556	1935-1960	45.00 to 125.00
Jester, Small, Marked A	D.5556	1935-1960	75.00 to 90.00

Jockey represents the horseman of racetrack fame.

Jockey, Large	D.6625	1971-1975	85.00 to 160.00
Jockey, Large, Marked A	D.6625	1971-1975	125.00

Jarge, Large D.6288

Jester, Small D.5556

John Barleycorn, Large D.5327

John Barleycorn, Signed Doulton,
Large D.5327

John Barleycorn was a figure from early English ballads. He was the personification of barley used for whiskey or liquor.

John Barleycorn, Large*	D.5327	1933-1960	70.00 to 125.00
John Barleycorn, Large, Marked A	D.5327	1933-1960	125.00 to 425.00
John Barleycorn, Miniature	D.6041	1938-1960	33.00 to 55.00
John Barleycorn, Miniature, Marked A	D.6041	1938-1960	35.00 to 65.00
John Barleycorn, Signed Doulton, Large*	D.5327	1978	125.00 to 150.00
John Barleycorn, Small	D.5735	1936-1960	45.00 to 65.00
John Barleycorn, Small, Marked A	D.5735	1936-1960	50.00 to 70.00

John Peel was a man who liked fox hunting and was the subject of the song "D'ye ken John Peel" written in 1866.

John Peel, Large*	D.5612	1935-1960	95.00 to 145.00
John Peel, Large, Marked A	D.5612	1935-1960	195.00 to 425.00
John Peel, Miniature	D.6130	1939-1960	55.00 to 80.00
John Peel, Miniature, Marked A	D.6130	1939-1960	37.50 to 75.00
John Peel, Small	D.5731	1936-1960	37.00 to 55.00
John Peel, Small, Marked A	D.5731	1936-1960	50.00 to 70.00
John Peel, Tiny	D.6259	1946-1960	140.00 to 190.00

Johnny Appleseed was the nickname of New Englander John Chapman, who traveled the Midwest planting apple seeds in the early nineteenth century.

Johnny Appleseed, Large*	D.6372	1952-1969	150.00 to 225.00

Lawyer represents the typical British lawyer who appears in court wearing a wig.

Lawyer, Large*	D.6498	1957-Present	35.00 to 75.00

John Peel, Large D.5612

Johnny Appleseed, Large D.6372

Long John Silver, Large
D.6335

Lawyer, Large D.6498

| Lawyer, Miniature | D.6524 | 1957-Present | 16.95 to 21.95 |
| Lawyer, Small | D.6504 | 1957-Present | 15.00 to 29.95 |

Lobster man represents the fisherman who sets the pots and traps the lobsters.

| Lobster Man, Large* | D.6617 | 1967-Present | 35.00 to 44.95 |
| Lobster Man, Small | D.6620 | 1967-Present | 22.50 to 29.95 |

Long John Silver is a character in the book "Treasure Island" by Robert Louis Stevenson.

Long John Silver, Large*	D.6335	1951-Present	25.00 to 44.95
Long John Silver, Large, Marked A	D.6335	1951-Present	28.00
Long John Silver, Miniature	D.6512	1960-Present	16.95 to 21.95
Long John Silver, Small	D.6386	1951-Present	22.50 to 29.95

Lumberjack, Large
D.6610

Mad Hatter, Large
D.6598

Lord Nelson was an English naval hero who died at the Battle of Trafalgar in 1805.

Lord Nelson, Large	D.6336	1957-1968	169.00 to 245.00

Lumberjack represents the loggers of the United States and Canada.

Lumberjack, Large*	D.6610	1966-Present	30.00 to 44.95
Lumberjack, Small	D.6613	1966-Present	22.50 to 29.95

Mad Hatter is a character from the book "Alice's Adventures in Wonderland" by Lewis Carroll.

Mad Hatter, Large*	D.6598	1964-Present	30.00 to 44.95
Mad Hatter, Miniature	D.6606	1964-Present	16.95 to 21.95
Mad Hatter, Small	D.6602	1964-Present	22.50 to 29.95

McCallum represents a Scottish Highlander. The jug was made for the whisky distillers D & J McCallum.

McCallum, White*		1930	650.00

Mephistopheles is a legendary character of medieval lore. He is one of the second of the fallen archangels; only Satan is more important. The more modern association for Mephistopheles is a character in the book "Faust" by Goethe.

Mephistopheles, Large	D.5757	1936-1948	625.00 to 925.00
Mephistopheles, Large, Marked A	D.5757	1936-1948	925.00
Mephistopheles, Small	D.5758	1936-1948	350.00 to 650.00

McCallum, White 1930

Merlin is a legendary magician and prophet of the fifth century. He is part of the King Arthur series.

Merlin, Large	D.6529	1959-Present	35.00 to 44.95
Merlin, Miniature	D.6543	1959-Present	16.95 to 21.95
Merlin, Small	D.6536	1959-Present	22.50 to 29.95

Mikado represents the Japanese Emperor, perhaps the one famous in the Gilbert and Sullivan operetta of 1885 called "The Mikado."

Mikado, Large	D.6501	1958-1968	178.00 to 240.00
Mikado, Small	D.6507	1958-1968	150.00 to 200.00

Mine Host represents the typical English host of nineteenth-century England.

Mine Host, Large*	D.6468	1957-Present	35.00 to 44.95
Mine Host, Miniature	D.6513	1960-Present	16.95 to 21.95
Mine Host, Small	D.6470	1957-Present	15.00 to 29.95

Monty was the nickname for Field Marshal Montgomery who was commander of the British Forces during Allied invasion of Europe.

Monty, Large*	D.6202	1945-Present	27.00 to 44.95
Monty, Large, Marked A	D.6202	1945-Present	45.00 to 225.00

Motorist, see Veteran Motorist

Mr. Micawber is a character from the book "David Copperfield" by Charles Dickens.

Mr. Micawber, Miniature*	D.6138	1939-1960	40.00 to 95.00
Mr. Micawber, Miniature, Marked A	D.6138	1939-1960	35.00 to 40.00
Mr. Micawber, Small	D.5843	1937-1960	50.00 to 115.00
Mr. Micawber, Small, Marked A	D.5843	1937-1960	45.00 to 65.00
Mr. Micawber, 4 1/2 In.	D.5843	1938-1948	110.00
Mr. Micawber, 4 1/2 In., Marked A	D.5843	1938-1948	100.00

Monty, Large D.6202

Mr. Micawber, Miniature D.6138

Mr. Pickwick, Large D.6060

Mr. Pickwick is a character from the book "Pickwick Papers" by Charles Dickens.

Mr. Pickwick, Large*	D.6060	1939-1960	80.00 to 100.00
Mr. Pickwick, Large, Marked A	D.6060	1939-1960	70.00 to 115.00
Mr. Pickwick, Miniature	D.6254	1947-1960	30.00 to 50.00
Mr. Pickwick, Miniature, Marked A	D.6254	1947-1960	40.00
Mr. Pickwick, Small	D.5839	1947-1960	43.00 to 60.00
Mr. Pickwick, Tiny	D.6260	1947-1960	135.00 to 180.00

Neptune is a Roman god of the springs and sea, later considered the god of the sea.

Neptune, Large*	D.6548	1960-Present	35.00 to 44.95
Neptune, Miniature	D.6555	1960-Present	16.95 to 21.95
Neptune, Small	D.6552	1960-Present	22.50 to 29.95

Night Watchman is a character from the Williamsburg series depicting the eighteenth-century town inhabitants.

Night Watchman, Large*	D.6569	1962-Present	35.00
Night Watchman, Miniature	D.6583	1962-Present	16.95
Night Watchman, Small	D.6576	1962-Present	18.00 to 22.50

North American Indian represents a chief of the Blackfoot tribe.

North American Indian, Large*	D.6611	1966-Present	32.50 to 44.95
North American Indian, Small	D.6614	1966-Present	22.50 to 29.95

Night Watchman, Large D.6569

Old Charley, Large D.5420

Old Charley represents the night watchman of the nineteenth century.

Old Charley, Large*	**D.5420**	**1934-Present**	**65.00 to 115.00**
Old Charley, Miniature	**D.6046**	**1938-Present**	**21.95 to 35.00**
Old Charley, Miniature, Marked A	**D.6046**	**1938-Present**	**20.00 to 65.00**
Old Charley, Small	**D.5527**	**1934-Present**	**20.00 to 115.00**
Old Charley, Small, Marked A	**D.5527**	**1934-Present**	**30.00 to 65.00**
Old Charley, Tiny	**D.6144**	**1939-Present**	**69.00 to 110.00**
Old Charley, Tiny, Marked A	**D.6144**	**1939-1960**	**69.00**

Old King Cole is the "merry old soul" of the nursery rhyme.

Old King Cole, Large*	**D.6036**	**1938-1960**	**125.00 to 135.00**
Old King Cole, Large, Marked A	**D.6036**	**1938-1960**	**100.00**
Old King Cole, Small	**D.6037**	**1939-1960**	**65.00 to 89.50**
Old King Cole, Small, Marked A	**D.6037**	**1938-1960**	**65.00**

Old Salt represents the aging fisherman.

Old Salt, Large*	**D.6551**	**1960-Present**	**30.00 to 44.95**
Old Salt, Small	**D.6554**	**1960-Present**	**22.50 to 29.95**
Owd Mac, see also Auld Mac			
Owd Mac, Large, Early Name Of Auld Mac			
	D.5823	**1938-1945**	**85.00**

Old King Cole, Large D.6036

Old Salt, Large D.6551

Paddy, Large D.5753

Parson Brown, Large D.5486

Pied Piper, Large D.6403

Paddy represents the typical Irishman.

Paddy, Large*	D.5753	1936-1960	66.00 to 100.00
Paddy, Miniature	D.6042	1939-1960	33.00 to 58.00
Paddy, Miniature, Marked A	D.6042	1938-1960	33.00 to 45.00
Paddy, Small	D.5768	1936-1960	50.00 to 55.00
Paddy, Small, Marked A	D.5768	1936-1960	40.00 to 70.00
Paddy, Tiny	D.6145	1939-1960	65.00 to 100.00

Parson Brown represents the typical Anglican parson of the nineteenth century.

Parson Brown, Large*	D.5486	1934-1960	80.00 to 95.00
Parson Brown, Small	D.5529	1934-1960	38.00 to 65.00
Parson Brown, Small, Marked A	D.5529	1934-1960	47.00 to 65.00
Pearly Boy, Large	D.6207		600.00
Pearly Boy, Small	D.6235		325.00
Pearly Girl, Large	D.6208		700.00
Pearly Girl, Miniature	D.6250		275.00
Pearly Girl, Small	D.6236		325.00

Pied Piper is the legendary character the Pied Piper of Hamelin who charmed the rats and children with his music.

Pied Piper, Large*	D.6403	1953-Present	30.00 to 44.95
Pied Piper, Miniature	D.6514	1960-Present	16.95 to 25.00
Pied Piper, Small	D.6462	1957-Present	22.50 to 29.95

Poacher represents the fish or game hunter who steals the catch illegally from private property.

Poacher, Large*	D.6429	1954-Present	30.00 to 44.95
Poacher, Miniature	D.6515	1960-Present	17.00 to 21.95
Poacher, Small	D.6464	1957-Present	22.50 to 29.95

Porthos is one of the characters from the book "The Three Musketeers" by Alexandre Dumas.

Porthos, Large*	D.6440	1955-Present	35.00 to 44.95
Porthos, Miniature	D.6516	1960-Present	16.95 to 21.95
Porthos, Small	D.6453	1955-Present	18.00 to 29.95

Punch and Judy Man represents the man who gives the puppet shows still popular with English children.

Punch & Judy Man, Large	D.6590	1963-1968	290.00 to 375.00
Punch & Judy Man, Miniature	D.6596	1963-1968	260.00 to 300.00
Punch & Judy Man, Small	D.6593	1963-1968	275.00 to 285.00

Regency Beau represents the fashionable, fun-loving gentleman of nineteenth-century England. Best known of this type of man was Beau Brummell, whose name still indicates fashion.

Regency Beau, Small	D.6562	1962-1967	270.00 to 350.00

Rip Van Winkle is a character in a story in "Sketch Book" by Washington Irving.

Rip Van Winkle, Large*	D.6438	1954-Present	35.00 to 44.95

Poacher, Large D.6429

Porthos, Large D.6440

Rip Van Winkle, Large D.6438

Rip Van Winkle, Miniature	D.6517	1960-Present	16.95 to 21.95
Rip Van Winkle, Small	D.6462	1957-Present	22.50 to 29.95

Robin Hood is a legendary character who robbed from the rich to feed the poor.

Robin Hood, Bow Handle, Small	D.6534	1959-Present	22.50 to 29.95
Robin Hood, Feather Handle, Large	D.6205	1946-1960	35.00 to 110.00
Robin Hood, Feather Handle, Small	D.6234	1946-1960	38.00 to 55.00
Robin Hood, Miniature, Marked A	D.6252	1946-1960	52.00 to 65.00
Robin Hood, Small, Marked A*	D.6234	1946-1960	35.00 to 55.00

Robinson Crusoe is a character in the book "Robinson Crusoe" by Daniel Defoe.

Robinson Crusoe, Large*	D.6532	1959-Present	30.00 to 44.95
Robinson Crusoe, Miniature	D.6546	1959-Present	16.95 to 21.95
Robinson Crusoe, Small	D.6539	1959-Present	18.00 to 29.95

Sairey Gamp is a character from the book "Martin Chuzzlewit" by Charles Dickens.

Sairey Gamp, Large*	D.5451	1934-Present	35.00 to 44.95
Sairey Gamp, Large, Marked A	D.5451	1934-Present	38.00 to 125.00
Sairey Gamp, Miniature	D.6045	1938-Present	29.00 to 65.00
Sairey Gamp, Small	D.5528	1934-Present	20.00 to 29.95
Sairey Gamp, Tiny, Marked A	D.6146	1939-1960	65.00 to 110.00

*Robin Hood, Small, Marked
A D.6234*

Robinson Crusoe, Large D.6532

Sairey Gamp, Large D.5451

Sam Johnson, Large D.6289

Sam Weller, Large D.6064

Samuel Johnson was the English writer who is best known for his "Dictionary of the English Language," completed in 1756.

Sam Johnson, Large*	D.6289	1949-1960	170.00 to 225.00
Sam Johnson, Small	D.6296	1949-1960	132.00 to 145.00
Sam Johnson, Small, Marked A	D.6296	1949-1960	155.00

Sam Weller is a character from the book "Pickwick Papers" by Charles Dickens.

Sam Weller, Large*	D.6064	1939-1960	68.00 to 125.00
Sam Weller, Large, Marked A	D.6064	1939-1960	79.00 to 425.00
Sam Weller, Miniature	D.6140	1939-1960	27.50 to 65.00
Sam Weller, Miniature, Marked A	D.6140	1939-1960	35.00 to 75.00
Sam Weller, Small	D.5841	1948-1960	50.00 to 110.00
Sam Weller, Small, Marked A	D.5841	1948-1960	50.00
Sam Weller, Tiny	D.6147	1939-1960	69.00 to 100.00
Sam Weller, 4 1/2 In.	D.5841	1938-1948	110.00

Sancho Panza is a character from the book "Don Quixote" by Miguel de Cervantes.

Sancho Panza, Large*	D.6456	1956-Present	35.00 to 44.95
Sancho Panza, Miniature	D.6518	1960-Present	16.95 to 21.95
Sancho Panza, Small	D.6461	1956-Present	22.50 to 29.95

Scaramouche was a character in the old Italian comedy who was a cowardly buffoon and ne'er-do-well.

Scaramouche, Large	D.6558	1961-1967	300.00 to 310.00

Sancho Panza, Large
D.6456

| Scaramouche, Miniature | D.6564 | 1961-1967 | 210.00 to 250.00 |
| Scaramouche, Small | D.6561 | 1961-1967 | 235.00 to 285.00 |

Sergeant Buz Fuz, Buz Fuz, or Mr. Sergeant is a barrister or trial lawyer in the book "Pickwick Papers" by Charles Dickens.

| Sergeant Buz Fuz, Small* | D.5838 | 1948-1960 | 65.00 to 95.00 |
| Sergeant Buz Fuz, Small, Marked A | D.5838 | 1948-1960 | 45.00 to 95.00 |

Simon the Cellarer was a man in charge of the wine cellar who was part of a popular drinking song of the nineteenth century.

Simon The Cellarer, Large*	D.5504	1934-1960	65.00 to 100.00
Simon The Cellarer, Large, Marked A	D.5504	1934-1960	145.00 to 195.00
Simon The Cellarer, Small	D.5616	1935-1960	36.00 to 65.00

Simple Simon is a character in the well-known children's nursery rhyme about the pieman.

| Simple Simon, Large* | D.6374 | 1953-1960 | 379.00 to 500.00 |

Sir Winston Churchill was Prime Minister of Britain. The jug is a tribute to his leadership in 1940 during the Battle of Britain.

| Sir Winston Churchill, White, Large | D.6170 | 1939-1941 | 1200.00 |

Sleuth represents a character similar to Sherlock Holmes, the fictional detective.

Sleuth, Large*	D.6631	1973-Present	35.00 to 44.95
Sleuth, Miniature	D.6639	1973-Present	17.00 to 21.95
Sleuth, Small	D.6635	1973-Present	15.00 to 29.95

Smuggler represents the eighteenth-century thieves who brought goods into the country without paying duty.

| Smuggler, Small* | D.6619 | 1967-Present | 22.50 to 29.95 |

Smuts, see Field Marshal Smuts

St. George is a legendary character who saved the king's daughter by slaying a dragon during the time of the crusades. There was a real St. George who died in 1303 but little is known about him.

St. George, Large	D.6618	1967-1974	59.00 to 90.00
St. George, Small	D.6621	1967-1974	35.00 to 65.00
St. George, Small, Marked A	D.6621	1967-1974	70.00

Tam O'Shanter is a character in a 1790 poem by Robert Burns. He is a farmer who finds some witches and barely escapes.

Tam O'Shanter, Large*	D.6632	1973-Present	35.00 to 44.95
Tam O'Shanter, Miniature	D.6640	1973-Present	14.00 to 21.95
Tam O'Shanter, Small	D.6636	1973-Present	15.00 to 29.95

Sergeant Buz Fuz, Small
D.5838

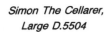

Simon The Cellarer,
Large D.5504

Simple Simon, Large
D.6374

Tam O'Shanter, Large
D.6632

Toby Philpots, Large
D.5736

Toby Philpots was a character in a song in 1761 but he had been a legendary drinker before that time. The toby jug, a full figure of a man, has been called a toby jug or a Toby Philpots since the eighteenth century.

Toby Philpots, Large*	D.5736	1936-1968	65.00 to 90.00
Toby Philpots, Large, Marked A	D.5736	1936-1968	115.00
Toby Philpots, Miniature	D.6043	1938-1968	33.00 to 55.00
Toby Philpots, Miniature, Marked A	D.6043	1938-1968	30.00 to 55.00
Toby Philpots, Small	D.5737	1936-1968	35.00 to 115.00
Toby Philpots, Small, Marked A	D.5737	1936-1968	45.00

Tony Weller, Large D.5531

Touchstone, Large D.5613

Tony Weller is a character from the book "Pickwick Papers" by Charles Dickens.

Tony Weller, Large*	D.5531	1935-1960	73.00 to 110.00
Tony Weller, Large, Marked A	D.5531	1935-1960	75.00
Tony Weller, Miniature	D.6044	1939-1960	29.00 to 50.00
Tony Weller, Miniature, Marked A	D.6044	1939-1960	35.00 to 75.00
Tony Weller, Small	D.5530	1935-1960	35.00 to 55.00

Touchstone is a character in the play "As You Like It" by Shakespeare. He is a clown.

Touchstone, Large*	D.5613	1936-1960	120.00 to 185.00
Touchstone, Large, Marked A	D.5613	1936-1960	155.00 to 175.00

Town Crier represents the eighteenth-century man who called the news for the town in the days before newspapers.

Town Crier, Large	D.6530	1960-1973	90.00 to 129.00
Town Crier, Miniature	D.6544	1960-1973	40.00 to 190.00
Town Crier, Small	D.6537	1960-1973	48.00 to 135.00

Trapper represents the North American man who trapped fur-bearing animals in the wild.

Trapper, Large*	D.6609	1966-Present	35.00 to 44.95
Trapper, Small	D.6612	1966-Present	18.00 to 29.95

Ugly Duchess is a character in the book "Alice in Wonderland" by Lewis Carroll.

Ugly Duchess, Miniature	D.6607	1964-1973	145.00 to 169.00
Ugly Duchess, Small	D.6603	1964-1973	135.00 to 150.00

Uncle Tom Cobbleigh is a character in a song from the 1800s which tells how he rode a horse to the Widdecombe Fair.

Uncle Tom Cobbleigh, Large*   **D.6337**   **1951-1960**   **235.00 to 300.00**

Veteran motorist represents the drivers of the motor cars of the pre-1905 period.

Veteran Motorist, Large*   **D.6633**   **1973-Present**   **35.00 to 44.95**
Veteran Motorist, Miniature   **D.6641**   **1973-Present**   **16.95 to 21.95**
Veteran Motorist, Small   **D.6637**   **1973-Present**   **22.50 to 29.95**

Trapper, Large D.6609

Uncle Tom Cobbleigh, Large
D.6337

Veteran Motorist, Large D.6633

Vicar of Bray is a character in an eighteenth-century song. He was a country parson.

Vicar Of Bray, Large*	D.5615	1936-1960	120.00 to 185.00
Vicar Of Bray, Large, Marked A	D.5615	1936-1960	120.00 to 425.00

Viking represents the Scandinavian seafarers of the eighth to tenth centuries.

Viking, Large	D.6496	1958-1975	59.00 to 79.50
Viking, Miniature	D.6526	1959-1975	100.00 to 150.00
Viking, Small	D.6502	1958-1975	32.00 to 70.00
Viking, Small, Marked A	D.6502	1958-1975	85.00

Walrus and Carpenter are characters in the book "Through the Looking Glass" by Lewis Carroll.

Walrus And Carpenter, Large*	D.6600	1964-Present	35.00 to 44.95
Walrus And Carpenter, Miniature	D.6608	1964-Present	16.95 to 21.95
Walrus And Carpenter, Small	D.6604	1964-Present	22.50 to 29.95

Yachtsman represents the modern sailing man.

Yachtsman, Large*	D.6622	1970-Present	27.00 to 44.95

Vicar Of Bray, Large D.5615

Walrus And Carpenter, Large D.6600

ANIMALS AND BIRDS

ANIMALS AND BIRDS

Animal and bird figures have been an important part of the Royal Doulton line for many years. A few animal figures were made before 1912, but it was not until that date that Charles Noke's models were produced in great numbers. Very realistic figures of wild and domestic animals, stylized figures, and birds were made. Animal figurines were made and the same animals were used to decorate ashtrays, bookends, and other small pieces. This was done in much the same manner that the character-jug designs were adapted to miscellaneous pieces.

Several special groups of animals have been made. The Championship Dog series started about 1939. They were realistic portrayals of champions of the breed and are listed in the catalogs with the abbreviation "Ch." at the beginning of each title. The HN numbers used were all between 1007 and 2667, although other types of animals are also included in these numbers. At least forty-one models have been made and many are still in production. Character dogs depict dogs playing, running, sitting, hunting, or in typical poses. Thirty-nine miniature dog, bird, cat and rabbit models were made. Earthenware goats, calves, and deer were made in small numbers about 1936. The Chatcull Range animals started in 1940. The Chatcull Range was named for Mr. Joe Ledger's home, Chatcull Hall. He was the artist who designed the animal figures for the series. These figures were given the HN numbers 2655 to 2667. Most of them are now out of production. A few whimsical figures were also made, such as the Huntsman Fox which depicts a fox dressed in a red hunting coat. Flambé animals and birds were made and are listed in the rouge flambé chapter. The Jefferson sculptures were designed by Robert Jefferson and produced in limited numbers after 1973.

ART SCULPTURES BY ROBERT JEFFERSON

Figurine	HN Number	Date Issued	Edition Limit
Black-Throated Loon	3500	1974	150
Chipping Sparrow	3511	1976	200
Colorado Chipmunks	3506	1974	75
Downy Woodpecker	3509	1975	unlimited
Fledgling Bluebird	3510	1976	250
Golden-Crowned Kinglet	3504	1974	unlimited
Harbor Seals	3507	1975	75
King Eider	3502	1974	150
Puffins	2668	1974	250
Roseate Terns	3503	1974	150
Snowshoe Hares	3508	1975	75
Snowy Owl, Female	2670	1974	150
Snowy Owl, Male	2669	1974	150
White-Winged Cross Bills	3501	1974	250
Winter Wren	3505	1974	unlimited

Name	HN Number	Price
Airedale, Cotsford Top Sail, Medium*	HN 1023	40.00 to 65.00
Alsatian, Benign Of Picardy, Medium*	HN 1116	37.50 to 65.00
Alsatian, Benign Of Picardy, Small	HN 1117	90.00
American Foxhound, Large	HN 2524	225.00
American Foxhound, Medium	HN 2525	125.00
Bloodhound	HN 176	265.00
Boxer, Warlord Of Mazelaine, Medium*	HN 2643	40.00 to 80.00
Brown Bear, Chatcull Range, 4 1/8 In.	HN 2659	75.00
Budgerigar, Birds, 6 In., Pair	HN 2547	98.50
Bull Pup	K 2	20.00
Bull Terrier, Brown, White, Medium	HN 1143	190.00
Bull Terrier, White, Medium	HN 1132	190.00
Bulldog, Brindle, Large	HN 1042	135.00 to 310.00
Bulldog, Brown & White, Small	HN 1047	22.50 to 40.00
Bulldog, Old Bill, Helmet & Haversack	HN 146	250.00
Bulldog, Union Jack, 2 3/4 In.	HN 6407	120.00 to 150.00
Cairn	K 11	20.00
Cairn, Charming Eyes, Medium	HN 1034	150.00

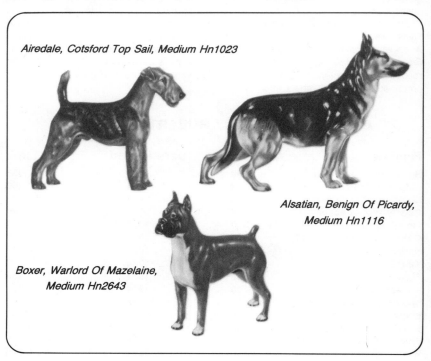

Airedale, Cotsford Top Sail, Medium Hn1023

Alsatian, Benign Of Picardy,
Medium Hn1116

Boxer, Warlord Of Mazelaine,
Medium Hn2643

Cat, Persian, Grey Hn 999

Chipping Sparrow, Jefferson,
7 1/2 In. Hn3511

Cocker & Pheasant, Liver & White, Med. Hn1028

Cat, Persian, Grey*	HN 999	22.50 to 45.00
Character Dog Lying	HN 1101	75.00
Character Dog On Back	HN 1098	75.00
Character Dog Running With Ball	HN 1097	19.95
Character Dog Standing	HN 2509	80.00
Character Dog With Ball*	HN 1103	13.00 to 19.95
Character Dog With Bone	HN 1159	16.95 to 19.95
Character Dog With Plate	HN 1158	16.95 to 19.95
Character Dog With Slipper*	HN 2654	16.95 to 19.95
Character Dog Yawning	HN 1099	13.00 to 19.95
Chestnut Mare With Foal, Large	HN 2522	300.00
Chipping Sparrow, Jefferson, 7 1/2 In.*	HN 3511	950.00
Cocker & Pheasant	HN 2632	60.00 to 70.00
Cocker & Pheasant, Black & White, Medium	HN 1138	60.00 to 70.00
Cocker & Pheasant, Liver & White, Large	HN 1001	225.00
Cocker & Pheasant, Liver & White, Medium *	HN 1028	70.00 to 100.00
Cocker & Pheasant, Liver & White, Small*	HN 1029	100.00

Cocker Spaniel, Black & White, Medium	HN 1109	55.00 to 65.00
Cocker Spaniel, Black & White, Small	HN 1078	70.00
Cocker Spaniel, Golden, Medium	HN 1187	55.00 to 65.00
Cocker Spaniel, Golden, Small	HN 1188	60.00
Cocker Spaniel, Liver & White, Large	HN 1002	210.00
Cocker, Spaniel, Liver & White, Medium*	HN 1036	55.00 to 65.00
Cocker Spaniel, Liver & White, Small	HN 1037	80.00 to 125.00
Cocker Spaniel, Lucky Star, Black, Medium*	HN 1020	40.00 to 125.00
Cocker Spaniel, Lucky Star, Large	HN 1000	195.00 to 210.00
Cocker Spaniel, 2 1/2 In.	K 9	25.00
Cocker Spaniels Sleeping	HN 2590	29.95 to 35.00
Collie, Ashstead Applause, Medium	HN 1058	55.00 to 70.00
Collie, Ashstead Applause, Small	HN 1059	70.00 to 225.00
Colorado Chipmunks, Jefferson, 13 In.*	HN 3506	2500.00
Dachshund, Black, Shrewd Saint, Medium	HN 1128	40.00 to 65.00
Dachshund, Black, Shrewd Saint, Small	HN 1129	125.00
Dachshund, Brown, Medium	HN 1140	110.00 to 175.00
Dachshund, Brown, Small	HN 1141	68.00
Dachshund, Large	HN 1127	200.00

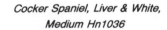

Cocker Spaniel, Liver & White, Medium Hn1036

Cocker Spaniel, Lucky Star, Black, Medium Hn1020

Colorado Chipmunks, Jefferson, 13 In. Hn3506

Dalmatian, Goworth Victor, Medium Hn1113

Doberman Pinscher, Rancho, Medium Hn2645

Dachshund, 2 3/8 In.	K 17	18.00 to 25.00
Dalmatian, Goworth Victor, Medium*	HN 1113	55.00 to 65.00
Dalmatian, Goworth Victor, Small	HN 1114	95.00
Doberman Pinscher, Rancho, Medium*	HN 2645	55.00 to 65.00
Downy Woodpecker, Jefferson, 7 1/2 In.	HN 3509	525.00
Drake, Mallard	HN 2591	50.00
Drake, Purple, 2 1/2 In.*	HN 807	25.00
Drake, White, Miniature	HN 806	50.00
Elephant	HN 2644	50.00 to 52.00

Character Dog With Slipper Hn2654

Character Dog With Ball Hn1103

Drake, Purple, 2 1/2 In. Hn807

English Setter & Pheasant Hn2529

English Setter, Maesydo Mustard, Medium Hn1050

English Setter & Pheasant*	HN 2529	187.50 to 300.00
English Setter, Maesydo Mustard, Medium*	HN 1050	50.00 to 65.00
English Setter, Maesydo Mustard, Small	HN 1051	75.00
Fighter Elephant, Prestige, 12 X 9 In.	HN 2640	450.00
Fledgling Bluebird, Jefferson, 6 In.*	HN 3510	600.00
Fox On Rock, Brown & Tan, 4 3/4 In.	HN 147	85.00 to 135.00
Fox, Prestige Figure	HN 2634	550.00
Fox, Red Frock Coat	HN 100	200.00
Foxhound	K 7	18.00
Foxhound, Medium	HN 1026	225.00
French Poodle, Medium	HN 2631	40.00 to 65.00
Golden Kinglet, Jefferson, 8 1/4 In.	HN 3504	525.00
Greyhound, Brown, Medium	HN 1066	190.00
Greyhound, Small	HN 1077	125.00
Gude Grey Mare, Medium	HN 2569	225.00
Harbor Seals, Jefferson, 8 1/2 In.*	HN 3507	1600.00

Fledgling Bluebird, Jefferson, 6 In. Hn3510

Harbor Seals, Jefferson, 8 1/2 In. Hn3507

King Eider, Jefferson, 11 In. Hn3502

Hare, Lying, Small*	**HN 2594**	25.00 to 30.00
Huntsman Fox	**HN 6448**	18.75 to 30.00
Irish Setter, Medium	**HN 1055**	55.00 to 65.00
Irish Setter, Small	**HN 1056**	55.00 to 70.00
King Eider, Jefferson, 11 In.*	**HN 3502**	1800.00
Kitten, Lying On Back, Brown	**HN 2579**	25.00 to 30.00
Kitten, Sitting On Haunches, Tan*	**HN 2582**	25.00 to 30.00
Kitten, Sitting, Licking Front Paw, Tan	**HN 2583**	25.00 to 30.00
Kitten, Sitting, Licking Hind Paw, Brown*	**HN 2580**	25.00 to 30.00
Kitten, Sitting, Surprised, Tan	**HN 2584**	25.00 to 30.00
Kitten, Sleeping, Brown	**HN 2581**	25.00 to 30.00
Labrador, Bumblikite, Mansergh, Medium*	**HN 2667**	55.00 to 65.00

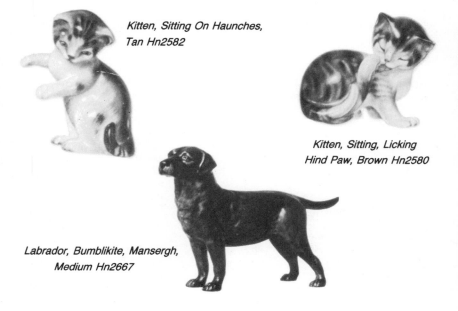

Kitten, Sitting On Haunches, Tan Hn2582

Kitten, Sitting, Licking Hind Paw, Brown Hn2580

Labrador, Bumblikite, Mansergh, Medium Hn2667

Leopard On Rock, Prestige, 11 1/2 In. Hn2638

Lion On Rock, Prestige, 11 In. Hn2641

Pekinese K 6

Langur Monkey, Chatcull Range, 4 3/8 In.	**HN 2657**	150.00
Leopard On Rock, Prestige, 11 1/2 In.*	**HN 2638**	1200.00
Lion On Rock, Prestige, 11 In.*	**HN 2641**	1200.00
Peacock	**HN 2577**	80.00
Pekinese*	**K 6**	20.00
Pekinese, Biddie Of Ifield, Small	**HN 1012**	25.00 to 40.00
Pekinese, Large	**HN 1011**	230.00
Pheasant	**HN 2545**	225.00
Pig	**HN 2650**	45.00
Pig	**HN 2653**	45.00
Pig, Asleep, Medium	**HN 800**	95.00
Pointer	**HN 2624**	146.25 to 225.00
Polar Bear On Ice Cube, 4 In.	**HN 119**	150.00
Pride Of The Shires, Brown, Small	**HN 2564**	200.00
Puffins, Jefferson, 11 In.*	**HN 2668**	1600.00
Puppies In Basket*	**HN 2588**	22.50 to 35.00
Puppy Begging, Cairn	**HN 2589**	20.00 to 35.00

Puppies In Basket Hn2588

Puffins, Jefferson, 11 In. Hn2668

Puppy In Basket, Cocker	HN 2585	29.95 to 35.00
Puppy In Basket, Cocker	HN 2586	29.95 to 35.00
Puppy In Basket, Terrier	HN 2587	29.95 to 35.00
River Hog, Chatcull Range	HN 2663	40.00
Roseate Terns, Jefferson, 12 1/4 In.*	HN 3503	2500.00
Rough-Haired Terrier, Crackley, Small	HN 1014	25.00 to 40.00
Rough-Haired Terrier, Startler, Medium	HN 1013	135.00
Scotch Terrier, Albourne Arthur, Medium	HN 1015	150.00
Scotch Terrier, Albourne Arthur, Small	HN 1016	25.00 to 40.00
Sealyham	K 3	18.00
Siamese Cat, Lying	HN 2662	42.00 to 50.00
Siamese Cat, Sitting	HN 2655	42.00 to 50.00
Siamese Cat, Standing	HN 2660	42.00 to 50.00
Smooth-Haired Terrier, Medium	HN 1069	190.00
Snowshoe Hares, Jefferson, 13 In.*	HN 3508	2750.00

Hare, Lying, Small Hn2594

*Roseate Terns, Jefferson,
12 1/4 In. Hn3503*

Snowshoe Hares, Jefferson, 13 In. Hn3508

Snowy Owl, Female, Jefferson, 9 1/2 In. Hn2670

Snowy Owl, Male, Jefferson, 16 In. Hn2669

Snowy Owl, Female, Jefferson, 9 1/2 In.*	HN 2670	2150.00
Snowy Owl, Male, Jefferson, 16 In.*	HN 2669	1750.00
Springer Spaniel, Dry Toast, Medium	HN 2516	150.00
Springer Spaniel, Dry Toast, Small	HN 2517	22.50 to 75.00
St. Bernard	K 19	20.00
Terrier, Seated	HN 997	195.00
Tiger On Rock, Prestige, 11 In.*	HN 2639	395.00
Welsh Corgi	K 16	20.00
Welsh Corgi, Medium	HN 2558	110.00
Welsh Corgi, Spring Robin, Small	HN 2559	33.00 to 40.00
White Winged Crossbills, Jefferson*	HN 3501	1450.00
Winter Wren, Jefferson, 4 3/4 In.	HN 3505	3750.00

Tiger On Rock, Prestige, 11 In. Hn2639

White-Winged Crossbills, Jefferson Hn3501

LIMITED EDITIONS

LIMITED EDITIONS

The term "limited edition" has had a special meaning since the early 1970s when many companies including the Doulton Company began making plates and other pieces in announced limited numbers. Before this time, the Doulton factory made several special commemorative jugs and presentation pieces that we would refer to as limited editions. The first of these was a jug called "Regency Coach" made in 1931 and limited to 500 pieces. Each piece was signed and numbered. The jugs were made with scenes picturing people and places. The decorations were three-dimensional. The following is a list of the known jugs and loving cups and the number in each edition.

Title	Date	Edition
Apothecary Loving Jug	1934	600
Captain Cook Jug	1933	350
Charles Dickens Loving Cup	1970	500
Dickens Jug	1936	1000
Drake Jug	1933	500
Edward VIII Coronation	1936	1800
Elizabeth II Coronation Loving Cup	1953	2000
George VI Coronation Loving Cup	1937	2000
George Washington Jug	1932	1000
Guy Fawkes Jug	1934	600
John Peel Loving Cup	1933	500
Loving Cup (large)	1937	2000
Loving Cup (small)	1937	2000
Master of Fox Hunt MFH Presentation Jug	1930	500
Mayflower Loving Cup	1970	500
Nelson Loving Cup	1935	600
Pied Piper Jug	1934	600
Regency Coach Jug	1931	500
Shakespeare Jug	1933	1000
Silver Wedding Loving Cup	1935	1000
Three Musketeers Loving Cup	1936	600
Tower of London Jug	1933	500
Treasure Island Jug	1934	600
Village Blacksmith Jug	1936	590

In 1970, a black Charles Dickens loving cup and a black Mayflower loving cup were made. Limited pieces listed in other chapters of this book include: bust of Prince Charles, a pair of busts of Queen Elizabeth and the Duke of Edinburgh, listed in the Miscellaneous chapter; Indian Brave, Palio, Lady Musicians, Dancers of the World, and Soldiers of the Revolution, listed in the Figurines chapter; and Jefferson bird sculptures, listed with Animals and Birds.

The modern limited-edition plates, tankards, and plaques were first made in 1972. All of these series and the pieces included are listed in the price list by title and year.

Name	Date	Price
Jug, Captain Cook*	1933	545.00
Jug, Dickens*	1936	750.00
Jug, Drake*	1933	550.00
Jug, George Washington*	1932	225.00 to 275.00
Jug, Guy Fawkes	1934	400.00
Jug, M.F.H. Presentation,13 1/2 In.*	1930	550.00
Jug, Pied Piper	1934	750.00

Jug, Captain Cook

Jug, Dickens

Jug, Treasure Island

Jug, Regency Coach*	1931	425.00 to 550.00
Jug, Shakespeare*	1933	250.00 to 300.00
Jug, Tower Of London	1933	250.00 to 300.00
Jug, Treasure Island*	1934	550.00
Jug, Village Blacksmith*	1936	550.00
Loving Cup, Charles Dickens	1934	300.00
Loving Cup, Charles Dickens	1970	285.00

Loving Cup, Edward VIII Coronation, Large*	**1937**	**340.00**
Loving Cup, Edward VIII Coronation, Small*	**1937**	**165.00**

Jug, Regency Coach

Jug, M.F.H. Presentation, 13 1/2 In.

Jug, George Washington

Loving Cup, Three Musketeers

Jug, Drake

Loving Cup, Edward VIII Coronation, Large

Jug, Village Blacksmith   *Loving Cup, Elizabeth II Coronation*

Loving Cup, Elizabeth II Coronation*	1953	500.00
Loving Cup, George VI Coronation*	1937	365.00
Loving Cup, John Peel	1933	400.00
Loving Cup, King George & Mary Silver Wedding		
	1935	300.00
Loving Cup, Mayflower*	1970	285.00
Loving Cup, Nelson	1935	300.00
Loving Cup, Three Musketeers*	1936	750.00

Christmas plaques are limited to 13,000 each year.

Plaque, Christmas	1973	37.50
Plaque, Christmas, Christmas Carol	1972	35.00 to 40.00

Loving Cup, George VI Coronation

Loving Cup, Mayflower

Jug, Shakespeare

Plate, All God's Children, A Brighter Day

All God's Children series by Lisette De Winne is limited to 15,000 each year.

Plate, All God's Children, A Brighter Day*	**1978**	**60.00 to 100.00**
Plate, All God's Children, Village Children	**1979**	**65.00**

Plate, American Tapestries,
Pumpkin Patch

Plate, American Tapestries, Sleigh Bells

American Tapestries series by C. A. Brown is limited to 10,000 each year.

Plate, American Tapestries, Pumpkin Patch*	**1979**	**70.00 to 75.00**
Plate, American Tapestries, Sleigh Bells*	**1978**	**45.00 to 70.00**

Annual Christmas series decorated with Victorian Era drawings is limited to the period of issue each year.

Plate, Annual Christmas, Annual Christmas Day*	**1979**	**29.95**
Plate, Annual Christmas, Victorian Girl	**1978**	**20.00 to 33.00**
Plate, Annual Christmas, Winter Fun*	**1977**	**36.00 to 55.00**

Plate, Annual Christmas, Annual
Christmas Day

Plate, Annual Christmas, Winter Fun

Christmas Around the World series was produced by Royal Doulton from 1972 to 1978 and is limited to 15,000 each year.

Plate, Christmas, Christmas In America	1978	55.00 to 70.00
Plate, Christmas, Christmas In Bulgaria	1974	40.00
Plate, Christmas, Christmas In England*	1972	35.00 to 40.00
Plate, Christmas, Christmas In Holland*	1976	55.00 to 60.00
Plate, Christmas, Christmas In Mexico**	1973	37.50 to 50.00
Plate, Christmas, Christmas In Norway*	1975	45.00 to 47.00
Plate, Christmas, Christmas In Poland	1977	50.00 to 55.00

Plate, Christmas, Christmas In England

Plate, Christmas, Christmas In Holland

Commedia Dell' Arte series by Leroy Neiman is limited to 15,000 each year.

Plate, Commedia Dell' Arte, Columbine*	1977	70.00
Plate, Commedia Dell' Arte, Harlequin*	1974	75.00

Plate, Commedia Dell' Arte, Punchinello

Plate, Commedia Dell' Arte, Harlequin   *Plate, Commedia Dell' Arte, Columbine*

Plate, Commedia Dell' Arte, Pierrot	**1976**	**65.00**
Plate Commedia Dell' Arte, Punchinello*	**1978**	**70.00**
Plate, Commedia Dell' Arte, Winning Color	**1980**	**80.00**

Flower Garden series by Hahn Vidal is limited to 15,000 each year.

Plate, Flower Garden, Country Bouquet*	**1978**	**45.00 to 70.00**
Plate, Flower Garden, Dreaming Lotus*	**1976**	**42.00 to 70.00**
Plate, Flower Garden, From Mother's Garden	**1979**	**85.00**
Plate, Flower Garden, Poet's Garden*	**1977**	**45.00 to 70.00**
Plate, Flower Garden, Spring Harmony*	**1975**	**49.00 to 75.00**

I Remember America series by Eric Sloane is limited to 15,000 each year.

Plate, I Remember America, Four Corners*	**1979**	**75.00**
Plate, I Remember America, Lovejoy Bridge*	**1978**	**45.00 to 70.00**
Plate, I Remember America, Pennsylvania*	**1977**	**45.00 to 85.00**

Plate, Flower Garden,
Dreaming Lotus

Plate, Flower Garden,
Poet's Garden

Plate, Flower Garden,
Country Bouquet

Plate, Flower Garden,
Spring Harmony

Plate, I Remember America,
Four Corners

Plate, I Remember America,
Lovejoy Bridge

Plate, I Remember America, Pennsylvania

Plate, Log Of Dashing Wave,
Rounding Horn

Plate, Log Of Dashing
Wave, Running Free

Jungle Fantasy series by Gustavo Novoa is limited to 10,000 each year.

Plate, Jungle Fantasy, Compassion	1980	**75.00**
Plate, Jungle Fantasy, The Ark**	1979	**75.00**

Kate Greenaway Almanack series is limited to the period of issue each year.

Plate, Kate Greenaway, Almanack	1978	**25.00 to 29.95**

Log of the Dashing Wave series by John Stobart is limited to 15,000 each year.

Plate, Log Of Dashing Wave, Hong Kong	1979	**75.00**
Plate, Log Of Dashing Wave, Rounding Horn*	1978	**45.00 to 70.00**
Plate, Log Of Dashing Wave, Running Free*	1977	**70.00**
Plate, Log Of Dashing Wave, Sailing With Tide	1976	**70.00 to 80.00**

Mother and Child series by Edna Hibel is limited to 15,000 each year.

Plate, Mother And Child, Colette & Child*	1973	**400.00 to 500.00**
Plate, Mother And Child, Kristina & Child	1975	**80.00 to 130.00**
Plate, Mother And Child, Lucia & Child	1977	**79.00 to 120.00**
Plate, Mother And Child, Marilyn & Child	1976	**75.00 to 100.00**
Plate, Mother And Child, Sayuri & Child*	1974	**105.00 to 140.00**

Plate, Mother And Child,
Colette & Child

Plate, Mother And Child, Sayuri & Child

Plate, Ports Of Call, New Orleans   *Plate, Ports Of Call, Venice*

Ports of Call series by Dong Kingman is limited to 15,000 each year.

Plate, Ports Of Call, Montmartre	**1978**	**45.00 to 70.00**
Plate, Ports Of Call, New Orleans*	**1976**	**42.00 to 70.00**
Plate, Ports Of Call, San Francisco	**1975**	**49.00 to 80.00**
Plate, Ports Of Call, Venice*	**1977**	**45.00 to 70.00**

Reflections on China series by Chen Chi is limited to 15,000 each year.

Plate, Reflections On China, Garden*	**1976**	**45.00 to 70.00**
Plate, Reflections On China, Imperial Palace	**1977**	**75.00 to 80.00**

Plate, Reflections On China,
Imperial Palace

Plate, Reflections On China,
Temple Of Heaven

*Plate, Reflections On China,
Tranquility Garden*

Plate, Reflections On China, Temple Of Heaven*	**1978**	**45.00 to 75.00**
Plate, Reflections On China, Tranquility Garden*	**1976**	**45.00 to 70.00**

Valentine series is limited to the period of issue each year.

Plate, Valentine, Heart & Flowers	**1977**	**18.00 to 78.00**
Plate, Valentine, If I Loved You	**1978**	**25.00 to 50.00**
Plate, Valentine, My Valentine**	**1979**	**20.00 to 30.00**
Plate, Valentine, Victorian Boy & Girl	**1976**	**50.00 to 99.00**

Christmas tankards series is limited from 13,000 the first year to 15,000 in later years.

Tankard, Christmas, Carolers	**1972**	**37.50 to 42.00**
Tankard, Christmas, Cratchit & Scrooge	**1971**	**35.00 to 54.00**
Tankard, Christmas, Ghost Of Christmas Future	**1979**	**60.00**
Tankard, Christmas, Ghost Of Christmas Past	**1975**	**47.50**
Tankard, Christmas, Ghost Of Christmas Present	**1977**	**50.00**
Tankard, Christmas, Ghost Of Christmas Present	**1978**	**55.00**
Tankard, Christmas, Ghost Of Christmas Present*		
	1976	**60.00**
Tankard, Christmas, Marley's Ghost*	**1974**	**45.00**
Tankard, Christmas, Solicitation**	**1973**	**40.00**

*Tankard, Christmas, Ghost Of
Christmas Present 1976*

Tankard, Christmas, Marley's Ghost

ROUGE FLAMBÉ

ROUGE FLAMBÉ

Rouge flambé is the name given to the blood red color that was found in the early Chinese glazes. Many potters have tried to duplicate the color, and during the 1890s the Doulton potters also tried. Charles J. Noke experimented with various red glazes, as did John Salter, Cuthbert Bailey, and Bernard Moore, a potter from another factory. The red glaze, a transmutation glaze, is created by the proper combination of copper oxide and other chemicals and the amount of oxygen admitted to the kiln at various times during the firing.

Doulton perfected a rouge flambé glaze and it received instant acclaim. The factory had many artists work on designs for flambé wares, and several types of the ware were made. The first of the Doulton flambé wares was shown in the St. Louis exhibition of 1904.

Experimentation continued for several years and required special kilns. Two types of decoration were selected. The veined sung, first made about 1920, is a glazed piece that depends upon the results of the kiln to determine the exact coloring of the glaze. No two pieces were exactly alike but each had shadings of red to purple. The woodcut flambé, started in 1964, combines the red glaze and woodcut vignettes based on Thomas Beswick drawings that picture the English landscape. A special series of rouge flambé animals was also made. Some pieces in all of these lines are still being made.

Bowl, Veined Sung	600.00
Buddha, Veined Sung	900.00
Cat, Rouge, No. 9, 4 3/4 In.	32.50 to 56.00
Dragon, Veined Sung	550.00
Drake, Rouge, No.137, 6 In.	33.00 to 68.00
Duck, Rouge, No.112, 1 1/2 In.	25.00 to 34.00
Duck, Rouge, No. 395, 2 1/2 In.	20.00 to 34.00
Elephant, Rouge, No. 489a, 5 1/2 In.*	80.00 to 195.00

Elephant, Rouge, No. 489a, 5 1/2 In.

Hare, Ear Up, Rouge, No.113, 2 1/2 In.

Fish	850.00
Fox, Lying, Rouge, No. 29b, 1 In.	27.50 to 38.00
Fox, Lying, 12 In.	350.00
Fox, Sitting, Rouge, No.14, 4 In.	32.50 to 42.00
Fox, Sitting, 6 In.	50.00
Hare, Ear Up, Rouge, No.113, 2 1/2 In.*	37.50 to 60.00
Hare, Lying, Rouge, No. 656a, 1 3/4 In.	20.00 to 38.00
Hare, Sitting, Rouge, No.1157, 2 3/4 In.	32.50 to 42.00
Hare, Sitting, 5 In.	50.00
Monkeys	250.00
Penguin, Rouge, No. 84, 6 In.	30.00 to 60.00
Puppy With Big Feet	175.00
Rhino, Veined Sung	600.00
Tiger, Rouge, No. 809, 6 In.	275.00 to 435.00
Tray, Veined Sung, No.1620	15.95
Vase, Desert Scene, Camels, Riders, 8 1/2 In.	345.00
Vase, Landscape, No. 7754, 7 1/2 In.	245.00
Vase, Veined Sung, No.1605, 4 1/4 In.	41.50 to 50.00
Vase, Veined Sung, No.1612, 8 In.*	75.00
Vase, Veined Sung, No.1618, 9 1/2 In.	129.95
Vase, Veined Sung, No. 925, 7 In.	65.00
Vase, Woodcut, No. 1603, 7 1/4 In.	37.50
Vase, Woodcut, No. 1606, 4 1/4 In.*	29.50
Vase, Woodcut, No. 1613, 6 1/2 In.	47.50 to 65.00
Vase, Woodcut, No. 1619	129.95

Vase, Veined Sung, No.1612, 8 In.

Vase, Woodcut, No.1606, 4 1/4 In.

SERIES WARES

SERIES WARES

Early in the 1900s, Charles J. Noke had still another idea for the Royal Doulton factory. He designed or had others design a line called series wares. The first of these seemed to be the series called Eglinton Tournament, first made in 1902. Other series followed, and by 1906 advertisements for them appeared in papers throughout the United States. Many of the series pictured scenes from literary or historic events. Some were based on illustrations that had appeared in books. Several series pictured scenes or characters from Shakespearean plays. Many of the series wares had special borders and special backstamps.

The Dickens ware was probably the most popular series. A huge selection of dishes for luncheon and dinner sets was made, as well as many types of serving pieces, pitchers, vases, humidors, toothbrush holders, butter pats, and match holders. There were at least thirty-six different characters pictured.

The Doulton factory made a special plate for the Dickens centennial in 1911. It had a picture of Dickens's head in the center and a border of his characters. The factory made similar-style plates, called "head rack plates," in the late 1940s. They pictured British historical and literary figures, including head portraits of celebrities. Most of them have special borders. Another series, called "scenic rack plates," pictures animals, scenery, or people and their way life in the United Kingdom.

ALICE IN WONDERLAND

Alice in Wonderland, produced 1906 to 1932, pictures scenes from Lewis Carroll's book "Alice in Wonderland."

Plate, Bowl, Creamer, Queen Of Hearts
65.00

BABES IN WOODS

Babes in Woods was produced from the late 1880s until 1928. It is sometimes called Blue Children. It is a flow blue ware. There is no special mark.

Bowl, Two Girls Sitting Under Tree, 9 1/2 In.
195.00

Jardiniere, Lady & Girl, 10 In.
500.00

Plate, 9 In.
125.00

Vase, Girl Playing Violin, 8 In.
185.00

Vase, Girl Sitting On Rock, Gold-Plated Handles, 6 In.
175.00

Vase, Two Children Under Tree, 8 3/4 In.
125.00

Vase, Two Girls Sitting, 10 In.
495.00

Vase, Woman Walking In Snow, 8 1/2 In.
250.00

Vase, 6 In.
275.00

BAYEUX TAPESTRY

Bayeux Tapestry, 1906 to about 1928, is a famous embroidery depicting William the Conquerer's expedition to England. The tapestry is preserved at Bayeux in Normandy and is attributed to William's wife. The ware is marked with the words "The Battle of Hastings 1066 from the Bayeux Tapestry." Some have a green and brown border; others have battle scenes.

Candlestick, Battle Of Hastings, 8 3/4 In., Pair
175.00

Creamer, Battle Of Hastings, 1910
40.00

Match Holder, Battle Of Hastings, 2 7/8 In.
40.00

Pitcher, Battle Of Hastings, Bulbous, 6 In.
75.00

Sugar & Creamer, Battle Of Hastings, Open
75.00 to 150.00

Tobacco Jar, Battle Of Hastings, Covered
90.00

Blue Children, see Babes in Woods

BOBBY BURNS

Bobby Burns was a Scottish poet who lived from 1759 to 1796. He was famous for his poem "Auld Lang Syne." The plates picture Burns and others accompanied by sayings from his poems.

Bowl, Here's A Health To Charlie, 1926, 9 1/2 In.
35.00

Mug, Take Ye A Cup O' Kindness
35.00

Plate, Heres A Health To Them Thats Awa, 10 1/2 In.
55.00

BUNNYKINS

Bunnykins was produced from 1934 to the present. There are over 150 designs on children's ware including mush sets, cereal bowls, etc. Pieces are marked with three bunnies and the name, some with Barbara Vernon and some with the "A" mark. Some pieces also have a running bunny border.

Bank, 9 1/2 In.
35.00

Bowl And Mug, Marked A
85.00

Egg, Opens, 2 3/4 In.
15.00

Egg, Opens, 3 3/4 In.
19.00

Saucer, Santa Bunny
35.00

CANTERBURY PILGRIMS

Canterbury Pilgrims was produced from 1902 to the 1920s. It features scenes from the book "Canterbury Tales" by Geoffrey Chaucer. They have a decorative border with lion and bird shields. They are marked "Canterbury Pilgrims."

Cup & Saucer
35.00

Pitcher, 7 1/2 In.
65.00

Plate, 10 1/2 In.
45.00 to 50.00

CAVALIERS

Cavaliers, sometimes called Three Musketeers, was produced from 1908 to the 1930s. The plates have a lion, cross, and shield border. There is no special mark.

Plate, 8 In.
20.00

Tankard, 6 In.
52.00

Tobacco Jar, Here's A Health Unto His Majesty, Blue & White
85.00

CHARACTER PLATES

Character Plates are illustrated with Royal Doulton figurines. They are hand-painted, embossed and sculpted. The back of the plates has information about the figurines.

Balloon Man, 1980, 10 In.
100.00

Old Balloon Seller, 1979, 10 In.
100.00

COACHING DAYS IN OLD ENGLAND

Coaching Days In Old England was made about 1906. Each is decorated with a single figure. They have a coaching scene border. There is no special mark.

Pitcher, Old Bob Ye Guard, 8 3/4 In.
125.00

Plate, Old Bob Ye Guard, 10 In.
55.00

COACHING DAYS

Coaching Days was made of bone china or earthenware about 1906. The early pieces are pastel and have no special mark. Later wares made around 1920 were produced in brighter colors and were marked with the words "Old English Coaching Scenes." Some were also signed "Grace." It is very similar to the Fox-Hunting series. The plates have a dark green border.

Bowl, 10 In.
150.00

Coffee Pot
45.00

Cup & Saucer
24.00 to 50.00

Milk & Mush Set
70.00

Pitcher, Bone China, 5 In.
75.00

Pitcher, 5 1/2 In.
65.00

Plate, 7 In.
15.00

Plate, 8 In.
20.00 to 22.00

Plate, 10 In.*
35.00 to 65.00

Saucer*
30.00

Tumbler, 4 1/4 In.
40.00

Vase, 4 3/8 In.
48.00

Vase, 8 1/2 In.
59.00

Coaching Days, Plate, 10 In.

DAVID TENIERS FLEMISH PAINTINGS

David Teniers Flemish Paintings picture paintings of David Teniers II, who lived from 1610 to 1690. The wares are decorated with deep colors.

Pitcher, Deep Tones, 8 In.
95.00

DESERT SCENES

Desert Scenes picture camels, palm trees, pyramids, and Arabs. The plates are decorated with pastel colors and a yellow color sand. They are marked "Desert Scenes."

Pitcher, 12 In.
50.00

Plate, Nappy Handle, 10 In.
25.00

Sugar, Covered
55.00

DICKENS WARE

Mr Macawber
D. 6327

Mr Pickwick.
D. 6327.

Dickens Ware was produced from 1908 to 1931 in one version and 1931 to 1974 in another. They all feature characters from various stories by Charles Dickens. The early wares are marked in brown and the later wares which are decorated in brighter colors are marked in black. There is also a line marked Australia. These are decorated with figures in relief.

Dickens Ware, see also listings in miscellaneous chapter

Bowl, Artful Dodger, 7 In.
65.00

Bowl, Barkis, 6 In.
65.00

Bowl, Bill Sykes, Handled, 6 3/4 In.
35.00

Bowl, Cap'n Cuttle, 9 1/2 In.
75.00

Bowl, Mr. Pickwick
25.00

Bowl, Sam Weller, Handled, 6 3/4 In.
35.00

Bowl, Tony Weller, 6 In.
65.00

Cache Pot, Mr. Micawber, 5 In.
60.00

Charger, Dick Swiveller, 13 In.
85.00

Charger, Mrs. Micawber, 13 In.
85.00

Creamer, Bill Sykes, 5 In.
75.00

Creamer, Tony Weller, 4 In.
70.00

Cup & Saucer, Alfred Jingle
75.00

Cup & Saucer, Bill Sykes
75.00

Cup & Saucer, Cap'n Cuttle
75.00

Napkin Ring, Fat Boy
85.00

Pin Tray, David Copperfield, Marked Australia, 8 In.*
58.00

Pin Tray, Mr. Pickwick, 8 In.
33.00

Pitcher, Barkis, Black Mark, 6 In.
85.00

Pitcher, Cap'n Cuttle, 7 1/4 In.
75.00 to 125.00

Pitcher, Fagin, Brown Mark, 6 3/4 In.
70.00

Pitcher, Poor Jo, 12 In.
125.00

David Copperfield,
Dickensware, Pin Tray,
Marked Australia, 8 In.

Pitcher, Tony Weller, Brown Mark, 5 1/8 In.
65.00

Pitcher, Tony Weller, 12 In.
95.00 to 125.00

Plate, Alfred Jingle, 6 In.
39.00

Plate, Barkis, 10 In.
55.00

Plate, Bill Sykes, Square, 5 3/4 In.
32.00

Plate, Cap'n Cuttle, 10 In.
55.00

Plate, Dick Swiveller, 10 In.
55.00

Plate, Fagin, 9 1/2 In.
35.00

Plate, Fat Boy, 8 In.
45.00

Plate, Mr. Micawber, 8 In.
50.00

Plate, Mr. Pickwick, 12 In.
55.00

Plate, Mr. Squeers, Square, 8 In.
60.00

Plate, Old Charlie, 10 In.
110.00

Plate, Sam Weller, 7 1/2 In.
32.00

Plate, Tom Pinch, 10 In.
55.00

Plate, Tony Weller, 8 In.
27.50 to 60.00

Sauce, Cap'n Cuttle
95.00

Sugar, Fat Boy, Open
100.00

Sugar, Sairey Gamp
60.00

Sugar, Tony Weller
59.00

Teapot, Fagin
77.50

Toothpick, Sairey Gamp, 3 In.
75.00 to 95.00

Tray, Bread, Oliver, Brown Mark
125.00

Tray, Mr. Squeers, 9 X 7 1/2 In.
60.00

Votes For Women Hn2816

Jester Hn71, Hn1295

Falstaff Hn1606

Flower Seller's Children Hn1206

Shepherdess, Purple Bodice,
  Blue Skirt Hn 735
Shepherd Hn 751

Sweet & Twenty Hn1298
Sweet & Twenty Hn1360
Sweet & Twenty Hn1589

Proposal, Lady, Red Dress Hn 715
Proposal, Male, Red Coat Hn 725

La Sylphide Hn2138
Giselle Hn2139
Giselle, Forest Glade Hn2140

Bather, Painted Bathing Suit Hn1708

Southern Belle Hn2229

Harmony Hn2824

Mask, Black With Blue, Yellow Dots Hn1271
Mask, White With Black Trim Hn 657
Mask, Red With Black Squares Hn 729

St.George Hn2067

Princess Badoura Hn2081   *St.George Hn2051*

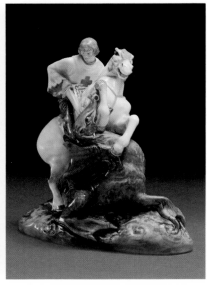

The Admiral, Head Rack Plate

Don Quixote, Large D.6455

*North American Indian,
Large D.6611*

Sleuth, Large D.6631

Mine Host, Large D.6468

Falconer, Large D.6533

Smuggler, Small D.6619

Athos, Large D.6439

Neptune, Large D.6548

Golfer, Large D.6623

Merlin, Large D.6529

Gaoler, Large D.6570

Yachtsman, Large D.6622

Lobster Man, Large D.6617

Bootmaker, Large D.6572

Vase, Barkis, Handled
175.00

Vase, Dick Swiveller, Tony Weller
275.00

Vase, Fat Boy, Brown Mark, 6 1/4 In.
55.00

Vase, Fat Boy, Handled
100.00

Vase, Fat Boy, Poor Jo, Relief, Marked Australia, 7 5/8 In.
135.00

Vase, Mr. Micawber, 9 1/2 In.
90.00

DON QUIXOTE

Don Quixote is a famous character in the book "Don Quixote" by
Miguel de Cervantes. The plates have a greenish grey background.
Some have a tree and windmill border. There is no special mark.

Pitcher, Quixote & Sancho Panza, Ironstone, 7 1/2 In.
65.00

Plate, Sancho, Windmill, Pasture, 10 In.
55.00

DUTCH

Dutch, sometimes called Holland, was produced from 1905. It pictures scenes of Dutch families and children in their surroundings. The
wares are decorated with a yellow sky, green grass, sailboats, and
sometimes brick walls. Some have a tulip border. There is no special
mark.

Beaker, Dutch Family, 3 1/2 In.
55.00

Cookie Jar, Made For McVitie Biscuit Co.
145.00

Pitcher, People, Boats And Windmill, Handled, 5 1/2 In.
44.00

Teapot, Windmill
350.00

Toothpick, Dutch People, 4 In.
16.00

Trivet*
55.00

Vase, Handled, 5 In.
38.00

Vase, 7 In.
45.00

Dutch, Trivet

EGLINTON TOURNAMENT

Eglinton Tournament, 1902 to about 1914, was held by Archibald, the 13th Earl of Eglinton in 1839. The wares picture knights on horseback, jousting, and other tournament events. It has no special mark.

Plate, Knights Jousting, 10 In.
37.50

EGYPTIAN TOUR

Egyptian Tour pictures scenes of Egypt. The plates have a brown, beige and orange border. There is no special mark.

Plate, Tutankhamin's Treasures, 10 In.
65.00

ENGLISH OLD PROVERBS

English Old Proverbs, about 1914, are decorated with a tree border, picture and two proverbs. They are marked with the words "English Old Proverbs."

Plate, Count Not Your Chickens
30.00 to 35.00

ENGLISH OLD SCENES

English Old Scenes is divided into two series, the Gipsies and the Gleaners. The Gipsies life-style is featured in bright colors and the harvest-working people of the fields are pictured in the Gleaners.

They have a tree border. They are marked with the words "English Old Scenes," and "Gipsies," or "Gleaners."

Bowl, The Gleaners, 8 1/2 In.
65.00

Pitcher, The Gleaners, 7 In.
185.00

Plaque, The Gipsies, 13 In.
140.00

Plaque, The Gleaners, 13 In.
140.00 to 175.00

Plate, The Gipsies, 10 In.
30.00

Vase, The Gleaners, 6 1/2 In.
65.00

FAIRY TALES

Fairy Tales was produced about 1933. The plates are decorated with characters from stories such as the Pied Piper or Rip Van Winkle. There is no special mark.

Cup, Rip Van Winkle
50.00

FALCONRY

Falconry is an early Royal Doulton-Burslem ware produced at the Nile St. factory. It pictures equestrian scenes. It has a decorative border. The mark is a prize ribbon with the word "Falconry."

Plate, Ladies And Gent On Horseback, 10 In.
60.00

FAMOUS SHIPS

Famous Ships pictures ships in relief on a pastel background. The
plates have a special mark which includes the name of the ship and
the Australian mark.

Pitcher, The Hydra, 5 1/2 In.
65.00

Plate, HMS Victory, 10 In.
55.00

Plate, The Revenge, 12 In.
40.00 to 50.00

FOX-HUNTING

Fox-Hunting, about 1906, is similar to Coaching Days. It has a scalloped edge and a dark green border. The words "Fox-Hunting" are
the special mark.

Beaker, Brown & Tan, Raised Figures, 4 In.
40.00

Mug
25.00

Plate, Hunters In Tavern, 10 In.
40.00

Punch Set, Bowl, 12 Mugs
780.00

GAFFERS

Gaffers, about 1923, pictures elderly country men and printed sayings. The plates are decorated in bright colors. They are marked with a crossed umbrella and cane and the word "Gaffers."

Plate, All The Way From Zummerset, 10 In.
45.00

GALLANT FISHERS

Gallant Fishers pictures fishing scenes and sayings from Isaac Walton's book "The Compleat Angler." It has a special mark showing a hanging fish sign and the words "The Gallant Fishers."

Pitcher, And When The Timrous Trout, 5 In.
65.00 to 80.00

GIBSON GIRL

Gibson Girl plates were made in the early 1900s. Twenty-four 10 1/2-inch plates picture episodes from the book "A Widow And Her Friends" by the artist Charles Dana Gibson in black and blue. There is no special mark.

Plate, Arriving At Journey's End, 10 1/2 In.
55.00 to 78.00

Plate, Disturbed By A Vision, 10 1/2 In.
55.00 to 78.00

Plate, Does Not Improve Her Spirits, 10 1/2 In.
55.00 to 78.00

Plate, Fails To Find Rest, 10 1/2 In.
55.00 to 65.00

Plate, Finds Consolation In Mirror, 10 1/2 In.
55.00 to 78.00

Plate, Message From Outside World, 10 1/2 In.
55.00 to 78.00

Plate, Miss Babbles Authoress, 10 1/2 In.
55.00 to 78.00

Plate, Miss Babbles Brings Paper, 10 1/2 In.
55.00 to 78.00

Plate, Morning Run, 10 1/2 In.
55.00 to 78.00

Plate, Mr. Waddles Finds Card, 10 1/2 In.
55.00 to 78.00

Plate, Mrs. Diggs Safety Of Child, 10 1/2 In.
55.00 to 78.00

Plate, Quiet Dinner With Dr. Bottles, 10 1/2 In.
55.00 to 78.00

Plate, Remained In Retirement, 10 1/2 In.
55.00 to 78.00

Plate, She Becomes A Nurse, 10 1/2 In.
55.00 to 78.00

Plate, She Contemplates The Cloister, 10 1/2 In.
55.00 to 78.00

Plate, She Decides To Die, 10 1/2 In.
55.00 to 78.00

Plate, She Goes Into Colors, 10 1/2 In.
55.00 to 78.00

Plate, She Goes To Fancy Dress Ball, 10 1/2 In.
55.00 to 78.00

Plate, She Is The Subject, 10 1/2 In.
55.00 to 78.00

Plate, She Longs For Seclusion, 10 1/2 In.
55.00 to 78.00

Plate, She Looks For Relief, 10 1/2 In.
55.00 to 78.00

Plate, They All Go Fishing, 10 1/2 In.
55.00 to 78.00

Plate, They All Go Skating, 10 1/2 In.
55.00 to 78.00

Plate, Winning New Friends, 10 1/2 In.
55.00 to 78.00

GOLFING

Golfing, about 1905 to the 1920s, pictures men golfing, with sayings printed around the plate. It has no special mark.

Plate, Every Dog Has His Day, Every Man His Hour, 10 In.
65.00

Plate, Good Judgement, 10 In.
75.00

Plate, Nothing Venture, Nothing Win, 10 In.
30.00

GONDOLIERS

Gondoliers are the singing boatmen of Venice. The plates are decorated in bright colors and have no special mark.

Plate, Venetian Gondola, 8 1/2 In.
25.00

HEAD RACK PLATES

Head Rack Plates feature prominent characters of England, such as The Admiral, The Mayor, and The Doctor. The borders on the plates vary. Each is marked with the character's name. They were produced at three different times in earthenware or china. Charles Dickens and William Shakespeare were made in flow blue.

Admiral, 10 In.
35.00 to 65.00

Bobby Burns, 10 In.*
35.00

Cobbler, 10 In.
35.00

Dickens, Character Border, 10 In.*
35.00 to 90.00

Head Rack Plate, Bobby Burns, 10 In.

Doctor, 10 In.
35.00 to 37.00

Falconer, 10 In.
35.00 to 68.00

Hunting Man, 10 In.
35.00 to 55.00

Jester, 10 In.
35.00 to 65.00

Mayor, 10 In.*
35.00 to 68.00

Head Rack Plate, Dickens, Character Border, 10 In.

Head Rack Plate, Mayor, 10 In.

Head Rack Plate, Shakespeare, 10 In.

Parson, 10 In.
35.00 to 65.00

Shakespeare, 10 In.*
35.00

Squire, 10 In.
35.00 to 65.00

Town Crier, 10 In.
35.00 to 45.00

HISTORIC CHARACTERS

Historic Characters pictures the bust of a famous character. They
have a sailing ship border and no special mark.

Plate, Sir Walter Raleigh, 10 In.
45.00

HISTORIC ENGLAND

Historic England features famous people and places of England. The
plates are beige with multi color scenes. They are marked with a
castle, tree, title and the Australian mark.

Bowl, Dr. Johnson at Temple Bar, 9 1/4 in.
50.00

Charger, Dr. Johnson at the Cheshire Cheese, 14 in.
185.00

Plaque, 1930s, 13 in.
140.00

Plate, Dr. Johnson at Temple Bar, 10 in.
45.00

Plate, Dr. Johnson at the Cheshire Cheese, 10 in.
40.00

Plate, King Henry VIII at Hampton Court, 10 in.
55.00

Plate, Queen Elizabeth at Kenilworth Castle, 10 in.
45.00

HISTORICAL BRITAIN

Historical Britain features famous places in Britain. The plates are
made of translucent china. There are 5 designs in the series. It has
no special mark.

Lighter, Tower of London
65.00

Pin tray, Tower of London, marked Australia, 66 in.
55.00

Plate, Anne Hathaway Cottage, 10 in.
35.00

Historical Britain, Plate, Clovelly, North Devon, 10 In.

Plate, Clovelly, North Devon, 10 In.*
35.00 to 40.00

Plate, Tudor Mansion, 10 In.*
40.00 to 50.00

Historical Britain, Plate, Tudor Mansion, 10 In.

Holland, see Dutch

ISAAC WALTON

Isaac Walton, 1906 to 1930s, is based on the same theme as "Gallant Fishers." They are decorated in greens and browns. Some have a saying on the plate. The plates have a tree border. The mark is round and says "Isaac Walton Ware" and pictures a tree, lake, and setting sun.

Pitcher, Where In A Brook, 10 In.
80.00

Plate, Man Fishing, Signed Noke, 10 In.
47.50 to 57.50

Plate, Of Recreation There Is None So Free, 9 1/2 In.
65.00

Trivet
55.00

JACKDAW OF RHEIMS

Jackdaw of Rheims, 1905 to 1925, is the chief character in a poem from "The Ingoldsby Legends." The lower half of the plate pictures a brick wall with ivy; the upper half, a scene and a line from the poem. Some have a bird border. There is no special mark.

Bowl, By The Name Of Jim Crow
59.00 to 79.00

Creamer, The Cardinal, 4 In.
50.00 to 75.00

Cup & Saucer, Cardinal Drew Off Each Plum-Colored Shoe
100.00

Humidor, Cardinal Archbishop Of Rheims
100.00

Pitcher, That Rascally Thief
88.00

Pitcher, The Cardinal, 4 In.
75.00

Plate, 10 In.
55.00

Plate, 13 1/2 In.
145.00

Sugar, Covered, 5 In.
45.00

Vase, Cardinal Archbishop, 10 In., Pair
195.00

Vase, Cardinal Drew Off Each Plum-Colored Shoe, 10 In.
85.00

Vase, Return Of The Ring, Handled,
8 3/4 In.
85.00

Vase, That Rascally Thief, Handled, 5 3/8 In.
55.00

Vase, That Rascally Thief, 8 1/2 In.
75.00 to 85.00

KING ARTHUR'S KNIGHTS

King Arthur's Knights, about 1908, pictures scenes from "The Knights of the Round Table."

Plate, Lancelot, 10 In.
30.00

MAY DAY CHILDREN

May Day Children pictures scenes of children carrying baskets of
flowers and dancing around the maypole celebrating the European
holiday. It has no special mark.

Breakfast Set, 3 Piece
65.00

Mush & Milk
85.00

Plate, 7 In.
22.00

MONKS

Monks were produced in three different series. Humorous monks
pictures monks enjoying such activities as fishing, and includes a
saying. The other series was produced in two color combinations,
blue and tan, or green and tan. They have no special mark.

Mustard Pot, Hinged Silver-Plated Top, 2 3/4 In.
40.00

Plate, Gold, Black Silhouette Of Monk Drinking, 10 In.
110.00

Plate, Green And Tan, 10 In.*
55.00

Plate, Monk Serving Buccaneer, Blue And Tan, 10 In.
30.00

Vase, Blue And Tan, 6 In.
60.00

**Vase, Monk In Sandals, Humorous, Relief, Handled, 11 1/2
In.**
400.00

Monks, Plate, Green And Tan, 10 In.

MOTOR SERIES

Motor Series was produced 1906 to 1911. Eight different motor car
scenes are pictured in shades of green and brown. It has a scenic
border of trees, hills, and clouds. It has no special mark.

Motor, Plate, Room For One, 10 In.

Plate, Itch Yer On Guvnor, 10 In.
120.00 to 125.00

Plate, Room For One, 10 In.*
115.00

MUNCHKINS

Munchkins is a ware that pictures elves. It is decorated with blues,
maroons, and golds, resembling Fairyland luster. It has no special
mark.

Bowl, 9 In.
100.00

Plate, 6 In.
85.00

NIGHT WATCHMAN

Night Watchman pictures the night watchman performing his nightly
duties. There is no special mark.

Plate, 10 In.
35.00 to 55.00

Tankard
75.00

NURSERY RHYMES

Nursery Rhymes was produced in 1903 in earthenware and 1917 to about 1925 in creamware. Little Bo Peep and Mary Had A Little Lamb are still in production. They are decorated with scenes and a verse from the rhyme. Some are marked "Nursery Rhymes."

Bowl, Cat & The Fiddle, 5 In.
15.00

Bowl, Old Mother Goose, 6 In.
16.00

Box, Advertising Candy Coffers, Peter Piper
125.00

Cup & Saucer, Pretty Milkmaid
20.00

Plate, Pretty Milkmaid, 8 In.
26.00

Old English Coaching Scenes, see Coaching Days

OLD ENGLISH INNS

Old English Inns pictures well-known taverns of England. It has a special mark of a tavern, the words "Old English Inns" and the Australian mark.

Plate, Boars Head Inn, 10 In.
32.00

Old Moreton, see Queen Elizabeth at Moreton Hall

OLD SEA DOGS

Old Sea Dogs illustrates the life of Jack, a typical sailor. The mark is a sailboat with the words "Old Sea Dogs."

Vase, Jack's The Lad For Work, 7 1/2 In.
475.00

POLAR BEAR

Polar Bear pieces are decorated with a border of polar bears in blues, greys, and greens. It has a crackle glaze and no special mark.

Creamer
50.00 to 75.00

Syrup
60.00

PROVERBS

Proverbs are very similar to English Old Proverbs. Each plate is decorated with a grapevine border, a picture, and two proverbs. There is no special mark.

Plate, Sultan, A Bird In The Hand, 10 In.
40.00

QUEEN ELIZABETH AT OLD MORETON HALL

Queen Elizabeth at Old Moreton Hall, 1915 to 1925, pictures Elizabethan court scenes and says "Queen Elizabeth at Old Moreton 1589." The plates have an architectural border. They are marked with a shield, and the words "Old Moreton 1589" are inside a circle.

Pitcher, 4 In.
75.00

Plate, 10 In.*
42.50 to 55.00

Tankard, 6 In.
16.00

Queen Elizabeth At Moreton Hall, Plate, 10 In.

REYNARD THE FOX

Reynard the Fox was produced in a bone china, made only in coffee wares. A picture of a fox and a yellow border is on each piece.

Demitasse Set, 6 Piece
600.00

RUSTIC ENGLAND

Rustic England pictures country scenes and homes. They are marked with the Australian mark and the words "Rustic England."

RUSTIC ENGLAND
D 5694
REG^D. AUSTRALIA 16306/7/8

Plate, 10 In.*
45.00

Rustic England, Plate, 10 In.

SAILING VESSELS

Sailing Vessels pictures sailboats, whale boats, and ships in full sail. The plates have a green border.

Pitcher, Vessels Large May Venture More, 3 X 4 In.
45.00

Plate, 10 In.
45.00

Vase, Blue & White Border, Bulbous
80.00

SAYINGS WARE

Sayings Ware, 1911 to 1914, pictures old ladies drinking tea with sayings such as "The Cup That Cheers." The sayings are written in grey and black letters. There is a brown border picturing hanging tea cups. It has no special mark.

Plate, A Merry Heart, 10 1/4 In.
20.00 to 35.00

Plate, Bread At Pleasure, 10 In.
35.00

SCENIC RACK PLATES

Scenic Rack Plates picture scenes of animals and scenic places around the world, such as "Koala Bears," "Vermillion Lake," and "Bow Valley." The plates are 10 inches in diameter. They are marked with a title.

Australian Aborigine*
22.50

Bow Valley, 10 In.*
25.00

Koala Bears, 10 In.*
30.00

Scenic Rack Plate, Australian Aborigine, 10 In.

Scenic Rack Plate, Bow Valley, 10 In.

Scenic Rack Plate, Koala Bears, 10 In.

Lake Louise, 10 In.*
22.50

Young Kookaburras*
25.00

Scenic Rack Plate, Young Kookaburras, 10 In.
Scenic Rack Plate, Lake Louise, 10 In.

SHAKESPEARE CHARACTERS

Shakespeare Characters, about 1906, pictures characters in the appropriate setting. The plates are pastel. The character's name is on the back of the plate. There is another Shakespeare Characters series with a green and brown cobblestone background.

Berry Set, Pastel, 9 Bowls
200.00

Plate, Falstaff, Brown & Green, 10 In.*
55.00

Plate, Falstaff, Pastel, 10 In.*
55.00

Plate, Hamlet, Pastel, 8 1/2 In.
85.00

Plate, Ophelia, Pastel, 10 In.*
55.00

Plate, Portia, Pastel, 8 1/2 In.
48.00

Plate, Romeo, Pastel, Square, 6 In.
48.00

Plate, Sir Andrew Aguecheek, Brown, Green, 7 1/2 In.
30.00

Tray, Cardinal Wolsey, Pastel, 11 In.
39.00 to 45.00

Shakespeare Characters, Plate,
Falstaff, Brown & Green, 10 In.

Shakespeare Characters, Plate,
Falstaff, Pastel, 10 In.

Shakespeare Characters, Plate,
Ophelia, Pastel, 10 In.

SHAKESPEARE FLOW BLUE

Shakespeare Flow Blue, about 1925, pictures scenes from Shakespeare's plays in flow blue.

Plate, 10 1/2 In.
55.00 to 78.00

Shakespeare Plays, Plate, Merry Wives
Of Windsor, 10 1/2 In.

SHAKESPEARE PLAYS

Shakespeare Plays, 1914 to 1940s pictures scenes from nine of
Shakespeare's plays. They have a geometric border. They are marked
with the act, scene, and title of play.

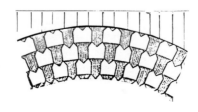

Jug, Midsummer Night's Dream, 5 3/4 In.
85.00

Pitcher, Midsummer Night's Dream, 7 In.
65.00

Plate, Merry Wives Of Windsor, 10 1/2 In.*
60.00

Salt & Pepper, Macbeth
89.00

Tea Tile, Much Ado About Nothing
47.50

*Shakespeare Plays, Plate, Falstaff
And Dame Quickly, 10 In.*

SIR ROGER DE COVERLEY

Sir Roger De Coverley was a character created by Addison and Steele, for "The Spectator," published 1711 to 1712. He represented a well-mannered and cultivated country gentleman of the eighteenth century. The name was originally from an old country tune. The mark is a fox head with a crop and a trumpet.

Plate, 10 In.
35.00

Three Musketeers, see Cavaliers

UNDER THE GREENWOOD TREE

Under The Greenwood Tree, about 1909, pictures the adventures of Robin Hood and his merry men. The scalloped plates are marked in a circle with a tree and the words "Under The Greenwood Tree."

Ashtray, Robin Hood Slays Guy Gisborne
25.00

Charger, 15 In.
150.00

Cup, Two Handled, Relief, 9 In.
300.00

Dresser Tray
15.00

Plate, Robin Hood, 10 In.*
45.00

Tray, Robin Hood, 5 In.
50.00 to 75.00

Vase, Handled, Friar Tuck Joins Robin Hood, 6 In.
70.00

Wall Plaque
175.00

Under The Greenwood Tree, Plate, Robin Hood, 10 In.

WELSH LADIES

Welsh Ladies pictures four or five ladies in their native country dress,
black hats and long black dresses. It has no special mark.

Candlestick, Pair
125.00

Cup & Saucer
55.00

Sugar & Creamer
125.00

Vase, 5 3/4 In.
65.00

Vase, 8 In.
45.00 to 85.00

TOBY JUGS

TOBY JUGS

Jugs shaped like human figures became popular in England during the eighteenth century, and they were possibly inspired by the medieval and ancient jugs of similar form. The vessel often pictured a seated man holding a drink. The name "Toby" was in common use by the 1770s, probably referring to a character in a song of 1761 named "Toby Phillpot."

The tradition of the Toby jug was continued when the first of the Royal Doulton Tobies were offered in 1939. Sixteen were made for sale to the general market. These include The Best Is Not Too Good, Cap'n Cuttle, Double XX, Falstaff, Fat Boy, Happy John, Honest Measure, Huntsman, Jolly Toby, Mr. Micawber, Mr. Pickwick, Old Charley, Sairey Gamp, Sam Weller, Sir Winston Churchill, and Squire. The Tobies were made in a variety of sizes.

Several other Toby jugs were made as advertising premiums for various companies. The Charrington Tobies, several versions of similar jugs, were made after 1954 for a brewery. The Cliff Cornell jugs were made in at least two sizes and two colors for the Cleveland Flux Company of Cleveland, Ohio. Brown and blue examples are known but there may have been a few gray Tobies made. A special mark was used. The Hoare Toby jug was made in 1930s, a George Robey jug was made in about 1910, and possibly a Charlie Chaplin Toby too. A prototype Toby of John Wesley is also known.

Name	Number	Date	Price
Best Is Not Too Good, 4 1/2 In.*	**D.6107**	**1939-1960**	**175.00 to 225.00**

Cap'n Cuttle or Captain Edward Cuttle is a character in the book "Dombey and Son" by Charles Dickens.

Name	Number	Date	Price
Cap'n Cuttle, 4 1/2 In.*	**D.6266**	**1948-1960**	**180.00**

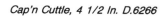

Cap'n Cuttle, 4 1/2 In. D.6266

Best Is Not Too Good, 4 1/2 In. D.6107

Cliff Cornell was a Cleveland, Ohio, businessman who ordered special toby jugs in 1956 to give to friends for Christmas. The jug is a portrait of Mr. Cornell.

Cliff Cornell, Blue, 5 1/2 In.**		1956	**225.00 to 400.00**
Cliff Cornell, Brown, 5 1/2 In.**		1956	**300.00**
Double XX Or Man On The Barrel*	D.6088	1939-1969	**200.00**

Cliff Cornell, Blue, 5 1/2 In.
Cliff Cornell, Brown, 5 1/2 In.

*Double XX Or Man On
The Barrel D.6088*

Falstaff or Sir John Falstaff is a character in the plays "Henry IV" and "The Merry Wives of Windsor" by Shakespeare.

Falstaff, 5 1/4 In.*	D.6063	1939-Present	**35.00**
Falstaff, 8 1/2 In.	D.6062	1939-Present	**50.00**

Falstaff, 5 1/4 In. D.6063

Fat Boy is a character in the book "Pickwick Papers" by Charles Dickens.

Fat Boy, 4 1/2 In.*	D.6264	1948-1960	180.00
Happy John, 5 1/2 In.*	D.6070	1939-Present	35.00
Happy John, 9 In.	D.6031	1939-Present	50.00
Honest Measure, 4 1/2 In.*	D.6108	1939-Present	35.00
Huntsman, 7 1/2 In.*	D.6320	1950-Present	50.00
Jolly Toby, 6 1/2 In.*	D.6109	1939-Present	75.00

Fat Boy, 4 1/2 In.
D.6264

Happy John, 5 1/2 In.
D.6070

Honest Measure, 4 1/2 In.
D.6108

Huntsman, 7 1/2 In.
D.6320

Jolly Toby, 6 1/2 In.
D.6109

Mr. Micawber is a character from the book "David Copperfield" by Charles Dickens.

Mr. Micawber, 4 1/2 In.*   D.6262 1948-1960   **180.00**

Mr. Pickwick is a character from the book "Pickwick Papers" by Charles Dickens.

Mr. Pickwick, 4 1/2 In.*   D.6261 1948-1960   **180.00**

Old Charley represents the night watchman of the nineteenth century.

Old Charley, 5 1/2 In.*   D.6069 1939-1960   **100.00**
Old Charley, 8 3/4 In.   D.6030 1939-1960   **125.00**

Sairey Gamp is a character from the book "Martin Chuzzlewit" by Charles Dickens.

Sairey Gamp, 4 1/2 In.*   D.6263 1948-1960   **180.00**

Mr. Pickwick, 4 1/2 In.
D.6261

Sairey Gamp, 4 1/2 In.
D.6263

Mr. Micawber, 4 1/2 In.
D.6262

Old Charley, 5 1/2 In.
D.6069

Sam Weller is a character from the book "Pickwick Papers" by Charles Dickens.

Sam Weller, 4 1/2 In., Marked A* D.6265 1948-1960   **180.00**

Sam Weller, 4 1/2 In.,
Marked A D.6265

Sir Winston Churchill was Prime Minister of Britain. The jug is a tribute to his leadership in 1940 during the Battle of Britain.

Sir Winston Churchill, 4 In.*	**D.6175**	**1941-Present**	**35.00**
Sir Winston Churchill, 5 1/2 In.	**D.6172**	**1941-Present**	**40.00**
Sir Winston Churchill, 9 In.	**D.6171**	**1941-Present**	**50.00**
Squire, 6 In.*	**D.6319**	**1950-1969**	**225.00 to 250.00**

Sir Winston Churchill, 4 1/2 In.
D.6175

Squire, 6 In. D.6319

MISCELLANEOUS

MISCELLANEOUS

Royal Doulton made a variety of wares that resemble the character jugs. Some seem to be made in the molds that were used for the character jugs but slightly adapted for other uses. Most of the miscellaneous "character" pieces were based on Dickens characters. Ash bowls were made in at least six styles in the years from 1938 to 1960. The tops of the bowls had cigarette-rest indentations. Ashtrays with ash pots were made during the same years in at least four styles. The pot had an open top and probably held wooden matches. The English call these "match stands." Several tobacco jars, figural teapots, small busts, wall vases, toothpick holders, and a set of napkin rings were made. They were all discontinued by the 1960s. A group of about thirteen table cigarette lighters were made from 1958 to 1973. Musical jugs were made from about 1938 to 1948. Some special, small stoppered bottles were made in the character-jug shapes for liquor companies during the 1960s. A paper Bols liquor label is found on many.

A series of six embossed jugs and a tankard were made starting in 1935 and continuing until 1960. These pieces pictured scenes from Dickens stories. Large busts of the royal family were made—HRH Prince Charles in 1969 and Her Majesty Queen Elizabeth II and H.R.H. The Duke of Edinburgh in 1972—and cups to commemorate coronations were made. Lamps were made from mounted figurines.

Name	Price
Ash Bowl, Auld Mac	75.00
Ash Bowl, Farmer John, Marked A	45.00 to 70.00
Ash Bowl, Old Charley	60.00
Ash Bowl, Paddy	60.00
Ash Bowl, Parson Brown, Marked A	60.00
Ash Bowl, Sairey Gamp	59.00 to 70.00
Ash Pot, Auld Mac	85.00
Ash Pot, Dick Turpin	59.00
Ash Pot, Old Charley, Marked A	44.00 to 59.00
Ash Pot, Paddy	47.00
Ash Pot, Sairey Gamp	50.00
Ashtray, Army Club	45.00
Ashtray, Auld Mac, Marked A, 3 In.	47.50
Ashtray, Mr. Pickwick, Marked A	65.00 to 95.00
Ashtray, Old Charley	45.00 to 65.00
Ashtray, Tony Weller, Square	34.00
Bols Liqueur, Falstaff, 6 1/4 In.	55.00
Bols Liqueur, Poacher, 6 1/4 In.	55.00
Bols Liqueur, Rip Van Winkle, 6 1/4 In.	55.00
Bottle, Figural, Old Crow	110.00

Bust, Elizabeth & Duke Of Edinburgh

Bust, Prince Charles

Bust, Elizabeth & Duke Of Edinburgh*	500.00 to 1000.00
Bust, Prince Charles*	400.00
Bust, Princess Anne	55.00 to 200.00
Bust, Sairey Gamp	55.00
Bust, Sam Weller	55.00
Bust, Sgt.Buz Fuz	55.00
Bust, Sir Winston Churchill	200.00
Bust, Tony Weller	55.00
Cup, Commemorating Coronation Of Queen Elizabeth	59.00
Cup, Commemorating King Edward VII And Queen Alexandra	45.00
Cup, King George V, Silver Jubilee, 2 Handled	119.00

Figure, Dickens, listed in figurine chapter

Jug, Old Curiosity Shop, Marked A, Figures In Relief*	90.00 to 150.00
Jug, Old London, Figures In Relief	189.00 to 750.00
Jug, Old Peggotty, Figures In Relief*	175.00 to 250.00

Jug, Old Curiosity Shop,
Marked A, Figures In Relief

Jug, Oliver Asks For More, Figures In Relief*	175.00 to 185.00
Jug, Oliver Twist, Figures In Relief	100.00 to 139.00
Jug, Pickwick Papers, Figures In Relief	85.00 to 165.00
Jug, Pied Piper, No. 7	700.00
Lamp, Fox Hunt Scene, Maroon, 22 In.	150.00
Lamp, Old Balloon Seller, Original Shade	140.00
Lamp, Polly Peachum	200.00
Lighter, Bacchus	60.00 to 85.00
Lighter, Beefeater	59.00 to 65.00
Lighter, Captain Ahab	75.00
Lighter, Falstaff	52.00 to 75.00
Lighter, Granny	100.00
Lighter, Lawyer	75.00
Lighter, Long John Silver	60.00
Lighter, Mr. Pickwick	75.00 to 100.00
Lighter, Old Charley	60.00
Lighter, Poacher	49.00 to 60.00

Jug, Old Peggotty, Figures In Relief

Jug, Oliver Asks For More, Figures In Relief

Lighter, Sgt. Buz Fuz	100.00
Pitcher, Jolly Drinker, Signed Noke, 8 In.	295.00
Plate, Areo, Hudson, Fulton Celebration, 1909	50.00
Plate, Black Scottie Dog, Pastel Landscape, Marked, 10 In.	60.00
Plate, Churchill, 4 In.	75.00
Plate, Churchill, 5 1/2 In.	95.00
Plate, Churchill, 9 In.	145.00
Plate, Granny, Marked A, 6 1/2 In.	125.00

Roger Salem El Cobler, see Head Rack Plate, Cobbler

Tankard, Oliver, Figures In Relief	139.00 to 200.00
Toothpick, Paddy	85.00
Vase, Woman With Flower Basket, L. J. Burgess, 11 In.	450.00
Wall Mask, Marlene Deitrich	375.00
Wall Mask, Sweet Anne, HN 1590, 8 In.	450.00

APPENDIX

Many different animal and bird figurines have been made. The following is a list of many of these figurines, and the HN numbers assigned by the factory. The list is divided into several sections, by animal type, to aid the reader.

*miniature
**character
***miniature character

BIRDS

HN 103	Two Penguins		HN 167	Tern Duck
HN 104	Penguin		HN 168	Tern Drake
HN 111	Cockerel		HN 169	Owl
HN 113	Penguin		HN 171	Baby Birds
HN 114	Drake (green)		HN 173	Owl**
HN 115	Drake (blue)		HN 175	Great Crested Grebe
HN 116	Drake		HN 178	Cockerel
HN 117	Turtle Doves		HN 180	Cockerel
HN 123	Pelican		HN 184	Cockerel
HN 124	Sitting Cockerel		HN 185	Parrot
HN 125	Guinea Fowl		HN 187	Owl**
HN 131	Kingfisher		HN 188	Duckling
HN 132	Drake		HN 189	Duckling
HN 133	Penguins		HN 190	Duckling
HN 134	Penguin		HN 191	Parrot
HN 135	Raven		HN 192	Parrot
HN 136	Robin		HN 195	Tern Duck
HN 137	Blue Tit		HN 196	Toucan
HN 139	Falcon		HN 197	Bird Standing on Rock
HN 143	Chaffinch		HN 198	Penguin and Chick
HN 144	Wren		HN 199	Budgerigar
HN 145	Yellow Bird		HN 200	Baby Parrot
HN 145A	Yellow Bird		HN 205	Ducklings
HN 148	Drakes		HN 206	Ducklings
HN 149	Swallow		HN 208	Toucan**
HN 150	Duck		HN 211	Black-Headed Gull
HN 152	Kingfisher		HN 212	Black-Headed Gull
HN 155	Owl		HN 214	Bird and Chicks
HN 157	Cockerel		HN 215	Bird and Chicks
HN 158	Toucan		HN 216	Bird and Chicks
HN 159	Toucan		HN 220	Bird
HN 160	Owl and Owlette		HN 222	Owl with Boat**
HN 161	Thrush Chicks		HN 224	Kingfisher
HN 163	Budgerigar		HN 229	Teal Duck
HN 164	Crowing Cockerel		HN 235	Duckling
HN 165	Kingfisher		HN 236	Baby Birds

HN 239	Ducks	HN 862A	Kingfisher
HN 240	Bird	HN 862B	Kingfisher
HN 241	Eagle	HN 863–865	Ducks**
HN 242	Eagle	HN 867–874	Birds**
HN 247	Guinea Fowl	HN 875	Kingfisher
HN 248	Drake	HN 877	Baby Parrot
HN 249	Mallard Drake	HN 878	Cockerel
HN 250	Heron	HN 879	Cockerel
HN 251	Heron	HN 880	Cockerel
HN 252	Drake	HN 882	Penguin
HN 256–266	Puffins and Penguins***	HN 884	Cockatoo
HN 267	Cockerel	HN 885	Cockatoo
HN 268	Kingfisher	HN 886	Cockatoo
HN 269	Bluebird	HN 888	Cockatoo
HN $ 271	Duck	HN 913–918	Toucan (bowls)
HN 272	Bird with Chicks	HN 928	Toucan (bowl)
HN 274	Green Bird	HN 936	Teal
HN 275	Orange Birds	HN 946	Penguin Chick
HN 277	Wren	HN 947	Penguin Chick
HN 278	Green Birds	HN 956	Mallard Drake
HN 279	Green Bird	HN 973	Duck**
HN 280	Chicks	HN 974	Duck**
HN 281	Yellow Bird	HN 977	Duck
HN 282	Bluebird	HN 998	Penguin and Chick
HN 283–293	Puffins and Penguins***	HN1004	Blue Tit
HN 294	Toucan	HN1005	Thrush
HN 295	Toucan	HN1189	King Penguin
HN 295A	Toucan	HN1190	Penguin
HN 296	Penguin	HN1191	Mallard
HN 297	Penguin and Chick	HN1192	Duck
HN 298	Duck	HN1193	Tern
HN 299	Drake	HN1194	Tern
HN 806	Drake*	HN1195	Seagull
HN 807	Drake*	HN1196	Seagull
HN 813	White Bird*	HN1197	Gannet
HN 840–845	Ducks**	HN1198	Drake
HN 846	Toucan	HN1199	Penguin
HN 847	Yellow Bird	HN2540	Kingfisher
HN 849	Ladybird and Duck	HN2541	Kingfisher, 3¼ in.
HN 850	Duck	HN2542	Baltimore Oriole
HN 851	Bird	HN2543	Bluebird, 5¾ in.
HN 852	Penguin	HN2544	Mallard
HN 853	Mallard Drake	HN2545	Pheasant
HN 854	Budgerigar	HN2546	Yellow-Throated Warbler, 4½ in.
HN 855	Bird	HN2547	Budgerigars
HN 856	Penguin	HN2548	Golden-Crested Wren
HN 858	Kingfisher	HN2549	Robin
HN 860	Bird	HN2550	Chaffinch, 2¼ in.

HN2551	Bullfinch	HN2612	Baltimore Oriole
HN2552	Baby Thrushes	HN2613	Golden-Crested Wren
HN2553	Baby Robins	HN2614	Bluebird
HN2554	Cardinal	HN2615	Cardinal
HN2555	Drake Mallard, 6 in.	HN2616	Bullfinch
HN2556	Mallard	HN2617	Robin
HN2572	Mallard	HN2618	Yellow-Throated Warbler
HN2573	Kingfisher	HN2619	Grouse
HN2574	Seagull	HN2632	Cock Pheasant
HN2575	Swan	HN2633	Penguin
HN2576	Pheasant	HN2634	Pheasant
HN2577	Peacock	HN2635	Mallard
HN2591	Drake Mallard	HN2636	Drake, Indian Runner
HN2610	Hen Pheasant	HN2647	Drake
HN2611	Chaffinch		

BUTTERFLIES

HN 162	Blue and Gold Butterfly	HN2607	Red Admiral Butterfly
HN2604	Peacock Butterfly	HN2608	Copper Butterfly
HN2605	Camberwell Beauty Butterfly	HN2609	Tortoiseshell Butterfly
HN2606	Swallowtail Butterfly		

CATS

HN 109	Cat (white)
HN 120	Cat (white)
HN 154	Cat**
HN 201	Cat (tabby) with Mouse
HN 202	Cat (black) with Mouse
HN 203	Cat (tortoiseshell)
HN 204	Cat (tortoiseshell)
HN 210	Cat (black and white)
HN 221	Cat (black and white)
HN 227	Cat (tabby)
HN 233	Kitten
HN 234	Cats
HN 244	Cat (black and white) with Mouse
HN 245	Cat (black) with Mouse
HN 818	Cat, Lucky (black and white)**

*miniature
**character

HN 819 Cat, Lucky (black and white)***
HN 820 Kitten*
HN 821 Kitten*
HN 822 Kitten*
HN 823 Kitten*
HN 824 Kitten*
HN 825 Kitten*
HN 827 Cat (tortoiseshell)**
HN 828 Cat (tabby)**
HN 829 Cat (black and white)**
HN 967 Cat (tabby)
HN 971 Cat, Lucky (ashtray)
HN 993 Cat, sleeping
HN 999 Cat, Persian (black and white), 5 in.
HN2539 Cat, Persian (white)
HN2579 Cat, Lying, Licking Front Paws, 1½ in.**
HN2580 Cat, Licking Hind Paw, 2¼ in.**
HN2581 Cat, Sleeping, 1½ in.**
HN2582 Cat, Sitting Up, 2¾ in.**
HN2583 Cat, Licking Front Paw, 2 in.**
HN2584 Cat, Sitting, 2 in.**

CHATCULL RANGE

HN2655 Siamese Cat, Sitting, 5½ in.
HN2656 Pine Marten, 4¼ in.
HN2657 Langur Monkey, 4⅜ in.
HN2658 White-Tailed Deer, 5⅝ in.
HN2659 Brown Bear, 4⅛ in.
HN2660 Siamese Cat, Standing, 5 in.

HN2661 Mountain Sheep, 5¼ in.
HN2662 Siamese Cat, Lying, 3¾ in.
HN2663 River Hog, 3½ in.
HN2664 Nyala Antelope, 5⅝ in.
HN2665 Llama, 6½ in.
HN2666 Badger, 3 in.

DOGS

HN 105 Alsatian (gray)
HN 106 Alsatian (white and gray)
HN 112 Alsatian (light gray)
HN 127 Pekinese
HN 128 Puppy
HN 129 Bulldog
HN 146 Bulldog, "Old Bill" (helmet and haversack)
HN 153 Bulldog, "Old Bill" (tammy)
HN 166 Beagle
HN 176 Bloodhound
HN 194 Puppy, Terrier

*miniature

HN 231	St. Bernard
HN 232	Puppy (bone)
HN 804	Puppy (orange)*
HN 805	Puppy (green and purple)*
HN 831	Puppy, Beagle
HN 832	Puppy, Pekinese
HN 833	Puppy, Pekinese
HN 834	Puppy, Pekinese (brown and black)
HN 835	Puppy, Pekinese (light brown)
HN 836	Puppy, Pekinese
HN 837	Chow (brown)
HN 838	Chow (light brown)
HN 839	Chow (gray and white)
HN 881	Bulldog
HN 889	Doberman (black and white)
HN 890	Doberman (brown)
HN 898	Alsatian (head only)
HN 899	Alsatian
HN 900	Fox Terrier (brown and white)
HN 901	Fox Terrier (black and white)
HN 904	Puppy, Terrier
HN 906	Puppy, Spaniel (white and black)
HN 907	Puppy, Spaniel (white and brown)
HN 908	Puppy, Spaniel (head only)
HN 909	Fox Terrier
HN 910	Fox Terrier
HN 921	Alsatian
HN 923	Fox Terrier
HN 924	Fox Terrier
HN 927	Pekinese Dogs
HN 929	Puppy, Terrier*
HN 930	Alsatian*
HN 931	Puppy, Terrier*
HN 932	Scotch Terrier*
HN 933	Scotch Terrier*
HN 934	Scotch Terrier*
HN 942	Terrier
HN 943	Terrier
HN 944	Fox Terrier
HN 945	Fox Terrier
HN 948	Bulldog (brown)
HN 953	Puppy, Terrier (black and brown)
HN 954	Puppy, Terrier (black and dark brown)
HN 957	Spaniel (white and liver)
HN 958	Spaniel (white and black)
HN 962	Terrier (head only)
HN 964	Scotch Terrier (black)
HN 965	Scotch Terrier (brown)
HN 970	Dachshund

HN 975   Collie (gray)
HN 976   Collie (brown)
HN 980   Scotch Terrier (black)
HN 981   Scotch Terrier (brown and gray)
HN 982   Sealyham Terrier (black)
HN 983   Sealyham Terrier (brown)
HN 986   Alsatian (bowl)
HN 987   Bulldog (bowl)
HN 988   Airedale Terrier (brown)
HN 989   Sealyham Terrier (gray)
HN 992   Sealyham Terrier (black)
HN 995   Pekinese (brown)
HN 996   Airedale Terrier (blue, brown, and black)
HN 997   Terrier (brown and black)
HN1000   Cocker Spaniel (black)
HN1001   Cocker Spaniel and Pheasant, 6½ in.
HN1002   Cocker Spaniel, 6½ in. (white and liver)
HN1003   Pekinese
HN1017   Scottish Terrier (black)
HN1018   Scottish Terrier (black)
HN1019   Scottish Terrier (black)
HN1028   Cocker Spaniel and Pheasant, 5¼ in.
HN1029   Cocker Spaniel and Pheasant, 3¾ in.
HN1036   Cocker Spaniel, 5 in. (white and liver)
HN1037   Cocker Spaniel, 3½ in. (white and liver)
HN1038   Scottish Terrier
HN1039   Pekinese
HN1040   Pekinese
HN1041   Sealyham
HN1042   Bulldog (brindle)
HN1043   Bulldog (brindle)
HN1044   Bulldog, 3 in. (brindle)
HN1045   Bulldog (white and brown)
HN1046   Bulldog (white and brown)
HN1047   Bulldog, 3 in. (white and brown)
HN1048   West Highland Terrier (white)
HN1052   Sealyham
HN1053   Sealyham
HN1054   Irish Setter, 7½ in.
HN1055   Irish Setter, 5¼ in.
HN1056   Irish Setter, 3¾ in.
HN1062   Cocker Spaniel and Pheasant, 3¾ in.
HN1063   Cocker Spaniel and Hare (white and liver)
HN1064   Cocker Spaniel and Hare (white and liver)
HN1065   Greyhound (brown)
HN1066   Greyhound (brown)
HN1067   Greyhound (brown)
HN1068   Smooth-Haired Fox Terrier

HN1069 Smooth-Haired Fox Terrier
HN1072 Bulldog, 5½ in. (white)
HN1073 Bulldog, 4¾ in. (white)
HN1074 Bulldog, 3 in. (white)
HN1075 Greyhound (white and black)
HN1076 Greyhound (white and black)
HN1077 Greyhound (white and black)
HN1078 Cocker Spaniel, 3½ in. (white and black)
HN1079 Gordon Setter
HN1080 Gordon Setter
HN1081 Gordon Setter
HN1104 Cairn (black)
HN1105 Cairn (black)
HN1106 Cairn (black)
HN1107 Cairn (black) (earthenware)
HN1108 Cocker Spaniel (white and black)
HN1109 Cocker Spaniel, 5 in (white and black)
HN1131 Staffordshire Bull Terrier
HN1132 Staffordshire Bull Terrier
HN1133 Staffordshire Bull Terrier
HN1134 Cocker Spaniel (white and liver)
HN1135 Cocker Spaniel (white and liver)
HN1136 Cocker Spaniel (white and liver)
HN1137 Cocker Spaniel and Pheasant, 6½ in. (white and black)
HN1138 Cocker Spaniel and Pheasant, 5¼ in. (white and black)
HN1139 Dachshund
HN1140 Dachshund, 4 in.
HN1141 Dachshund, 3 in.
HN1186 Cocker Spaniel (light brown)
HN1187 Cocker Spaniel, 5 in. (light brown)
HN1188 Cocker Spaniel (light brown)
HN2524 American Foxhound
HN2525 American Foxhound
HN2526 American Foxhound
HN2529 English Setter and Pheasant, 8 in.
HN2557 Welsh Corgi
HN2558 Welsh Corgi
HN2559 Welsh Corgi, 3⅝ in.
HN2560 Great Dane
HN2561 Great Dane
HN2562 Great Dane
HN2599 English Setter and Pheasant
HN2600 Cocker Spaniel and Pheasant
HN2601 American Great Dane
HN2602 American Great Dane
HN2603 American Great Dane
HN2620 English Setter (white and liver)
HN2621 English Setter (white and liver)

HN2622   English Setter (white and liver)
HN2624   Pointer, 5⅜ in.
HN2625   Poodle
HN2626   Poodle
HN2627   Poodle
HN2628   Chow
HN2629   Chow
HN2630   Chow
HN2631   French Poodle, 5¼ in.
HN2645   Doberman Pinscher, 6¼ in.

DOG MODELS CHAMPION

HN1007   Rough-Haired Terrier, Crackley Startler
HN1008   Scottish Terrier, Albourne Arthur
HN1010   Pekinese, Biddee of Ifield
HN1011   Pekinese, Biddee of Ifield
HN1012   Pekinese, Biddee of Ifield, 3⅛ in.
HN1013   Fox Terrier, Crackley Hunter
HN1014   Fox Terrier, Crackley Hunter, 4 in.
HN1015   Scottish Terrier, Albourne Arthur
HN1016   Scottish Terrier, Albourne Arthur, 3½ in.
HN1020   Cocker Spaniel, Lucky Pride of Ware, 5 in.
HN1021   Cocker Spaniel, Lucky Pride of Ware, 3½ in.
HN1022   Airedale Terrier, Cotsfold Topsail, 8 in.
HN1023   Airedale Terrier, Cotsfold Topsail, 5¼ in.
HN1024   Airedale Terrier, Cotsfold Topsail, 3¾ in.
HN1025   Foxhound, Tring Rattler
HN1026   Foxhound, Tring Rattler
HN1027   Foxhound, Tring Rattler
HN1030   Sealyham, Scotia Stylist
HN1031   Sealyham, Scotia Stylist
HN1032   Sealyham, Scotia Stylist
HN1033   Cairn, Charming Eyes
HN1034   Cairn, Charming Eyes
HN1035   Cairn, Charming Eyes, 3¼ in.
HN1049   English Setter, Maesydd Mustard, 8 in.
HN1050   English Setter, Maesydd Mustard, 5¼ in.
HN1051   English Setter, Maesydd Mustard, 3¾ in.
HN1057   Collie, Ashstead Applause, 7½ in.
HN1058   Collie, Ashstead Applause, 5 in.
HN1059   Collie, Ashstead Applause, 3½ in.
HN1111   Dalmatian, Goworth Victor
HN1113   Dalmatian, Goworth Victor, 5¾ in.
HN1114   Dalmatian, Goworth Victor, 4¼ in.
HN1115   Alsatian, Benign of Picardy
HN1116   Alsatian, Benign of Picardy, 6¼ in.

HN1117 Alsatian, Benign of Picardy, 4¼ in.
HN1127 Dachshund, Shrewd Saint, 6 in.
HN1128 Dachshund, Shrewd Saint, 4 in.
HN1129 Dachshund, Shrewd Saint, 3 in.
HN1142 Bull Terrier, Bokus Brock
HN1143 Bull Terrier, Bokus Brock
HN1144 Bull Terrier, Bokus Brock
HN2512 Smooth-Haired Terrier, Chosen Dan of Notts
HN2513 Smooth-Haired Terrier, Chosen Dan of Notts
HN2514 Smooth-Haired Terrier, Chosen Dan of Notts
HN2515 Springer Spaniel, Dry Toast
HN2516 Springer Spaniel, Dry Toast
HN2517 Springer Spaniel, Dry Toast, 3¾ in.
HN2643 Boxer, Warlor of Mazelaine, 6½ in.
HN2667 Labrador, Bumblikite of Manserge, 5 in. (black)

CHARACTER, DOGS

HN 808 Puppy
HN 809 Puppy
HN 810 Puppy
HN 811 Puppy
HN 812 Puppy
HN 814 Puppy
HN 815 Puppy
HN 826 Puppy
HN1097 Dog, Yawning, 4¼ in.
HN1098 Dog
HN1099 Dog, Running with Ball, 2¼ in.
HN1100 Dog
HN1101 Dog
HN1103 Dog, Ball in Mouth, 2½ in.
HN1158 Dog, Eating, 3¼ in.
HN1159 Dog, Toy in Mouth, 3¾ in.
HN2508 Dog
HN2509 Dog
HN2510 Dog
HN2511 Dog
HN2585 Pup in Basket, 2 in.
HN2586 Pup in Basket, 2½ in.
HN2587 Pup in Basket, 3 in.
HN2588 Puppies in Basket, 3¼ in.
HN2589 Dog, Standing, 4 in.
HN2590 Dogs, Sleeping, 1¾ in.
HN2654 Dog, Slipper in Mouth, 3¼ in.

HORSES

HN2518	Pride of the Shires with Mare and Foal (brown)
HN2519	Gude Grey Mare and Foal, 5 in.
HN2520	Farmers Boy, Dappled Shire, 8½ in.
HN2521	Dapple Grey, with Girl
HN2522	Chestnut Mare and Foal, 6½ in.
HN2523	Pride of the Shires with Mare and Foal (dapple gray)
HN2528	Pride of the Shires, 9 in. (brown)
HN2530	Merely a Minor, 12 in. (brown)
HN2531	Merely a Minor, 12 in. (gray)
HN2532	Gude Grey Mare and Foal
HN2533	Chestnut Mare and Foal
HN2534	Pride of the Shires, Mare and Foal (brown)
HN2536	Pride of the Shires with Mare and Foal (gray)
HN2537	Merely a Minor (brown)
HN2538	Merely a Minor (gray)
HN2563	Pride of the Shires (brown)
HN2565	Chestnut Mare, 6 in. (brown)
HN2566	Chestnut Mare
HN2567	Merely a Minor (gray)
HN2568	Gude Grey Mare, 5 in.
HN2569	Gude Grey Mare
HN2570	Gude Grey Mare
HN2571	Merely a Minor (brown)
HN2578	Farmer's Boy, Dappled Shire, 8½ in. (no boy)
HN2623	Farmer's Boy, 8½ in. (no boy) (brown)

PIGS

HN 213	Pigs		HN 892–97	Pigs (clown costume)**
HN 238	Pigs		HN 902–3	Pigs**
HN 243	Pig (bowl)		HN 968	Black and White Pig
HN 246	Pig**		HN2648	Pig, Lying, Head Up, 1¾ in.**
HN 800	Sleeping Pig		HN2649	Pig, Standing, 1½ in.**
HN 801	Sleeping Pig		HN2650	Pig, Lying, 1¼ in.**
HN 802	Pigs		HN2651	Pig, Lying on Side, 1 in.**
			HN2652	Pig, Sitting, 2 in.**
			HN2653	Pig, Nose Down, 1½ in.**

RAOH SCHORR ANIMALS

HN1145	Standing Moufflon	HN1147	Standing Calf
HN1146	Sleeping Calf	HN1148	Buffalo

HN1149	Donkey	HN1169	Goat, Jumping
HN1150	Young Doe	HN1170	Donkey
HN1151	Swiss Goat	HN1171	Doe
HN1152	Horse	HN1172	Antelope
HN1153	Lying Moufflon	HN1173	Sleeping Calf
HN1154	Goat, Jumping	HN1174	Standing Calf
HN1155	Donkey	HN1175	Buffalo
HN1156	Doe	HN1176	Donkey
HN1157	Antelope	HN1177	Young Doe
HN1160	Standing Moufflon	HN1178	Swiss Goat
HN1161	Sleeping Calf	HN1179	Standing Moufflon
HN1162	Standing Calf	HN1180	Horse
HN1163	Buffalo	HN1181	Lying Moufflon
HN1164	Donkey	HN1182	Goat, Jumping
HN1165	Young Doe	HN1183	Donkey
HN1166	Swiss Goat	HN1184	Doe
HN1167	Horse	HN1185	Antelope
HN1168	Lying Moufflon		

WILD ANIMALS

HN 118	Monkey	HN 911	Tiger
HN 119	Polar Bear	HN 912	Tiger
HN 121	Polar Bear	HN 919	Leopard
HN 140	Ape	HN 939	Brown Bears
HN 141	Rhinoceros	HN 940	Brown Bears
HN 156	Monkey	HN 941	Elephant
HN 170	Brown Bear (Titanian)	HN 949	Baby Elephant
HN 172	Buffalo	HN 950	Baby Elephant
HN 177	Ape (bowl)	HN 951	Baby Elephant
HN 181	Elephant	HN 952	Baby Elephant
HN 182	Monkey**	HN 955	Brown Bear
HN 183	Monkey**	HN 960	Ape**
HN 186	Elephant	HN 961	Ape**
HN 223	Lion	HN 966	Elephant
HN 225	Tiger	HN 972	Ape**
HN 253	Ape	HN 990	Tiger
HN 254	Apes	HN 991	Tiger
HN 270	Brown Bear	HN1082	Tiger
HN 861	Polar Bear	HN1083	Tiger
HN 876	Tiger	HN1084	Tiger
HN 883	Monkeys	HN1085	Lion
HN 891	Elephant	HN1086	Lion
		HN1094	Leopard
*miniature		HN1112	Lion
**character		HN1118	Tiger

HN1119 Lion
HN1120 Elephant
HN1121 Elephant
HN1122 Elephant
HN1123 Elephant
HN1124 Elephant
HN1125 Lion
HN1126 Tiger
HN2500 Cerval
HN2501 Lynx

HN2506 Elephant
HN2507 Zebra
HN2535 Tiger
HN2637 Polar Bear
HN2638 Leopard (prestige figure)
HN2639 Tiger (prestige figure)
HN2640 Elephant (prestige figure)
HN2641 Lion (prestige figure)
HN2644 Elephant
HN2646 Tiger

K NUMBERS (MINIATURE ANIMALS)

1 Bulldog, 2¼ in.
2 Bull Pup, 1¾ in.
3 Sealyham, 2¾ in.
4 Sealyham
5 Airedale
6 Pekinese, 2 in.
7 Foxhound, 2½ in.
8 Terrier, 2½ in.
9 Cocker Spaniel, 2½ in.
10 Scottish Terrier, 3 in.
11 Cairn, 2½ in.
12 Cat, 2¾ in.
13 Alsatian, 3 in.
14 Bull Terrier
15 Chow Chow, 2¼ in.
16 Welsh Corgi, 2¼ in.
17 Dachshund, 2 in.
18 Scottish Terrier, 2¼ in.
19 St. Bernard, 1¾ in.
20 Penguin, 2¼ in.

21 Penguin, 2 in.
22 Penguin, 1¾ in.
23 Penguin, 1¼ in.
24 Penguin, 1¾ in.
25 Penguin, 2¼ in.
26 Mallard
27 Yellow-Throated Warbler
28 Cardinal Bird
29 Baltimore Oriole
30 Blue Bird
31 Bull Finch
32 Budgerigar
33 Golden-Crested Wren
34 Magpie
35 Jay
36 Goldfinch
37 Hare, 1¼ in.
38 Hare, 2¼ in.
39 Hare, 2¾ in.

FIGURINES

The following lists are for the miniature figurines, number M 1 to M 91 and the figurines for HN 1 to HN 2916.

The first column is the HN or M number; the second column is the name of the figurine. This is the name used by the Royal Doulton Company or its publications. The third column is the year the figurine was introduced, and the year the figurine was discontinued.

The fourth column lists the color description and the variations of the figurine model. The first time a specific figurine is mentioned all the HN number versions are included. Subsequent listings refer back to the first entry. The colors included are the most prominent colors used on the figurine. In most cases these colors are the ones that were changed for later versions of the figurine.

The name given to the figurine is, in most cases, the official name used by the Royal Doulton factory and written on the bottom of the figurine. In a few cases the name is not recorded by the factory and we have used the names given in the book, *Royal Doulton Figures,* published by Royal Doulton Tableware, Ltd., 1978. One group of figurines is not named with the official Doulton name. The figures called "One of the Forty" are listed here as "Forty Thieves." This is because most collectors and shops refer to them by that name.

Numbers	Title	Dates	Description Variations
		M (miniatures)	
M 1	Victorian Lady	1932–1945	Color, see M 2, 25
M 2	Victorian Lady	1932–1945	Color, see M 1, 25
M 3	Paisley Shawl	1932–1938	Color, see M 4, 26
M 4	Paisley Shawl	1932–1945	Color, see M 3
M 5	Sweet Anne	1932–1945	Color, see M 6, 27
M 6	Sweet Anne	1932–1945	Color, see M 5
M 7	Patricia	1932–1945	Color, see M 8, 28
M 8	Patricia	1932–1938	Color, see M 7
M 9	Chloe	1932–1945	Color, see M 10, 29
M 10	Chloe	1932–1945	Color, see M 9
M 11	Bridesmaid	1932–1938	Color, see M 12, 30
M 12	Bridesmaid	1932–1945	Color, see M 11
M 13	Priscilla	1932–1938	Color, see M 14, 24
M 14	Priscilla	1932–1945	Color, see M 13
M 15	Pantalettes	1932–1945	Color, see M 16, 31
M 16	Pantalettes	1932–1945	Color, see M 15
M 17	Shepherd	1932–1938	Color, see M 19
M 18	Shepherdess	1932–1938	Color, see M 20
M 19	Shepherd	1932–1938	Color, see M 17
M 20	Shepherdess	1932–1938	Color, see M 18
M 21	Polly Peachum	1932–1945	Color, see M 22, 23
M 22	Polly Peachum	1932–1938	Color, see M 21
M 23	Polly Peachum	1932–1938	Color, see M 21
M 24	Priscilla	1932–1945	Color, see M 13, 14
M 25	Victorian Lady	1932–1945	Color, see M 1
M 26	Paisley Shawl	1932–1938	Color, see M 3
M 27	Sweet Anne	1932–1945	Color, see M 5
M 28	Patricia	1932–1945	Color, see M 7
M 29	Chloe	1932–1945	Color, see M 9
M 30	Bridesmaid	1932–1938	Color, see M 11
M 31	Pantalettes	1932–1945	Color, see M 15
M 32	Rosamund	1932–1945	Color, see M 33
M 33	Rosamund	1932–1945	Color, see M 32
M 34	Denise	1933–1945	Color, see M 35
M 35	Denise	1933–1945	Color, see M 34

M 36	Norma	1933–1945	Color, see M 37
M 37	Norma	1933–1945	Color, see M 36
M 38	Robin	1933–1945	Color, see M 39
M 39	Robin	1933–1945	Color, see M 38
M 40	Ermine	1933–1945	
M 41	Mr. Pickwick	1932–present	
M 42	Mr. Micawber	1932–present	
M 43	Mr. Pecksniff	1932–present	
M 44	Fat Boy	1932–present	
M 45	Uriah Heep	1932–present	
M 46	Sairey Gamp	1932–present	
M 47	Tony Weller	1932–present	
M 48	Sam Weller	1932–present	
M 49	Fagin	1932–present	
M 50	Stiggins	1932–present	
M 51	Little Nell	1932–present	
M 52	Alfred Jingle	1932–present	
M 53	Buz Fuz	1932–present	
M 54	Bill Sykes	1932–present	
M 55	Artful Dodger	1932–present	
M 56	Tiny Tim	1932–present	
M 57	Dickens napkin ring		
M 58	Dickens napkin ring		
M 59	Dickens napkin ring		
M 60	Dickens napkin ring		
M 61	Dickens napkin ring		
M 62	Dickens napkin ring		
M 63	Not issued		
M 64	Veronica	1934–1949	Color, See M 70
M 65	June	1935–1949	Color, see M 71
M 66	Monica	1935–1949	Color, see M 72
M 67	Dainty May	1935–1949	Color, see M 73
M 68	Mirabel	1936–1949	Color, see M 74
M 69	Janet	1936–1949	Color, see M 75
M 70	Veronica	1934–1949	Color, see M 64
M 71	June	1936–1949	Color, see M 65
M 72	Monica	1936–1949	Color, see M 66
M 73	Dainty May	1936–1949	Color, see M 67
M 74	Mirabel	1936–1949	Color, see M 68
M 75	Janet	1936–1949	Color, see M 69
M 76	Bumble	1939–present	
M 77	Captain Cuttle	1939–present	
M 78	Windflower	1939–1949	Color, see M 79
M 79	Windflower	1939–1949	Color, see M 78
M 80	Goody Two Shoes	1939–1949	Color, see M 81
M 81	Goody Two Shoes	1939–1949	Color, see M 80
M 82	Bo-Peep	1939–1949	Color, see M 83

M 83	Bo-Peep	1939–1949	Color, see M 82
M 84	Maureen	1939–1949	Color, see M 85
M 85	Maureen	1939–1949	Color, see M 84
M 86	Mrs. Bardell	1949–present	
M 87	Scrooge	1949–present	
M 88	David Cooperfield	1949–present	
M 89	Oliver Twist	1949–present	
M 90	Dick Swiveller	1949–present	
M 91	Trotty Veck	1949–present	
HN 1	Darling	1913–1928	White Nightshirt. See HN 1319, 1371, 1372.
HN 2	Elizabeth Fry	1913–1938	
HN 2A	Elizabeth Fry	1913–1938	Blue base. See HN 2.
HN 3	Milking Time	1913–1938	See HN 306.
HN 4	Picardy Peasant (female)	1913–1938	White hat, blue skirt. See HN 5, 17A, 351, 513.
HN 5	Picardy Peasant (female)	1913–1938	Dove gray costume. See HN 4, 17A, 351, 513.
HN 6	Dunce	1913–1938	See HN 310, 357.
HN 7	Pedlar Wolf	1913–1938	
HN 8	Crinoline, The	1913–1938	Pale lilac dress. See HN 9, 9A, 21, 21A, 413, 566, 628.
HN 9	Crinoline, The	1913–1938	Pale green skirt with flower sprays. See HN 8.
HN 9A	Crinoline, The	1913–1938	Pale green skirt, no flower sprays. See HN 8.
HN 10	Madonna of the Square	1913–1938	Lilac dress. See HN 10A, 11, 14, 27, 326, 573, 576, 594, 613, 764, 1968, 1969, 2034.
HN 10A	Madonna of the Square	1913–1938	Blue dress. See HN 10.
HN 11	Madonna of the Square	1913–1938	Gray dress. See HN 10.
HN 12	Baby	1913–1938	
HN 13	Picardy Peasant (male)	1913–1938	Blue costume. See HN 17, 19.
HN 14	Madonna of the Square	1913–1938	Same as HN 10A.
HN 15	Sleepy Scholar, The	1913–1938	Blue dress. See HN 16, 29.
HN 16	Sleepy Scholar, The	1913–1938	Yellow dress. See HN 15.
HN 17	Picardy Peasant (male)	1913–1938	Green hat and green trousers. See HN 13.
HN 17A	Picardy Peasant (female)	1913–1938	Green costume. See HN 4, 5, 351, 513.
HN 18	Pussy	1913–1938	See HN 325, 507.
HN 19	Picardy Peasant (male)	1913–1938	Green costume. See HN 13.
HN 20	Coquette, The	1913–1938	Yellow green costume. See HN 37.

HN 21	Crinoline, The	1913–1938	Yellow Skirt with rosebuds. See HN 8.
HN 21A	Crinoline, The	1913–1938	Yellow skirt, no rosebuds. See HN 8.
HN 22	Lavender Woman, The	1913–1938	Pale aqua dress. See HN 23, 23A, 342, 569, 744.
HN 23	Lavender Woman, The	1913–1938	Green dress. See HN 22.
HN 23A	Lavender Woman, The	1913–1938	Blue and green dress. See HN 22.
HN 24	Sleep	1913–1938	Pale blue-green dress. See HN 24A, 25, 25A, 424, 692, 710.
HN 24A	Sleep	1913–1938	Dark blue dress. See HN 24.
HN 25	Sleep	1913–1938	Blue-green dress. See HN 24.
HN 25A	Sleep	1913–1938	See HN 24.
HN 26	Diligent Scholar, The	1913–1938	Brown and green costume.
HN 27	Madonna of the Square	1913–1938	Mottled green and blue costume. See HN 10.
HN 28	Motherhood	1913–1938	See HN 30, 303.
HN 29	Sleepy Scholar, The	1913–1939	Brown costume. See HN 15.
HN 30	Motherhood	1913–1938	Gray costume. See HN 28.
HN 31	Return of Persephone, The	1913–1938	Gray and ivory costumes.
HN 32	Child and Crab	1913–1938	Light blue robe.
HN 33	An Arab	1913–1938	Green robe, blue cloak. See HN 343, 378, 1308, 1366, 1425, 1657, 2082.
HN 34	Moorish Minstrel	1913–1938	Dark Blue robe. See HN 364, 415, 797.
HN 35	Charley's Aunt	1914–1938	Black dress. See HN 640.
HN 36	Sentimental Pierrot, The	1914–1938	Black and white costume. See HN 307.
HN 37	Coquette, The	1914–1938	Green costume with flower sprays. See HN 20.
HN 38	Carpet Vendor, The	1914–1938	See HN 38A, 348
HN 38A	Carpet Vendor, The	1914–1938	Persian-style carpet. See HN 38.
HN 39	Welsh Girl, The	1914–1938	Brown, purple, red costume. See HN 92, 456, 514, 516, 519, 520, 660, 668, 669, 701, 792.
HN 40	A Lady of the Elizabethan Period	1914–1938	Gray-green and white dress. See HN 40A, 73, 309, 411.

HN 40A	A Lady of the Elizabethan Period	1914–1938	Plain dress. See HN 40.
HN 41	A Lady of the Georgian Period	1914–1938	Rust overdress. See HN 331, 444, 690, 702.
HN 42	Robert Burns	1914–1938	Brown, black, rust, yellow plaid costume.
HN 43	A Woman of the Time of Henry VI	1914–1938	
HN 44	A Lilac Shawl	1915–1938	Lilac shawl with roses, cream skirt. See HN 44A, 339, 340, 362, 388, 442, 612, 765.
HN 44A	A Lilac Shawl	1915–1938	Printed pattern on shawl. See HN 44.
HN 45	A Jester	1915–1938	Black and white checkered costume. See HN 71, 320, 367, 412, 426, 446, 552, 616, 627, 1295, 1702, 2016.
HN 45A	A Jester	1915–1938	Green and white checkered costume. See HN 45B.
HN 45B	J Jester	1915–1938	Red and white checkered costume. See HN 55, 308, 630, 1333.
HN 46	Gainsborough Hat, The	1915–1938	Lilac dress. See HN 46N, 47, 329, 352, 383, 453, 675, 705.
HN 46A	Gainsborough Hat, The	1915–1938	Black patterned collar. See HN 46.
HN 47	Gainsborough Hat, The	1915–1938	Light green dress. See HN 46.
HN 48	Lady of the Fan	1916–1938	Lilac dress. See HN 52, 53, 53A, 335, 509.
HN 48A	Lady with Rose	1916–1938	Cream dress. See HN 52A, 68, 304, 336, 515, 517, 584, 624.
HN 49	Under the Gooseberry Bush	1916–1938	Nude child, green bush.
HN 50	A Spook	1916–1938	Blue-green robe, dark green cap. See HN 51, 51A, 51B, 58, 512, 625, 1218.
HN 51	A Spook	1916–1938	Red Cap. See HN 50.
HN 51A	A Spook	1916-1938	Black cap. See HN 50.
HN 51B	A Spook	1916-1938	Blue cloak. See HN 50.
HN 52	Lady of the Fan	1916–1938	Yellow dress. See HN 48.

HN 52A	Lady with Rose	1916–1938	Yellow dress. See HN 48A.
HN 53	Lady of the Fan	1916–1938	Dark blue dress. See HN 48.
HN 53A	Lady of the Fan	1916–1938	Green-blue dress. See HN 48.
HN 54	Lady Ermine	1916–1938	Blue coat. See HN 332, 671.
HN 55	A Jester	1916–1938	Black and lilac costume. See HN 45B.
HN 56	Land of Nod, The	1916–1938	Ivory Nightshirt. See HN 56A, 56B.
HN 56A	Land of Nod, The	1916–1938	Pale gray nightshirt, green candlestick. See HN 56.
HN 56B	Land of Nod, The	1916–1938	Pale gray nightshirt, red candlestick. See HN 56.
HN 57	Curtsey, The	1916–1938	See HN 57B, 66A, 327, 334, 363, 371, 518, 547, 629, 670.
HN 57A	Flounced Skirt, The	1916–1938	Orange dress. See HN 66, 77, 78, 333.
HN 57B	Curtsey, The	1916–1938	Lilac dress. See HN 57.
HN 58	A Spook	1916–1938	See HN 50.
HN 59	Upon Her Cheeks She Wept	1916–1938	Pale blue dress. See HN 511, 522.
HN 60	Shy Anne	1916–1938	Flowered blue dress. See HN 64, 65, 568.
HN 61	Katharine	1916–1938	Green dress. See HN 74, 341, 471, 615, 793.
HN 62	A Child's Grace	1916–1938	Green Coat, black pattern. See HN 62A, 510.
HN 62A	A Child's Grace	1916–1938	Without black patterning on coat. See HN 62.
HN 63	Little Land, The	1916–1938	See HN 67.
HN 64	Shy Anne	1916–1938	White dress. See HN 60.
HN 65	Shy Anne	1916–1938	Blue spotted dress, dark blue hem. See HN 60.
HN 66	Flounced Skirt, The	1916–1938	Lilac dress. See HN 57A.
HN 66A	Curtsey, The	1916–1938	Lilac Dress. See HN 57.
HN 67	Little Land, The	1916–1938	Blue costume. See HN 63.
HN 68	Lady with Rose	1916–1938	Green and yellow dress. See HN 48A.
HN 69	Pretty Lady	1916–1938	Flowered blue dress. See HN 70, 302, 330, 361, 384, 565, 700, 763, 783.
HN 70	Pretty Lady	1916–1938	Pale blue dress. See HN 69.

HN 71	A Jester	1917–1938	Black, green, and red costume. See HN 45.
HN 72	Orange Vendor	1917–1938	Black coat. See HN 508, 521, 1966.
HN 73	A Lady of the Elizabethan Period	1917–1938	Dark blue-green costume. See HN 40.
HN 74	Katharine	1917–1938	Pale blue dress, green spots. See HN 61.
HN 75	Blue Beard	1917–1938	See HN 410.
HN 76	Carpet Vendor, The	1917–1938	See HN 350.
HN 77	Flounced Skirt, The	1917–1938	Lemon yellow dress, black trimmings. See HN 57A.
HN 78	Flounced Skirt, The	1917–1938	Flowered yellow lustre dress. See HN 57A.
HN 79	Shylock	1917–1938	Multicolored cloak, yellow sleeves. See HN 317.
HN 80	Fisherwomen	1917–1938	Pink Shawl. See HN 349, 359, 631.
HN 81	A Shepherd	1918–1938	Earthenware. Tan coat. See HN 617, 632.
HN 82	Afternoon Call, The	1918–1938	
HN 83	Lady Anne, The	1918–1938	Yellow dress. See HN 87, 93.
HN 84	A Mandarin	1918–1938	Mauve shirt, green cloak. See HN 316, 318, 382, 611, 746, 787, 791.
HN 85	Jack Point	1918–1938	Red checkered costume. See HN 91, 99, 2080.
HN 86	Out For a Walk	1918–1938	Pink and gray dress. See HN 443, 748.
HN 87	Lady Anne, The	1918–1938	Green dress. See HN 83.
HN 88	Spooks	1918–1936	Pale blue-green robes, dark green caps. See HN 89, 372.
HN 89	Spooks	1920–1936	Red caps. See HN 88.
HN 90	Doris Keene as Cavallini	1918–1936	Black dress. See HN 467.
HN 91	Jack Point	1918–1938	Green and black costume. See HN 85.
HN 92	Welsh Girl, The	1918–1938	Blue-gray costume. See HN 39.
HN 93	Lady Anne, The	1918–1938	Blue dress. See HN 83.
HN 94	Young Knight, The	1918–1936	
HN 95	Europa and the Bull	1919–1938	
HN 96	Doris Keene ad Cavallini	1918–1938	Black dress, white shawl. See HN 345.

HN 97	Mermaid, The	1918–1936	Green seaweed in hair, beige base. See HN 300.
HN 98	Guy Fawkes	1918–1949	Red cloak. See HN 347, 445.
HN 99	Jack Point	1918–1938	Heraldic tunic. See HN 85.
HN 100–299	Animals and birds.		
HN 300	Mermaid, The	1918–1936	Red berries in hair, dark base. See HN 97.
HN 301	Moorish Piper Minstrel	1918–1938	Dark blue robe, red hat. See HN 328, 416.
HN 302	Pretty Lady	1918–1938	Patterned lilac dress. See HN 69.
HN 303	Motherhood	1918–1938	White dress, black pattern. See HN 28.
HN 304	Lady with Rose	1918–1938	Gray-lilac dress, brown pattern. See HN 48A.
HN 305	A Scribe	1918–1936	Olive-green robe. See HN 324, 1235.
HN 306	Milking Time	1913–1938	Pale costume, black markings, See HN 3.
HN 307	Sentimental Pierrot, The	1918–1938	Black and white costume. See HN 36.
HN 308	A Jester	1918–1938	Black and lilac costume. See HN 45B.
HN 309	A Lady of the Elizabethan Period	1918–1938	Raised pattern on dress. See HN 40.
HN 310	Dunce	1918–1938	Black and white costume, green base. See HN 6.
HN 311	Dancing Figure	1918–1938	
HN 312	Spring (The Seasons)	1918–1938)	Pale yellow dress. See HN 472.
HN 313	Summer (The Seasons)	1918–1938	Pale green dress. See HN 473.
HN 314	Autumn (The Seasons)	1918–1938	Pink dress. See HN 474.
HN 315	Winter (The Seasons)	1918–1938	Pale blue dress. See HN 475.
HN 316	A Mandarin	1918–1938	Black and yellow costume. See HN 84.
HN 317	Shylock	1918–1938	Dark multicolored cloak. See HN 79.
HN 318	A Mandarin	1920–1938	Gold and black costume. See HN 84.
HN 319	A Gnome	1918–1938	Pale blue costume. See HN 380, 381.
HN 320	A Jester	1918–1938	Green and black costume. See HN 45.

HN 321	Digger	1918–1938	New Zealand uniform.
HN 322	Digger	1918–1938	Australian uniform. See HN 353.
HN 323	Blighty	1918–1938	British uniform.
HN 324	A Scribe	1918–1938	Green hat, brown costume. See HN 305.
HN 325	Pussy	1918–1938	White dress, black pattern. See HN 18.
HN 326	Madonna of the Square	1918–1938	Earthenware, gray-blue costume. See HN 10.
HN 327	Curtsey, The	1918–1938	See HN 57.
HN 328	Moorish Pipe Minstrel	1918–1938	Green and brown striped robe. See HN 301.
HN 329	Gainsborough Hat, The	1918–1938	Patterned blue dress. See HN 46.
HN 330	Pretty Lady	1918–1938	Patterned lilac dress. See HN 69.
HN 331	A Lady of the Georgian Period	1918–1938	Brown and yellow dress. See HN 41.
HN 332	Lady Ermine	1918–1938	Red coat and hat, green and yellow patterned skirt. See HN 54.
HN 333	Flounced Skirt, The	1918–1938	Brown mottled dress. See HN 57A.
HN 334	Curtsey, The	1918–1938	Lilac dress, brown pattern, green trim. See HN 57.
HN 335	Lady of the Fan	1919–1938	Blue dress, brown pattern. See HN 48.
HN 336	Lady with Rose	1919–1938	Multicolored dress, brown pattern. See HN 48A.
HN 337	Parson's Daughter, The	1919–1938	Lilac dress, brown flowered pattern. See HN 338, 441, 564, 790, 1242, 1356, 2018.
HN 338	Parson's Daughter, The	1919–1938	Blue patterned dress, red cap and shawl. See HN 337.
HN 339	In Grandma's Days	1919–1938	Renamed version. See HN 44.
HN 340	In Grandma's Days	1919–1938	Yellow and lilac dress. See HN 44.
HN 341	Katharine	1919–1938	Red dress. See HN 6.
HN 342	Lavender Woman, The	1919–1938	Patterned dress, lilac shawl. See HN 22.
HN 343	An Arab	1919–1938	Striped yellow and purple cloak. See HN 33.

HN 344	Henry Irving as Cardinal Wolsey	1919–1949	Red robe.
HN 345	Doris Keene as Cavallini	1919–1949	Dark fur color, striped muff. See HN 96.
HN 346	Tony Weller	1919–1938	Green coat, blue rug. See HN 368, 684.
HN 347	Guy Fawkes	1919–1938	Brown cloak. See HN 98.
HN 348	Carpet Vendor, The	1919–1938	Blue-green costume, checkered base. See HN 38.
HN 349	Fisherwoman	1919–1968	Middle Woman with yellow shawl. See HN 80.
HN 350	Carpet Vendor, The	1919–1938	Blue costume, green and brown floral carpet. See HN 76.
HN 351	Picardy Peasant (female)	1919–1938	Pale blue hat and costume. See HN 4.
HN 352	Gainsborough Hat, The	1919–1938	Yellow dress, purple hat. See HN 46.
HN 353	Digger	1919–1938	Natural colors. See HN 322.
HN 354	A Geisha	1919–1938	Yellow Kimono. See HN 376, 387, 634, 741, 779, 1321, 1322.
HN 355	Dolly	1919–1938	Pale blue nightgown.
HN 356	Sir Thomas Lovell	1919–1938	Red, green, and black costume.
HN 357	Dunce	1919–1938	Gray costume, black pattern. See HN 6.
HN 358	An Old King	1919–1938	Red, purple, green costume. See HN 623, 1801, 2134.
HN 359	Fisherwoman	1919–1938	Middle woman with red shawl. See HN 80.
HN 360	Pretty Lady	1919–1938	Blue-green dress. See HN 69.
HN 362	In Grandma's Days	1919–1938	Blue patterned dress. See HN 44.
HN 363	Curtsey, The	1919–1938	Lilac and peach dress. See HN 57.
HN 364	A Moorish Minstrel	1920–1938	Blue, green, and orange striped costume. See HN 34.
HN 365	Double Jester	1920–1938	
HN 366	A Mandarin	1920–1938	Yellow and blue costume. See HN 455, 641.
HN 367	A Jester	1920–1938	Green, red, and yellow costume. See HN 45.

HN 368	Tony Weller	1920–1938	Blue coat, brown blanket. See HN 346.
HN 369	Cavalier	1920–1938	
HN 370	Henry VIII	1920–1938	See HN 673.
HN 371	Curtsey, The	1920–1938	Yellow dress. See HN 57.
HN 372	Spooks	1920–1936	Patterned green costume. brown cap. See HN 88.
HN 373	Boy on a Crocodile	1920–1938	
HN 374	Lady and Blackamoor	1920–1938	Blue and green dress. See HN 375, 377, 470.
HN 375	Lady and Blackamoor	1920–1938	Yellow dress. See HN 374.
HN 376	A Geisha	1920–1938	Blue and yellow mottled kimono. See HN 354.
HN 377	Lady and Blackamoor	1920–1938	Pink and green dress. See HN 374.
HN 378	An Arab	1920–1938	Green and yellow costume, dark cloak. See HN 33.
HN 379	Ellen Terry as Queen Catherine	1920–1949	Blue and lilac dress.
HN 380	A Gnome	1920–1938	Lilac costume. See HN 319.
HN 381	A Gnome	1920–1938	Green costume. See HN 319.
HN 382	A Mandarin	1920–1938	Blue and yellow costume. See HN 84.
HN 383	Gainsborough Hat, The	1920–1938	Striped dress. See HN 46.
HN 384	Pretty Lady	1920–1938	Red dress, striped skirt. See HN 69.
HN 385	St. George	1920–1938	Dapple gray horse, blue-green costume. See HN 386. 1800, 2067.
HN 386	St. George	1920–1938	Dark horse. See HN 385.
HN 387	A Geisha	1920–1938	Blue Kimono, yellow sleeves. See HN 354.
HN 388	In Grandma's Days	1920–1938	Blue patterned dress. See HN 44.
HN 389	Little Mother, The	1920–1938	Pink dress, blond hair. See HN 390, 469.
HN 390	Little Mother, The	1920–1938	Pink dress, dark hair. See HN 389.
HN 391	A Princess	1920–1938	Green cloak, lilac skirt. See HN 392, 420, 430, 431, 633.
HN 392	A Princess	1920–1938	Multicolored costume, striped skirt. See HN 391.

HN 393	Lady without Bouquet	1920–1938	Peach and blue dress. See HN 394.
HN 394	Lady without Bouquet	1920–1938	Blue and yellow dress. See HN 393.
HN 395	Contentment	1920–1938	Yellow skirt, blue blouse. See HN 396, 421, 468, 572, 685, 686, 1323.
HN 396	Contentment	1920–1938	Yellow and pink striped chair. See HN 395.
HN 397	Puff and Powder	1920–1938	Yellow skirt, brown bodice. See HN 398, 400, 432, 433.
HN 398	Puff and Powder	1920–1938	Pale blue skirt. See HN 397.
HN 399	Japanese Fan	1920–1938	Purple and dark multicolored costume. See HN 405, 439, 440.
HN 400	Puff and Powder	1920–1938	Green and blue bodice, yellow skirt. See HN 397.
HN 401	Marie	1920–1938	Pink dress, white, yellow, blue skirt. See HN 434, 502, 504, 505, 506.
HN 402	Betty	1920–1938	Pink dress. See HN 403, 435, 438, 477, 478.
HN 403	Betty	1920–1938	Green skirt, blue, yellow, white border. See HN 402.
HN 404	King Charles	1920–1951	Dark Costume, pink base. See HN 2084.
HN 405	Japanese Fan	1920–1938	Pale yellow dress. See HN 399.
HN 406	Bouquet, The	1920–1938	See HN 414, 422, 428, 429, 567, 794.
HN 407	Omar Khayyam and the Beloved	1920–1938	See HN 419, 459, 598.
HN 408	Omar Khayyam	1920–1938	Dark blue-green robe. See HN 409.
HN 409	Omar Khayyam	1920–1938	Black robe, yellow pants. See HN 408.
HN 410	Blue Beard	1920–1938	Blue costume. See HN 75.
HN 411	A Lady of the Elizabethan Period	1920–1938	Brown mottled dress. See HN 40.
HN 412	A Jester	1920–1938	Green and red striped tights. See HN 45.
HN 413	Crinoline, The	1920–1938	White and blue dress. See HN 8.

HN 414	Bouquet, The	1920–1938	Pink and yellow shawl. See HN 406.
HN 415	A Moorish Minstrel	1920–1938	Green and yellow striped costume. See HN 34.
HN 416	A Moorish Piper Minstrel	1920–1938	Green and yellow striped robe. See HN 301.
HN 417	Forty Thieves	1920–1938	See HN 490, 495, 501, 528, 648, 677, 1351, 1352.
HN 418	Forty Thieves	1920–1938	See HN 423, 427, 480, 481, 482, 483, 484, 491, 492, 493, 494, 496, 497, 498, 499, 500, 645, 646, 647, 649, 663, 664, 665, 666, 667, 704, 712, 713, 714, 1336, 1350, 1353, 1354.
HN 419	Omar Khayyam and the Beloved	1920–1938	Blue-green costumes. See HN 407.
HN 420	A Princess	1920–1938	Pink and green striped skirt, blue cloak. See HN 391.
HN 421	Contentment	1920–1938	Pale blue costume. See HN 395.
HN 422	Bouquet, The	1920–1938	Yellow and pink striped skirt. See HN 406.
HN 423	Forty Thieves	1921–1938	See HN 418.
HN 424	Sleep	1921–1938	Smaller in size. See HN 24.
HN 425	Goosegirl, The	1921–1938	Blue skirt, striped blue blouse. See HN 436, 437, 448, 559, 560.
HN 426	A Jester	1921–1938	Costume with pink pattern, black tights. See HN 45.
HN 427	Forty Thieves	1921–1938	See HN 418.
HN 428	Bouquet, The	1921–1938	Blue dress. See HN 406.
HN 429	Bouquet, The	1921–1938	Multicolored dress. See HN 406.
HN 430	A Princess	1921–1938	Green flowered dress, blue-green striped cloak. See HN 391.
HN 431	A Princess	1921–1938	Pink dress, blue-green cloak. See HN 391.
HN 432	Puff and Powder	1921–1938	Lilac skirt, orange spots. See HN 397.
HN 433	Puff and Powder	1921–1938	Yellow skirt, blue spots. See HN 397.

HN 434	Marie	1921–1938	Yellow skirt, orange stripes. See HN 401.
HN 435	Betty	1921–1938	Blue skirt, yellow spots. See HN 402.
HN 436	Goosegirl, The	1921–1938	Green skirt, blue spots, spotted blouse. See HN 425.
HN 437	Goosegirl, The	1921–1938	Checkered brown and blue dress. See HN 425.
HN 438	Betty	1921–1938	Green skirt. See HN 402.
HN 439	Japanese Fan	1921–1938	Blue dress, green spots. See HN 399.
HN 440	Japanese Fan	1921–1938	Yellow dress, orange spots. See HN 399.
HN 441	Parson's Daughter, The	1921–1938	Yellow dress, orange spots. See HN 337.
HN 442	In Grandma's Days	1921–1938	White spotted skirt, green shawl. See HN 44.
HN 443	Out for a Walk	1921–1936	See HN 86.
HN 444	A Lady of the Georgian Period	1921–1938	Green-blue spotted dress. See HN 41.
HN 445	Guy Fawkes	1921–1938	Green cloak. See HN 98.
HN 446	A Jester	1921–1938	Green sleeves, blue base. See HN 45.
HN 447	Lady with Shawl	1921–1938	Pale blue and white striped dress. See HN 458, 626, 678, 679.
HN 448	Goosegirl, The	1921–1938	Blue striped dress, blue hat. See HN 425.
HN 449	Fruit Gathering	1921–1938	Blue striped blouse, blue skirt. See HN 476, 503, 561, 562, 706, 707.
HN 450	A Mandarin	1921–1938	Red robe. See HN 460, 461, 601.
HN 451	An Old Man	1921–1938	
HN 452	Gainsborough Hat, The	1921–1938	Red, blue, and green dress. See HN 46.
HN 454	Smiling Buddha, The	1921–1938	Blue-green robe.
HN 455	A Mandarin	1921–1938	Green costume. See HN 366.
HN 456	Welsh Girl, The	1921–1938	Green blouse, brown skirt. See HN 39.
HN 457	Crouching Nude	1921–1938	Ivory, blue-green base.
HN 458	Lady with Shawl	1921–1938	Multicolored shawl, pink dress. See HN 447.

HN 459	Omar Khayyam and the Beloved	1921–1938	Multicolored costumes. See HN 407.
HN 460	A Mandarin	1921–1938	Blue costume. See HN 450.
HN 461	A Mandarin	1921–1938	Red costume. See HN 450.
HN 462	Woman Holding Child	1921–1938	Green dress, white apron. See HN 570, 703, 743.
HN 463	Polly Peachum	1921–1949	White dress. See HN 465, 550, 589, 614, 680, 693.
HN 464	Captain MacHeath	1921–1949	Red jacket. See HN 590, 1256.
HN 465	Polly Peachum	1921–1949	Red dress. See HN 463.
HN 466	Tulips	1921–1938	Green dress. See HN 488, 672, 747, 1334.
HN 467	Doris Keane as Cavallini	1921–1936	Gold jewelry. See HN 90.
HN 468	Contentment	1921–1938	Green spotted dress. See HN 395.
HN 469	Little Mother, The	1921–1938	White dress, brown hair. See HN 389.
HN 470	Lady and Blackamoor	1921–1938	Green and lilac dress. See HN 374.
HN 471	Katharine	1921–1938	Spotted blouse and dress. See HN 61.
HN 472	Spring (The Seasons)	1921–1938	Patterned robe. See HN 312.
HN 473	Summer (The Seasons)	1921–1938	Patterned robe. See HN 313.
HN 474	Autumn (The Seasons)	1921–1938	Patterned robe. See HN 314.
HN 475	Winter (The Seasons)	1921–1938	Patterned robe. See HN 315.
HN 476	Fruit Gathering	1921–1938	Green checkered blouse. See HN 449.
HN 477	Betty	1921–1938	Spotted green skirt. See HN 402.
HN 478	Betty	1921–1938	White spotted skirt. See Hn 402.
HN 479	Balloon Seller, The	1921–1938	Blue dress, white spots. See HN 486, 548, 583, 697.
HN 480	Forty Thieves	1921–1938	See HN 418.
HN 481	Forty Thieves	1921–1938	Dark spotted robes. See HN 418.
HN 482	Forty Thieves	1921–1938	Spotted waistband. See HN 418.

HN 483	Forty Thieves	1921–1938	Brown hat, green striped robes. See HN 418.
HN 484	Forty Thieves	1921–1938	Mottled green robes. See HN 418.
HN 485	Lucy Lockett	1921–1949	Green dress. See HN 524.
HN 486	Balloon Seller, The	1921–1938	Blue dress, no hat. See HN 479.
HN 487	Pavlova	1921–1938	White tutu, black base. See HN 676.
HN 488	Tulips	1921–1938	Ivory dress. See HN 466.
HN 489	Polly Peachum	1921–1938	Green dress. See HN 549, 620, 694, 734.
HN 490	Forty Thieves	1921–1938	Blue and brown checkered coat. See HN 417.
HN 491	Forty Thieves	1921–1938	See HN 418.
HN 492	Forty Thieves	1921–1938	See HN 418.
HN 493	Forty Thieves	1921–1938	Blue hat and waistband. See HN 418.
HN 494	Forty Thieves	1921–1938	See HN 418.
HN 495	Forty Thieves	1921–1938	Blue hat and waistband. See HN 417.
HN 496	Forty Thieves	1921–1938	Yellow hat and vase. See HN 418.
HN 497	Forty Thieves	1921–1938	Brown hat, checkered pants. See HN 418.
HN 498	Forty Thieves	1921–1938	Dark striped coat, pale striped pants. See HN 418.
HN 499	Forty Thieves	1921–1938	Cream costume, green hat. See HN 418.
HN 500	Forty Thieves	1921–1938	Checkered coat, red hat. See HN 418.
HN 501	Forty Thieves	1921–1938	Green striped coat. See HN 417.
HN 502	Marie	1921–1938	White dress, red and blue bodice. See HN 401.
HN 503	Fruit Gathering	1921–1938	Brown and blue checkered dress. See HN 449.
HN 504	Marie	1921–1938	Green and blue dress, red spots. See HN 401.
HN 505	Marie	1921–1938	Green and lilac skirt, blue spotted bodice. See HN 401.
HN 506	Marie	1921–1938	Blue and green striped bodice, spotted lilac skirt. See HN 401.
HN 507	Pussy	1921–1938	Spotted blue dress. See HN 18.

HN 508	Orange Vendor, The	1921–1938	Purple coat. See HN 72.
HN 509	Lady of the Fan	1921–1938	Green, lilac, and blue spotted dress. See HN 48.
HN 510	A Child's Grace	1921–1938	Checkered dress, green base. See HN 62.
HN 511	Upon Her Cheeks She Wept	1921–1938	Lilac dress. See HN 59.
HN 512	A Spook	1921–1938	Blue spotted costume. See HN 50.
HN 513	Picardy Peasant (female)	1921–1938	Blue blouse, spotted skirt. See HN 4.
HN 514	Welsh Girl, The	1921–1938	Green skirt, spotted apron. See HN 39.
HN 515	Lady with Rose	1921–1938	Green dress, lilac stripes. See HN 48A.
HN 516	Welsh Girl, The	1921–1938	Checkered lilac dress, black spotted cloak. See HN 39.
HN 517	Lady with Rose	1921–1938	Lilac dress, orange spots. See HN 48A.
HN 518	Curtsey, The	1921–1938	Lilac skirt, orange spots. See HN 57.
HN 519	Welsh Girl, The	1921–1938	Blue skirt, lilac skirt. See HN 39.
HN 520	Welsh Girl, The	1921–1938	Spotted lilac dress. See HN 39.
HN 521	Orange Vendor, The	1921–1938	Pale blue costume, black collar, purple hood. See HN 72.
HN 522	Upon Her Cheeks she Wept	1921–1938	Lilac dress, spots. See HN 59.
HN 523	Sentinel	1921–1938	
HN 524	Lucy Lockett	1921–1949	Yellow dress. See HN 485.
HN 525	Flower Seller's Children, The	1921–1949	Boy in green, girl in blue costume. See HN 551, 1206, 1342, 1406.
HN 526	Beggar, The	1921–1949	Blue trousers, red sash. See HN 591.
HN 527	Highwayman, The	1921–1949	Red costume, dark coat. See HN 592, 1257.
HN 528	Forty Thieves	1921–1938	See HN 417.
HN 529	Mr. Pickwick (miniature)	1922–1932	Yellow vest, black jacket.
HN 530	Fat Boy, The (miniature)	1922–1932	Blue jacket, white.
HN 531	Sam Weller (miniature)	1922–1932	Striped yellow vest.
HN 532	Mr. Micawber (miniature)	1922–1932	Yellow vest, red dotted tie.

HN 533	Sairey Gamp (miniature)	1922–1932	Green dress, black cape.
HN 534	Fagin (miniature)	1922–1932	Black coat.
HN 535	Pecksniff (miniature)	1922–1932	Red vest, black coat.
HN 536	Stiggins (miniature)	1922–1932	Black vest and coat.
HN 537	Bill Sykes (miniature)	1922–1932	Brown vest, black jacket.
HN 538	Buz Fuz (miniature)	1922–1932	Brown vest, black robe.
HN 539	Tiny Tim (miniature)	1922–1932	Blue scarf and socks.
HN 540	Little Nell (miniature)	1922–1932	Pink dress.
HN 541	Alfred Jingle (miniature)	1922–1932	Black jacket, tan trousers.
HN 542	Cobbler, The	1922–1939	Yellow shirt, dark green robe. See HN 543, 682.
HN 543	Cobbler, The	1922–1938	Special firing.
HN 544	Tony Weller (miniature)	1922–1932	Red vest, yellow dotted tie.
HN 545	Uriah Heep (miniature)	1922–1932	Yellow vest, black suit.
HN 546	Artful Dodger, The (miniature)	1922–1932	Red vest, blue tie.
HN 547	Curtsey, The	1922–1938	Green and yellow skirt, blue bodice. See HN 57.
HN 548	Balloon Seller, The	1922–1938	Black shawl, blue dress. See HN 479.
HN 549	Polly Peachum	1922–1949	Red dress. See HN 489.
HN 550	Polly Peachum	1922–1949	See HN 463.
HN 551	Flower Seller's Children, The	1922–1949	Boy in blue costume, girl in orange and yellow. See HN 525.
HN 552	A Jester	1922–1938	Black and red costume. See HN 45.
HN 553	Pecksniff	1922–1939	Tan vest, black trousers. See HN 1891.
HN 554	Uriah Heep	1923–1939	Black jacket, black trousers. See HN 1892.
HN 555	Fat Boy, The	1923–1939	Blue jacket, white scarf. See HN 1893.
HN 556	Mr. Pickwick	1923–1939	Blue jacket, yellow trousers. See HN 1894.
HN 557	Mr. Micawber	1923–1939	Brown jacket, black trousers. See HN 1895.
HN 558	Sairey Gamp	1923–1939	Black dress and cape. See HN 1896.
HN 559	Goosegirl, The	1923–1938	Pink spotted dress. See HN 425.
HN 560	Goosegirl, The	1923–1938	Red blouse. See HN 425.
HN 561	Fruit Gathering	1923–1938	Green blouse. See HN 449.
HN 562	Fruit Gathering	1923–1938	Pink blouse, spotted skirt. See HN 449.

HN 563	Man in Tudor Costume	1923–1938	
HN 564	Parson's Daughter, The	1923–1949	Multicolored skirt. See HN 337.
HN 565	Pretty Lady	1923–1938	Orange dress, green spots. See HN 69.
HN 566	Crinoline, The	1923–1938	Cream skirt, green spots, green blouse. See HN 406.
HN 567	Bouquet, The	1923–1938	Cream shawl, green and red spots. See HN 406.
HN 568	Shy Anne	1923–1938	Green dress. See HN 60.
HN 569	Lavender Woman, The	1924–1938	Red striped shawl. See HN 22.
HN 570	Woman Holding Child	1923–1938	Pink and green striped skirt, red striped blanket. See HN 462.
HN 571	Falstaff	1923–1938	Rust coat, green patterned cloth. See HN 575, 608, 609, 619, 638, 1216, 1606.
HN 572	Contentment	1923–1938	Pink blouse, spotted, cream skirt, spotted. See HN 395.
HN 573	Madonna of the Square	1923–1938	Orange skirt. See HN 10.
HN 574			
HN 575	Falstaff	1923–1938	Brown coat, yellow spotted cloth on base. See HN 571.
HN 576	Madonna of the Square	1923–1938	Green skirt, black patterned shawl. See HN 10.
HN 577	Chelsea Pair, The (female)	1923–1938	White flowered dress. See HN 578.
HN 578	Chelsea Pair, The (female)	1923–1938	Red blouse, yellow flowers. See HN 577.
HN 579	Chelsea Pair, The (male)	1923–1938	Red jacket, yellow flowers. See HN 580.
HN 580	Chelsea Pair, The (male)	1923–1938	Blue flowers. See HN 579.
HN 581	Perfect Pair, The	1923–1938	Pink dress, red jacket.
HN 582	Grossmith's Tsang Ihang Perfume of Tibet	1923–?	Yellow and blue multicolored costume.
HN 583	Balloon Seller, The	1923–1949	Green shawl, cream dress. See HN 479.
HN 584	Lady with Rose	1923–1938	Green and pink dress. See HN 48A.

HN 585	Harlequinade	1923–1938	Purple and green costume. See HN 635, 711, 780.
HN 586	Boy with Turban	1923–1938	See HN 587, 661, 662, 1210, 1212, 1213, 1214, 1225.
HN 587	Boy with Turban	1923–1938	See HN 586.
HN 588	Girl with Yellow Frock	1923–1938	Yellow dress.
HN 589	Polly Peachum	1924–1949	Pink dress, yellow underskirt. See HN 463.
HN 590	Captain MacHeath	1924–1949	Yellow cravat. See HN 464.
HN 591	Beggar, The	1924–1949	Different glaze. See HN 526.
HN 592	Highwayman, The	1924–1949	Different glaze. See HN 527.
HN 593	Nude on Rock	1924–1938	Pale blue-green glaze.
HN 594	Madonna of the Square	1924–1938	Green skirt, brown patterned shawl. See HN 10.
HN 595	Grief	1924–1938	
HN 596	Despair	1924–1938	
HN 597	Bather, The	1924–1938	Mottled gray robes, blue base. See HN 687, 781, 782, 1238, 1708.
HN 598	Omar Khayyam and the Beloved	1924–1938	Pink cloak, striped, blue dress, striped. See HN 407.
HN 599	Masquerade (male)	1924–1949	Red jacket. See HN 636, and 683.
HN 600	Masquerade (female)	1924–1949	Pink dress. See HN 637, 674.
HN 601	A Mandarin	1924–1938	Blue costume. See HN 450.
HN 602			
HN 603 A	Child Study	1924–1938	See HN 603B.
HN 603 B	Child Study	1924–1938	Kingcups on base. See HN 603A.
HN 604 A	Child Study	1924–1938	Primroses on base. See HN 604B.
HN 604 B	Child Study	1924–1938	See HN 604A.
HN 605 A	Child Study	1924–1938	
HN 605 B	Child Study	1924–1938	
HN 606 A	Child Study	1924–1938	See HN 606B.
HN 606 B	Child Study	1924–1938	Kingcups on base. See HN 606A.
HN 607			
HN 608	Falstaff	1924–1938	Red coat, red cloth. See HN 571.

HN 609	Falstaff	1924–1938	Green coat, green cloth. See HN 571.
HN 610	Henry Lytton as Jack Point	1924–1949	Black and gold striped costume.
HN 611	A Mandarin	1924–1938	Yellow patterned tunic. See HN 84.
HN 612	Poke Bonnet	1924–1938	Yellow skirt, green plaid shawl. See HN 44.
HN 613	Madonna of the Square	1924–1938	Striped pink skirt, orange spotted shawl. See HN 10.
HN 614	Polly Peachum	1924–1949	Pale pink dress, blue bows. See HN 463.
HN 615	Katharine	1924–1938	Pink skirt, green spots. See HN 61.
HN 616	A Jester	1924–1938	Quartered heraldic tunic. See HN 45.
HN 617	A Shepherd	1924–1948	China body, purple-blue pants and coat. See HN 81.
HN 618	Falstaff	1924–1938	Black collar, lilac blanket, green base. See HN 2054.
HN 619	Falstaff	1924–1938	Brown coat, green collar, yellow cloth. See HN 571.
HN 620	Polly Peachum	1924–1938	Pink dress, cream underskirt. See HN 489.
HN 621	Pan on Rock	1924–1938	See HN 622.
HN 622	Pan on Rock	1924–1938	Black base.
HN 623	An Old King	1924–1938	Gray, red, and green robe. See HN 358.
HN 624	Lady with Rose	1924–1938	Green-blue skirt, pink and black cuffs. See HN 48A.
HN 625	A Spook	1924–1938	Yellow robe. See HN 50.
HN 626	Lady with Shawl	1924–1938	Yellow shawl, pink spots, white dress, green spots. See HN 447.
HN 627	A Jester	1924–1938	Brown checkered costume. See HN 45.
HN 628	Crinoline, The	1924–1938	Yellow and blue bodice. See HN 8.
HN 629	Curtsey, The	1924–1938	Green dress, black trim. See HN 57.
HN 630	A Jester	1924–1938	Brown striped tights. See HN 45B.
HN 631	Fisherwomen	1924–1938	Middle woman with green shawl. See HN 80.

HN 632	A Shepherd	1924–1938	China body, white smock, blue pants. See HN 81.
HN 633	A Princess	1924–1938	Black and white dress. See HN 391.
HN 634	A Geisha	1924–1938	Black and white kimono. See HN 354.
HN 635	Harlequinade	1924–1938	Gold costume. See HN 585.
HN 636	Masquerade (male)	1924–1938	Gold costume. See HN 599.
HN 637	Masquerade (female)	1924–1938	Gold dress. See HN 600.
HN 638	Falstaff	1924–1938	Red coat, spotted cream cloth. See HN 571.
HN 639	Elsie Maynard	1924–1949	
HN 640	Charley's Aunt	1924–1938	Green and mauve spotted dress.
HN 641	A Mandarin	1924–1938	Onyx color. See HN 366.
HN 642	Pierrette	1924–1938	Red dress. See HN 643, 644, 691, 721, 731, 732, 784.
HN 643	Pierrette	1924–1938	Black and red dress. See HN 642.
HN 644	Pierrette	1924–1938	White and black dress. See HN 642.
HN 645	Forty Thieves	1924–1938	Blue, black, and white robes. See HN 418.
HN 646	Forty Thieves	1924–1938	Blue, black, and white robes. See HN 418.
HN 647	Forty Thieves	1924–1938	Blue, black, and white robes. See HN 418.
HN 648	Forty Thieves	1924–1938	Blue, black, and white robes. See HN 417.
HN 649	Forty Thieves	1924–1938	Blue, black, and white robes. See HN 418.
HN 650	Crinoline Lady (miniature)	1924–1938	Green overdress, white patterned skirt. See HN 651, 652, 653, 654, 655.
HN 651	Crinoline Lady (miniature)	1924–1938	Orange trim, green flowers. See HN 650.
HN 652	Crinoline Lady (miniature)	1924–1938	Purple dress. See HN 650.
HN 653	Crinoline Lady (miniature)	1924–1938	Gray and white striped dress. See HN 650.
HN 654	Crinoline Lady (miniature)	1924–1938	Orange and green mottled dress. See HN 650.
HN 655	Crinoline Lady (miniature)	1924–1938	Blue dress. See HN 650.
HN 656	Mask, The	1924–1938	Blue and purple costume. See HN 657, 729, 733, 785, 1271.

HN 657	Mask, The	1924–1938	Black and white costume. See HN 656.
HN 658	Mam'selle	1924–1938	White and black dress. See HN 659, 724, 786.
HN 659	Mamselle	1924–1938	Purple and red dress. See HN 658.
HN 660	Welsh Girl, The	1924–1938	Spotted white costume, blue-lined cloak. See HN 39.
HN 661	Boy with Turban	1924–1938	Blue costume. See HN 586.
HN 662	Boy with Turban	1924–1938	Black and white costume. See HN 586.
HN 663	Forty Thieves	1924–1938	Checkered yellow robes. See HN 418.
HN 664	Forty Thieves	1924–1938	Yellow patterned robes. See HN 418.
HN 665	Forty Thieves	1924–1938	See HN 418.
HN 666	Forty Thieves	1924–1938	Yellow patterned robes. See HN 418.
HN 667	Forty Thieves	1924–1938	Yellow patterned robes. See HN 418.
HN 668	Welsh Girl, The	1924–1938	Yellow checkered costume, pink lined cloak. See HN 39.
HN 669	Welsh Girl, The	1924–1938	Yellow spotted costume, checkered green lined cloak. See HN 39.
HN 670	Curtsey, The	1924–1938	Pink and yellow spotted dress. See HN 57.
HN 671	Lady Ermine	1924–1938	Green coat, yellow skirt. See HN 54.
HN 672	Tulips	1924–1938	Green shawl, cream dress. See HN 466.
HN 673	Henry VIII	1924–1938	Brown and lilac robe.
HN 674	Masquerade (female)	1924–1938	Orange and yellow checkered dress. See HN 600.
HN 675	Gainsborough Hat, The	1924–1938	Purple-blue dress, red and yellow spots. See HN 46.
HN 676	Pavlova	1924–1938	Green base. See HN 487.
HN 677	Forty Thieves	1924–1938	Orange, green, and red striped robes. See HN 417.
HN 678	Lady with Shawl	1924–1938	Black and white shawl, yellow and white dress. See HN 447.

HN 679	Lady with Shawl	1924–1938	Black, yellow, and blue shawl, black and white dress. See HN 447.
HN 680	Polly Peachum	1924–1949	White dress, black, yellow, and blue spots. See HN 463.
HN 681	Cobbler, The	1924–1938	Green costume, red skirt. See HN 1251, 1283.
HN 682	Cobbler, The	1924–1938	Red shirt, green robe. See HN 542.
HN 683	Masquerade (male)	1924–1938	Green coat. See HN 599.
HN 684	Tony Weller	1924–1938	Green coat, plaid rug. See HN 346.
HN 685	Contentment	1923–1938	Black and white floral dress. See HN 395.
HN 686	Contentment	1924–1938	Black and white striped chair. See HN 395.
HN 687	Bather, The	1924–1949	Purple and blue robe. See HN 597.
HN 688	A Yeoman of the Guard	1924–1938	Red uniform. See HN 2122.
HN 689	A Chelsea Pensioner	1924–1938	Red uniform.
HN 690	A Lady of the Georgian Period	1925–1938	See HN 41.
HN 691	Pierrette	1925–1938	Gold costume. See HN 642.
HN 692	Sleep	1925–1938	Gold dress. See HN 24.
HN 693	Polly Peachum	1925–1949	Rose-pink dress, green bows. See HN 463.
HN 694	Polly Peachum	1925–1949	Rose-pink dress, green bows. See HN 489.
HN 695	Lucy Lockett	1925–1949	Gold dress. See HN 696.
HN 696	Lucy Lockett	1925–1949	Light blue dress. See HN 695.
HN 697	Balloon Seller, The	1925–1938	Striped red shawl, blue dress. See HN 479.
HN 698	Polly Peachum (miniature)	1925–1949	Pink dress. See HN 699, 757, 758, 759, 760, 761, 762.
HN 699	Polly Peachum (miniature)	1925–1949	Blue dress. See HN 698.
HN 700	Pretty Lady	1925–1938	Yellow dress, black spots. See HN 69.
HN 701	A Welsh Girl	1925–1938	Striped costume, checkered blue-lined coat. See HN 39.
HN 702	A Lady of the Georgian Period	1925–1938	Striped pink skirt, green overdress. See HN 41.

HN 703	Woman Holding Child	1925–1938	Purple cloak, black and red skirt. See HN 462.
HN 704	Forty Thieves	1925–1938	Red checkered robe. See HN 418.
HN 705	Gainsborough Hat, The	1925–1938	Multicolored dress. See HN 46.
HN 706	Fruit Gathering	1925–1938	Purple blouse, yellow skirt. See HN 449.
HN 707	Fruit Gathering	1925–1938	Spotted skirt, red blouse. See HN 449.
HN 708	Shepherdess (miniature)	1925–1948	Red overskirt.
HN 709	Shepherd (miniature)	1925–1938	Green jacket.
HN 710	Sleep	1925–1938	Matt vellum finish. See HN 24.
HN 711	Harlequinade	1925–1938	Black and white costume. See HN 585.
HN 712	Forty Thieves	1925–1938	Red checkered robes. See HN 418.
HN 713	Forty Thieves	1925–1938	Red checkered robes. See HN 418.
HN 714	Forty Thieves	1925–1938	Red patterned robe. See HN 418.
HN 715	Proposal (lady)	1925–1938	Red dress. See HN 716, 788.
HN 716	Proposal (lady)	1925–1938	Cream dress, black squares. See HN 716.
HN 717	Lady Clown	1925–1938	White, red, and black costume. See HN 718, 738, 770, 1263.
HN 718	Lady Clown	1925–1938	White costume red stripes, black spots. See HN 717.
HN 719	Butterfly	1925–1938	Pink and apricot costume. See HN 720, 730, 1203, 1456.
HN 720	Butterfly	1925–1938	Black and red costume. See HN 719.
HN 721	Pierrette	1925–1938	Black and white striped costume. See HN 642.
HN 722	Mephisto	1925–1938	Black blouse. See HN 723.
HN 723	Mephisto	1925–1938	Red blouse. See HN 722.
HN 724	Mam'selle	1925–1938	Pink skirt. See HN 658.
HN 725	Proposal, The (male)	1925–1938	Red coat. See HN 1209.
HN 726	A Victorian Lady	1925–1938	Purple and pink multicolored dress. See HN 727, 728, 736, 740, 742, 745, 1208, 1258, 1276, 1277, 1345, 1452, 1529.

HN 727	A Victorian Lady	1925–1938	Yellow skirt, red shawl. See HN 726.
HN 728	A Victorian Lady	1925–1952	Red skirt, purple shawl. See HN 726.
HN 729	Mask, The	1925–1938	Red and black costume. See HN 656.
HN 730	Butterfly	1925–1938	Blue-black wings, yellow dress. See HN 719.
HN 731	Pierrette	1925–1938	Spotted black and white shirt. See HN 642.
HN 732	Pierrette	1925–1938	Black and white dress. See HN 642.
HN 733	Mask, The	1925–1938	White and black costume. See HN 656.
HN 734	Polly Peachum	1925–1949	White skirt, black spots and bodice. See HN 489.
HN 735	Shepherdess	1925–1938	Purple overdress, blue and red skirt. See HN 750.
HN 736	A Victorian Lady	1925–1938	Purple dress, light blue border design, red shawl. See HN 726.
HN 737			
HN 738	Lady Clown	1925–1938	Black and white pants, red spots. See HN 717.
HN 739	A Victorian Lady	1925–1938	Blue and yellow skirt, yellow scarf, mottled red. See HN 726.
HN 740	A Victorian Lady	1925–1938	Red dress, red and yellow shawl. See HN 726.
HN 741	A Geisha	1925–1938	Dark multicolored kimono, black trim. See HN 354.
HN 742	A Victorian Lady	1925–1938	Black and white checkered shawl, white dress, blue spots. See HN 726.
HN 743	Woman Holding Child	1925–1938	Blue and yellow striped apron. See HN 462.
HN 744	Lavender Woman, The	1925–1938	Blue spotted dress, striped shawl. See HN 22.
HN 745	A Victorian Lady	1925–1938	Pink roses patterned dress. See HN 726.
HN 746	A Mandarin	1925–1938	Black costume with green dragons. See HN 84.
HN 747	Tulips	1925–1938	Purple dress, green shawl. See HN 466.
HN 748	Out For a Walk	1925–1936	Dark multicolored dress, white muff. See HN 86.

HN 749	London Cry, Strawberries	1925–1938	Cream overdress, red skirt. See HN 772.
HN 750	Shepherdess	1925–1938	Pink bodice, yellow skirt. See HN 735.
HN 751	Shepherd	1925–1938	Green jacket, red cape.
HN 752	London Cry, Turnips and Carrots	1925–1938	Red bodice, purple skirt. See HN 771.
HN 753	Dandy, The	1925–1938	Red jacket, purple sash.
HN 754	Belle, The	1925–1938	Pastel multicolored dress. See HN 776.
HN 755	Mephistopheles and Marguerite	1925–1949	Orange dress, purple cloak. See HN 775.
HN 756	Modern Piper, The	1925–1938	Pale green cape, lavender jacket.
HN 757	Polly Peachum (miniature)	1925–1949	Red bodice, spotted skirt. See HN 698.
HN 758	Polly Peachum (miniature)	1925–1949	Pink skirt, orange stripes. See HN 698.
HN 759	Polly Peachum (miniature)	1925–1949	Yellow and white skirt, black spots. See HN 698.
HN 760	Polly Peachum (miniature)	1925–1949	Multicolored mottled skirt. See HN 698.
HN 761	Polly Peachum (miniature)	1925–1949	Blue and purple skirt. See HN 698.
HN 762	Polly Peachum	1925–1949	Pink roses on skirt. See HN 698.
HN 763	Pretty Lady	1925–1938	Orange dress. See HN 69.
HN 764	Madonna of the Square	1925–1938	Blue and purple striped shawl, yellow skirt. See HN 10.
HN 765	Poke Bonnet, The	1925–1938	Dark green, blue and purple mottled skirt. See HN 44.
HN 766	Irish Colleen	1925–1938	Red jacket. See HN 767.
HN 767	Irish Colleen	1925–1938	Green skirt, black jacket. See HN 766.
HN 768	Harlequinade Masked	1925–1938	Black, red, green checkered costume. See HN 769, 1274, 1304.
HN 769	Harlequinade Masked	1925–1938	Blue, red, and yellow costume. See HN 768.
HN 770	Lady Clown	1925–1938	Green masks and streamers painted on costume. See HN 717.
HN 771	London Cry, Turnips and Carrots	1925–1938	Multicolored dress and blouse. See HN 752.

HN 772	London Cry, Strawberries	1925–1938	Multicolored dress. See HN 749.
HN 773	Bather, The	1925–1938	Pink robe. See HN 774, 1227.
HN 774	Bather, The	1925–1938	Purple, red, and black robe. See HN 773.
HN 775	Mephistopheles and Marguerite	1925–1938	Red cloaks. See HN 755.
HN 776	Belle, The	1925–1938	See HN 754.
HN 777	Bo-Peep	1926–1938	Purple dress. See HN 1202, 1327, 1328.
HN 778	Captain	1926–1938	Red and white uniform.
HN 779	A Geisha	1926–1938	Red dress, purple spots. See HN 354.
HN 780	Harlequinade	1926–1938	Pink dress, blue, black, and orange markings. See HN 585.
HN 781	Bather, The	1926–1938	Blue and green robe. See HN597.
HN 782	Bather, The	1926–1938	Purple robe, black lining. See HN 597.
HN 783	Pretty Lady	1926–1938	Blue dress. See HN 69.
HN 784	Pierrette	1926–1938	Pink costume, black ruff. See HN 642.
HN 785	Mask, The	1926–1938	Blue costume pink striped skirt. See HN 656.
HN 786	Mam'selle	1926–1938	Pink and black dress. See HN 658.
HN 787	A Mandarin	1926–1938	Pink and orange tunic, black flowers. See HN 84.
HN 788	Proposal (lady)	1926–1938	Pink dress. See HN 715.
HN 789	Flower Seller, The	1926–1938	Green cape, cream skirt.
HN 790	Parson's Daughter, The	1926–1938	Patchwork skirt, dark multicolored shawl. See HN 337.
HN 791	A Mandarin	1926–1938	Yellow tunic, green and red markings. See HN 84.
HN 792	Welsh Girl, The	1926–1938	Pink checkered costume, blue cloak. See HN 39.
HN 793	Katharine	1926–1938	Lilac dress, green spots. See HN 61.
HN 794	Bouquet, The	1926–1938	Blue shawl, red and green spots. See HN 406.
HN 795	Pierrette (miniature)	1926–1938	Pink roses on skirt. See HN 796.

HN 796	Pierrette (miniature)	1926–1938	White skirt, silver spots. See HN 795.
HN 797	Moorish Minstrel, The	1926–1949	Purple costume. See HN 34.
HN 798	Tête-à-Tête	1926–1938	Mottled pink and blue dress. See HN 799.
HN 799	Tête-à-Tête	1926–1938	Purple and pink dress. See HN 798.
HN 800–1200	See Animal and bird list.		
HN1201	Hunts Lady	1926–1938	Gray jacket, rust boots.
HN1202	Bo-Peep	1926–1938	Purple skirt, green, pink, and black trim. See HN 777.
HN1203	Butterfly	1926–1938	Gold wings. See HN 719.
HN1204	Angela	1926–1938	Red and purple costume. See HN 1303.
HN1205	Miss 1926	1926–1938	Ermine trimmed coat. See HN 1207.
HN1206	Flower Seller's Children, The	1926–1949	Dark blue skirt. See HN 525.
HN1207	Miss 1926	1926–1938	Black fur collar. See HN 1205.
HN1208	A Victorian Lady	1926–1938	Red shawl, green dress. See HN 726.
HN1209	Proposal, The (male)	1926–1938	Blue coat, pink waistcoat. See HN 725.
HN1210	Boy with Turban	1926–1938	Black and red turban. See HN 586.
HN1211	Quality Street	1926–1938	Rose-red dress.
HN1212	Boy with Turban	1926–1938	Pink-purple and green pants. See HN 586.
HN1213	Boy with Turban	1926–1938	White costume, black squares. See HN 586.
HN1214	Boy with Turban	1926–1938	White costume, black and green markings. See HN 586.
HN1215	Pied Piper, The	1926–1938	Red hat and cape. See HN 2102.
HN1216	Falstaff	1926–1949	Multicolored costume. SEe HN 571.
HN1217	Prince of Wales, The	1926–1938	Red jacket, black hat.
HN1218	A Spook	1926–1938	Multicolored costume, blue cap. See HN50.
HN1219	Negligée	1916–1938	Dark blue hairband. See HN 1228, 1272, 1273, 1454.

HN1220	Lido Lady	1927–1938	Flowered blue costume. See HN 1229.
HN1221	Lady Jester	1027–1938	Pink and black costume. See HN 1222, 1332.
HN1222	Lady Jester	1927–1938	Black and white costume. See HN 122.
HN1223	A Geisha	1927–1938	Purple and red multicolored kimono. See HN 1234, 1292, 1310.
HN1224	Wandering Minstrel, The	1927–1938	Purple, pink, and red costume.
HN1225	Boy with Turban	1927–1938	Yellow pants, blue spots. See HN 586.
HN1226	Huntsman, The	1927–1938	Red jacket, black hat.
HN1227	Bather, The	1927–1938	Flowered pink robe. See HN 773.
HN1228	Negligée	1927–1938	Rust hairband. See HN 1219.
HN1229	Lido Lady	1927–1938	Flowered pink costume. See HN 1220.
HN1230	Baba	1927–1938	Yellow and purple striped trousers. See HN 1243, 1244, 1245, 1246, 1247, 1248.
HN1231	Cassim	1927–1938	Blue hat and pants. See HN 1232.
HN1232	Cassim	1927–1938	Brown vest, orange and white pants. See HN 1231.
HN1233	Susanna	1927–1938	Pink robe. See HN 1288, 1299.
HN1234	A Geisha	1927–1938	Green, red, yellow, multicolored kimono. See HN 1223.
HN1235	A Scribe	1927–1938	Brown coat, blue hat. See HN 305.
HN1236	Tête-à-Tête	1927–1938	Purple and pink dress. Miniature of HN 798. See HN 1237.
HN1237	Tête-à-Tête	1927–1938	Pink dress. See HN 1236.
HN1238	Bather, The	1927–1938	Red and black robe. See HN 597.
HN1239–1241	See Animal and bird list.		
HN1242	Parson's Daughter, The	1927–1938	Lilac shawl, patchwork skirt. See HN 337.

HN1243	Baba	1927–1927	Orange pants. See HN 1230.
HN1244	Baba	1927–1928	Yellow and green pants. See HN 1230.
HN1245	Baba	1927–1938	Black, white, and blue pants. See HN 1230.
HN1246	Baba	1927–1938	Green pants. See HN 1230.
HN1247	Baba	1928–1938	White and black pants. See HN 1230.
HN1248	Baba	1927–1938	Green and red pants. See HN 1230.
HN1249	Circe	1927–1938	Pink and green robe. See HN 1250, 1254, 1255.
HN1250	Circe	1927–1939	Orange and black robe. See HN 1249.
HN1251	Cobbler, The	1927–1938	Black pants, red shirt. See HN 681.
HN1252	Kathleen	1927–1938	Pale pink skirt. See HN 1253, 1275, 1279, 1291, 1357, 1512.
HN1253	Kathleen	1927–1938	Orange-red skirt. See HN 1252.
HN1254	Circe	1927–1938	Orange and red robe. See HN 1249.
HN1255	Circe	1927–1938	Blue robe. See HN 1249.
HN1256	Captain MacHeath	1927–1938	Earthenware. See HN 464.
HN1257	Highwayman	1927–1949	Earthenware. Wee HN 527.
HN1258	A Victorian Lady	1927–1938	Blue dress, purple shawl. See HN 726.
HN1259	Alchemist, The	1927–1938	Mottled robe, red hat. See HN 1282.
HN1260	Carnival	1927–1938	Pink tights. See HN 1278.
HN1261	Sea Sprite	1927–1938	Red and purple drape.
HN1262	Spanish Lady	1927–1938	Black dress, red flowers. See HN 1290, 1293, 1294, 1309.
HN1263	Lady Clown	1927–1938	Blue and red pants. See HN 717.
HN1264	Judge and Jury	1927–1938	Red, ermine-trimmed robe.
HN1265	Lady Fayre	1928–1938	Purple and red dress. See HN 1557.
HN 1266	Ko-Ko	1928–1949	Black and white costume. See HN 1286.
HN1267	Carmen	1928–1938	Red dress, black shawl. See HN 1300.
HN1268	Yum-Yum	1928–1938	White kimono, blue and pink pattern. See HN 1287.

HN1269	Scotch Girl	1928–1938	Red plaid costume.
HN1270	Swimmer, The	1928–1938	Black, floral print bathing suite. See HN 1326, 1329.
HN1271	Mask, The	1928–1938	Multicolored spotted costume. See HN 656.
HN1272	Negligée	1928–1938	Red and yellow mottled negligée. See HN 1219.
HN1273	Negligée	1928–1938	White negligée. See HN 1219.
HN1274	Harlequinade Masked	1928–1938	Red and black costume. See HN 768.
HN1275	Kathleen	1928–1938	Black floral shawl. See HN 1252.
HN1276	A Victorian Lady	1928–1938	Red, green and yellow skirt, purple shawl. See HN 726.
HN1277	A Victorian Lady	1928–1938	Red shawl, yellow and blue dress. See NH 726.
HN1278	Carnival	1928–1938	Pale green tights. See HN 1260.
HN1279	Kathleen	1928–1938	Pink-red skirt, red-orange shawl. See HN 1252.
HN1280	Blue Bird	1928–1938	Nude child on red-pink base.
HN1281	Scotties	1928–1938	Red dress. See HN 1349.
HN1282	Alchemist, The	1928–1938	Brown hat, red scarf. See HN 1259.
HN1283	Cobbler, The	1928–1949	Green robe, yellow and red shirt. See HN 681.
HN1284	Lady Jester	1928–1938	Blue vest, red tights. See HN 1285.
HN1285	Lady Jester	1928–1938	Red vest, blue and red tights. See HN 1284.
HN1286	Ko-Ko	1938–1949	Red robe. See HN 1266.
HN1287	Yum-Yum	1928–1939	Red, yellow, and orange kimono. See HN 1268.
HN1288	Susanna	1928–1938	Dark red robe. See HN 1233.
HN1289	Midinette	1928–1938	See HN 1306, Peach Skirt.
HN1290	Spanish Lady	1928–1938	Yellow dress. See HN 1262.
HN1291	Kathleen	1928–1938	Red shawl, yellow dress. See HN 1252.
HN1292	A Geisha	1928–1938	Blue-green collar, orange kimono. See HN 1223.
HN1293	Spanish Lady	1928–1938	Black dress, orange and red flowers. See HN 1262.

HN1294	Spanish Lady	1928–1938	Red mottled dress. See HN 1262.
HN1295	A Jester	1928–1949	Black, orange, and blue shirt. See HN 45.
HN1296	Columbine	1928–1938	Purple line border on orange and purple dress. See HN 1297, 1439.
HN1297	Columbine	1930–1938	White line border on dress. See HN 1296.
HN1298	Sweet and Twenty	1928–1969	Red and pink dress. See HN 1360, 1437, 1438, 1549, 1563, 1649.
HN1299	Susanna	1928–1938	Black, red, and blue robe. See HN 1233.
HN1300	Carmen	1928–1938	Light dress, green shoes. See HN 1267.
HN1301	Gypsy Woman with Child	1928–1938	Green shawl, blue skirt.
HN1302	Gypsy Girl with Flowers	1928–1938	Red jacket, cream and green striped skirt.
HN1303	Angela	1928–1938	Blue fan, spotted costume. See HN 1204.
HN1304	Harlequinade Masked	1928–1938	Black spotted costume. See HN 768.
HN1305	Siesta	1928–1938	Pink and lavender drape.
HN1306	Midinette	1928–1938	Red blouse, green skirt. See HN 1289.
HN1307	An Irishman	1928–1938	Green Jacket and Hat.
HN1308	Moor, The	1929–1938	Blue costume, red cloak. See HN 33.
HN1309	Spanish Lady	1929–1938	Multicolored skirt, black bodice. See HN 1262.
HN1310	A Geisha	1929–1938	Multicolored spotted kimono. See HN 1223.
HN1311	Cassim	1929–1938	Mounted on lid of pink bowl. See HN 1312.
HN1312	Cassim	1929–1938	Mounted on lid of green bowl. See HN 1311.
HN1313	Sonny	1929–1938	Pink clothes. See HN 1314.
HN1314	Sonny	1929–1938	Purple clothes. See HN 1313.
HN1315	Old Balloon Seller	1929–present	Green skirt and shawl, red jacket.
HN1316	Toys	1929–1938	Red jacket, green skirt.
HN1317	Snake Charmer, The	1929–1938	Green and black turban and robe.
HN1318	Sweet Anne	1929–1949	Blue jacket, pale green skirt. See HN 1330, 1331, 1453, 1496, 1631, 1701.

HN1319	Darling	1929–1959	Black base. See HN 1.
HN1320	Rosamund	1929–1938	Pink jacket, pale green skirt.
HN1321	A Geisha	1929–1938	Green kimono. See HN 354.
HN1322	A Geisha	1929–1938	Pink and blue kimono. See HN 354.
HN1323	Contentment	1929–1938	Red dress, blue chair. See HN 395.
HN1324	Fairy	1929–1938	Several related figures. See HN 1374, 1375, 1376, 1377, 1378, 1379, 1380, 1393, 1394, 1395, 1396, 1532, 1533, 1534, 1535, 1536.
HN1325	Orange Seller, The	1929–1949	Lavender jacket, green skirt.
HN1326	Swimmer, The	1929–1938	Orange and lilac costume. See HN 1270.
HN1327	Bo-Peep	1929–1938	Multicolored flowered dress. See HN 777.
HN1328	Bo-Peep	1929–1938	Pink dress, black and lilac squares. See HN 777.
HN1329	Swimmer, The	1929–1938	Pink costume. See HN 1270.
HN1330	Sweet Anne	1929–1949	Red, pink, and yellow skirt. See HN 1318.
HN1331	Sweet Anne	1929–1949	Blue and yellow skirt. See HN 1318.
HN1332	Lady Jester	1929–1938	Red, blue, and black skirt. See HN 1221.
HN1333	A Jester	1929–1949	Blue tunic, yellow and black stripes. See HN 45B.
HN1334	Tulips	1929–1938	Green dress, blue and pink shawl See HN 466.
HN1335	Folly	1929–1938	Green hat, pink dress. See HN 1750.
HN1336	Forty Thieves	1929–1938	Red, orange, and blue robes. See HN 418.
HN1337	Priscilla	1929–1938	Pale lavender and yellow dress. See HN 1340, 1495, 1501, 1559.
HN1338	Courtier, The	1929–1938	Rose-red costume.
HN1339	Covent Garden	1929–1938	Green dress, lavender apron.
HN1340	Priscilla	1929–1949	Red dress, purple collar. See HN 1337.

HN1341	Marietta	1929–1949	Black costume, red cape. See HN 1446, 1699.
HN1342	Flower Seller's Children, The	1929–present	Red and yellow roses. See HN 525.
HN1343	Dulcinea	1929–1938	Red and black dress, black shoes. See HN 1419.
HN1344	Sunshine Girl	1929–1938	Green and black bathing suit. See HN 1348.
HN1345	A Victorian Lady	1929–1949	Blue-green skirt, purple shawl. See HN 726.
HN1346	Iona	1929–1938	Green hat, white costume.
HN1347	Moira	1929–1938	Green hat, blue costume.
HN1348	Sunshine Girl	1929–1938	Black and orange bathing suit. See HN 1344
HN1349	Scotties	1929–1949	Light multicolored dress, white Scotties. See HN 1281.
HN1350	Forty Thieves	1929–1949	Multicolored robes. See HN 418.
HN1351	Forty Thieves	1920–1949	See HN 417.
HN1352	Forty Thieves	1920–1949	Multicolored robes. See HN 417.
HN1353	Forty Thieves	1929–1949	Multicolored robes. See HN 418.
HN1354	Forty Thieves	1929–1949	Multicolored robes. See HN 418.
HN1355	Mendicant, The	1929–1938	Black and brown robe. See HN 1365.
HN1356	Parson's Daughter, The	1929–1938	Red, blue and purple striped border on dress. See HN 337.
HN1357	Kathleen	1929–1938	Pink, orange, and yellow skirt. See HN 1252.
HN1358	Rosina	1929–1938	Red dress, ermine trim. See HN 1364, 1556.
HN1359	Two-A-Penny	1929–1938	
HN1360	Sweet and Twenty	1929–1938	Blue-pink-purple dress, blue-green couch. See HN 1298.
HN1361	Mask Seller	1929–1938	Black cape, red hat. See HN 2103.
HN1362	Pantalettes	1929–1938	Green skirt, red tie on hat. See HN 1412, 1507, 1709.
HN1363	Doreen	1929–1938	Pink dress. See HN 1389, 1390.

HN1364	Rosina	1929–1938	Red, purple, and pink dress and shawl. See HN 1358.
HN1365	Mendicant, The	1929–1969	Different glaze effects. See HN 1355.
HN1366	Moor, The	1930–1949	Red Costume. See HN 33.
HN1367	Kitty	1930–1938	White skirt, purple stripes.
HN1368	Rose	1930–present	Pink-red dress. See HN 1387, 1416, 1506, 1654.
HN1369	Boy on Pig	1930–1938	Nude child, dark mottled pig.
HN1370	Marie	1930–present	Lavender-purple dress. See HN 1388, 1417, 1489, 1531, 1635, 1655.
HN1371	Darling	1930–1938	Green nightshirt. See HN 1.
HN1372	Darling	1930–1938	Pink nightshirt. See HN 1.
HN1373	Sweet Lavender	1930–1949	Red and green plaid shawl, cream skirt.
HN1374	Fairy	1930–1938	Yellow flowers. See HN 1324.
HN1375	Fairy	1930–1938	Purple hat. See HN 1324.
HN1376	Fairy	1930–1938	As HN 1532, smaller, no mushroom. See HN 1324.
HN1377	Not issued (fairy)		
HN1378	Fairy	1930–1938	Orange flowers. See HN 1324.
HN1379	Fairy	1930–1939	Blue flowers, leaves overhead. See HN 1324.
HN1380	Fairy	1930–1938	Dark mottled mushroom. See HN 1324.
HN1381–1386	Not issued (fairies)		
HN1387	Rose	1930–1938	Blue and pink flowered dress, orange flowers. See HN 1368.
HN1388	Marie	1930–1938	Red and blue flowered dress. See HN 1370.
HN1389	Doreen	1930–1938	Green dress. See HN 1363.
HN1390	Doreen	1929–1938	Lilac dress. See HN 1363
HN1391	Pierrette	1930–1938	Red costume. See HN 1749.
HN1391	Paisley Shawl	1930–1949	White dress, red shawl. See HN 1460, 1707, 1739, 1987.
HN1393	Fairy	1930–1938	Yellow flowers. See HN 1324

HN1394	Fairy	1930–1938	Yellow flowers. See HN 1324.
HN1395	Fairy	1930–1938	Blue flowers. See HN 1324
HN1396	Fairy	1930–1938	Blue flowers. See HN 1324.
HN1397	Gretchen	1930–1938	Blue and white dress. See HN 1562.
HN1398	Derrick	1930–1938	Blue costume, red hat
HN1399	Young Widow, The	1930–1930	Light colored basket. See HN 1418, 1641 for renamed versions.
HN1400	Windmill Lady, The	1930–1938	Green and orange plaid shawl, green skirt.
HN1401	Chorus Girl	1930–1938	Red and Yellow costume.
HN1402	Miss Demure	1930–1975	Pale pink dress. See HN 1440, 1463, 1499, 1560.
HN1403	Not issued (Old Huntsman)		
HN1404	Betty	1930–1938	Pink and white dress. See HN 1405, 1435, 1436.
HN1405	Betty	1930–1938	Green dress. See HN 1404.
HN1406	Flower Seller's Children, The	1930–1938	Yellow dress, dark blue cloth over basket. See HN 525.
HN1407	Winner, The	1930–1938	
HN1408	John Peel	1930–1937	Red jacket, brown horse. See HN 1815 for renamed version.
HN1409	Hunting Squire	1930–1938	Red jacket, dappled gray horse. See HN 1814.
HN1410	Abdullah	1930–1938	Blue cushions, green turban. See HN 2104.
HN1411	Charley's Aunt	1930–1938	Black dress. See HN 1554.
HN1412	Pantalettes	1930–1949	Pink skirt, green tie on hat. See HN 1362.
HN1413	Margery	1930–1949	Red dress.
HN1414	Patricia	1930–1949	Yellow dress. See HN 1431, 1462, 1567.
HN1415			
HN1416	Rose	1930–1949	Blue-purple dress. See HN 1368.
HN1417	Marie	1930–1949	Orange dress. See HN 1370.
HN1418	Little Mother, The	1930–1938	Dark colored basket. See HN 1399.
HN1419	Dulcinea	1930–1938	Red and pink dress, green shoes. See HN 1343.

HN1420	Phyllis	1930–1949	Flowered overskirt and shawl. See HN 1430, 1486, 1698.
HN1421	Barbara	1930–1938	Flowered skirt. See HN 1432, 1461.
HN1422	Joan	1930–1949	Blue dress. See HN 2023.
HN1423	Babette	1930–1938	Yellow and red striped clothes. See HN 1424.
HN1424	Babette	1930–1938	Blue cloak and shorts. See HN 1423.
HN1425	Moor, The	1930–1949	Dark multicolored costume. See HN 33.
HN1426	Gossips, The	1930–1949	Blue and red dresses. See HN 1429, 2025.
HN1427	Darby	1930–1949	Mottled pink coat. See HN 2024.
HN1428	Calumet	1930–1949	Striped rug. See HN 1689, 2068.
HN1429	Gossips, The	1930–1949	Red dress, white dress. See HN 1426.
HN1430	Phyllis	1930–1938	Pink skirt, dark blue shawl. See HN 1420.
HN1431	Patricia	1930–1949	Pink-blue dress. See HN 1414.
HN1432	Barbara	1930–1938	Multicolored dress. See HN 1421.
HN1433	Little Bridesmaid, The	1930–1951	Pale yellow dress. See HN 1434, 1530.
HN1434	Little Bridesmaid, The	1930–1949	Yellow dress. See HN 1433.
HN1435	Betty	1930–1938	Multicolored dress. See HN 1404.
HN1436	Betty	1930–1938	Patterned green dress. See HN 1404.
HN1437	Sweet and Twenty	1930–1938	Red dress, dark couch. See HN 1298.
HN1438	Sweet and Twenty	1930–1938	Multicolored dress. See HN 1298.
HN1439	Columbine	1930–1938	Red multicolored dress. See HN 1296.
HN1440	Miss Demure	1930–1949	Pale blue dress. See HN 1402.
HN1441	Child Study	1931–1938	Flowers on base. See HN 1539.
HN1442	Child Study	1931–1938	Flowers on base. See HN 1540.
HN1443	Child Study	1931–1938	Flowers on base. See HN 1540.

HN1444	Pauline	1931-1938	Blue dress, green hat.
HN1445	Biddy	1931-1938	Green-yellow dress, blue shawl. See HN 1500, 1513.
HN1446	Marietta	1931-1949	Lilac costume, green cape. See HN 1341.
HN1447	Marigold	1931-1949	White and purple dress. See HN 1451, 1555.
HN1448	Rita	1931-1938	Yellow and pink dress. See HN 1450.
HN1449	Little Mistress, The	1931-1949	
HN1450	Rita	1931-1938	Blue dress. See HN 1448.
HN1451	Marigold	1931-1938	Yellow dress. See HN 1447.
HN1452	A Victorian Lady	1931-1949	Green dress and shawl. See HN 726.
HN1453	Sweet Anne	1931-1949	Green dress, blue hat. See HN 1318.
HN1454	Negligée	1931-1938	Pink negligée, red base. See HN 1219.
HN1455	Molly Malone	1931-1938.	
HN1456	Butterfly	1931-1938	Purple-pink cloak. See HN 719.
HN1457	All-A-Blooming	1931-?	Blue dress. See HN 1466.
HN1458	Monica	1931-1949	White flower-print dress. See HN 1459, 1467.
HN1459	Monica	1931-?	Lilac dress. See HN 1458.
HN1460	Paisley Shawl	1931-1949	Green dress and shawl, pink trim. See HN 1392.
HN1461	Barbara	1931-1938	Green dress. See HN 1421.
HN1462	Patricia	1931-1938	Green-yellow dress, pink hat. See HN 1414.
HN1463	Miss Demure	1931-1949	Green dress. See HN 1402.
HN1464	Carpet Seller, The	1931-1969	Gray-green robe.
HN1465	Lady Clare	1931-1938	Pink dress.
HN1466	All-A-Blooming	1931-1938	Red dress. See HN 1457.
HN1467	Monica	1931-present	Red hat. See HN 1458.
HN1468	Pamela	1931-1938	See HN 1469, 1564.
HN1469	Pamela	1931-1938	Yellow dress. See HN 1468.
HN1470	Chloe	1931-1949	Yellow dress. See HN 1476. 1479, 1498, 1765, 1956.
HN1471	Annette	1931-1938	Blue dress. See HN 1472, 1550.
HN1472	Annette	1931-1949	Green dress. See HN 1471.
HN1473	Dreamland	1931-1938.	Purple and red robe. See HN 1481.

HN1474	In the Stocks	1931–1938.	Red dress. See HN 1475.
HN1475	In the Stocks	1931–1938	Green dress. See HN 1474.
HN1476	Chloe	1931–1938	Blue–white dress. See HN 1470.
HN1477			
HN1478	Sylvia	1931–1938	
HN1479	Chloe	1931–1949	Pink-blue dress. See HN 1470.
HN1480	Newhaven Fishwife	1931–1938	
HN1481	Dreamland	1931–1938	Red-yellow nightgown, dark couch. See HN 1473.
HN1482	Pearly Boy	1931–1949	Red Jacket. See HN 1547.
HN1483	Pearly Girl	1931–1949	Red Jacket. See HN 1548.
HN1484	Jennifer	1931–1949	
HN1485	Greta	1931–1953	
HN1486	Phyllis	1931–1949	Blue shawl, pink skirt. See HN 1420.
HN1487	Suzette	1931–1950	Pink dress. See HN 1577, 1585, 1696, 2026.
HN1488	Gloria	1932–1938	Gray-blue cape and dress. See HN 1700.
HN1489	Marie	1932–1949	Yellow-green dress. See HN 1370.
HN1490	Dorcas	1932–1938	Beige dress. See HN 1491, 1558.
HN1491	Dorcas	1932–1938	Light green-blue dress. Se HN 1490.
HN1492	Old Lavender Seller	1932–1949	Green and orange cape. See HN 1571.
HN1493	Potter, The	1932–present	Dark red-brown cloak. See HN 1518, 1522.
HN1494	Gwendolen	1932–1938	Green and pink dress. See HN 1503, 1570.
HN1495	Priscilla	1932–1949	Blue dress, green hat, and umbrella. See HN 1337.
HN1496	Sweet Anne	1932–1967	Pink and purple dress and hat. See HN 1318.
HN1497	Rosamund	1932–1938	Red dress. See HN 1551.
HN1498	Chloe	1932–1938	Yellow dress. See HN 1470.
HN1499	Miss Demure	1932–1938	Pink dress, yellow hat. See HN 1402.
HN1500	Biddy	1932–1938	Yellow dress. See HN 1445.
HN1501	Priscilla	1932–1938	Yellow Dress. See HN 1337.

HN1502	Lucy Ann	1932–1951	Pale pink dress. See HN 1565.
HN1503	Gwendolen	1932–1949	Orange-yellow dress. See HN 1494.
HN1504	Sweet Maid	1932–1938	Blue dress. See HN 1505.
HN1505	Sweet Maid	1932–1938	Pink-red dress. See HN 1504.
HN1506	Rose	1932–1938	Yellow dress. See HN 1368.
HN1507	Pantalettes	1932–1949	Yellow dress. See HN 1362.
HN1508	Helen	1932–1938	Green dress. See HN 1509, 1572.
HN1509	Helen	1932–1938	White, blue and red dress. See HN 1508.
HN1510	Constance	1932–1938	Purple and yellow dress. See HN 1511.
HN1511	Constance	1932–1938	Pink dress, red purse. See HN 1510.
HN1512	Kathleen	1932–1938	Lilac Dress, blue hat. See HN 1252.
HN1513	Biddy	1932–1951	Red dress, blue shawl. See HN 1445.
HN1514	Dolly Vardon	1932–1938	Flowered cape. See HN 1515.
HN1515	Dolly Vardon	1932–1949	Red cape. See HN 1514.
HN1516	Cicely	1932–1949	Blue and white dress.
HN1517	Veronica	1932–1951	Red and white dress. See HN 1519, 1650, 1943.
HN1518	Potter, The	1932–1949	Green cloak. See HN 1492
HN1519	Veronica	1932–1938	Blue-white dress, red hat. See HN 1517.
HN1520	Eugene	1932–1938	Green and pink dress. See HN 1521.
HN1521	Eugene	1932–1938	Red and white dress. See HN 1520.
HN1522	Potter, The	1932–1949	Dark blue and green cloak. See HN 1492.
HN1523	Lisette	1932–1938	White and red dress. See HN 1524, 1684.
HN1524	Lisette	1932–1938	Multicolored dress. See HN 1523.
HN1525	Clarissa	1932–1938	Green dress, red shawl. See HN 1687.
HN1526	Anthea	1932–1938	Green dress. See HN 1527, 1669.
HN1527	Anthea	1932–1949	Purple dress, red umbrella. See HN 1526.

HN1528	Bluebeard	1932–1949	Red robe. See HN 2105.
HN1529	A Victorian Lady	1932–1938	Orange-yellow dress, green shawl. See HN 726.
HN1530	Little Bridesmaid, The	1932–1938	Yellow and green dress. See HN 1433.
HN1531	Marie	1932–1938	Yellow-green dress. See HN 1370
HN1532	Fairy	1932–1938	Yellow mushroom. See HN 1324.
HN1533	Fairy	1932–1938	Multicolored flowers. See HN 1324.
HN1534	Fairy	1932–1938	Large yellow flowers. See HN 1324.
HN1535	Fairy	1932–1938	Yellow and blue flowers. See HN 1324.
HN1536	Fairy	1932–1938	Light green base. See HN 1324.
HN1537	Janet	1932–present	Red dress. See HN 1538, 1652, 1737.
HN1538	Janet	1932–1949	Blue-red dress. See HN 1537.
HN1539	A Saucy Nymph	1933–1949	Nude child, green base. See HN 1441.
HN1540	'Little Child so Rare and Sweet'	1933–1949	Nude child, standing green base. See HN 1442.
HN1541	'Happy Joy, Baby Boy'	1933–1949	Blond child with drape. See HN 1443.
HN1542	'Little Child so Rare and Sweet'	1933–1949	Nude child sitting on blue base, brown hair.
HN1543	'Dancing Eyes and Sunny Hair'	1933–1949	Nude child sitting on blue base, brown hair.
HN1544	'Do You Wonder Where Fairies are that Folk Declare Have Vanished'	1933–1949	Child in lavendar shorts, beige base.
HN1545	'Called Love, a Little Boy, almost naked, Wanton, Blind, Cruel now, and then as kind'	1933–1949	Nude child, tan base, red and blue pail.
HN1546	'Here a Little Child I Stand'	1933–1949	Child in pale lavender dress, green base.
HN1547	Pearly Boy	1933–1949	Green coat, purple pants. See HN 1482.

HN1548	Pearly Girl	1933–1949	Purple bodice, green skirt. See HN 1483.
IN1549	Sweet and Twenty	1933–1949	Multicolored dress and couch. See HN 1298.
HN1550	Annette	1933–1949	Red blouse, green underskirt. See HN 1471.
HN1551	Rosamund	1933–1938	Blue dress. See HN 1497.
HN1552	Pinkie	1933–1938	Pink dress. See HN 1953.
HN1553	Pinkie	1933–1938	Yellow and blue dress. See HN 1552.
HN1554	Charley's Aunt	1933–1938	Purple dress. See HN 1411.
HN1555	Marigold	1933–1949	Pink dress, blue bow. See HN 1447.
HN1556	Rosina	1933–1938	Light-colored dress. See HN 1358
HN1557	Lady Fayre	1933–1938	Pink dress. See HN 1265.
HN1558	Dorcas	1933–1952	Red dress. See HN 1490.
HN1559	Priscilla	1933–1949	Pink and yellow skirt. See HN 1337.
HN1560	Miss Demure	1933–1949	Purple bow, red shawl. See HN 1402.
HN1561	Willy-Won't He	1933–1949	Blue jacket. See HN 1584, 2150.
HN1562	Gretchen	1933–1938	Red and purple dress. See HN 1397.
HN1563	Sweet and Twenty	1933–1938	Light pink dress, black couch. See HN 1298.
HN1564	Pamela	1933–1938	Pink dress. See HN 1468.
HN1565	Lucy Ann	1933–1938	Light green dress. See HN 1502.
HN1566	Estelle	1933–1938	Lavender and white dress. See HN 1802.
HN1567	Patricia	1933–1949	Red dress. See HN 1414.
HN1568	Charmian	1933–1938	Red and white dress. See HN 1569, 1651.
HN1569	Charmian	1933–1938	Light green-blue skirt. See HN 1568.
HN1570	Gwendolen	1933–1949	Pink dress. See HN 1494.
HN1571	Old Lavender Seller	1933–1949	Orange patterned cape. See HN 1492.
HN1572	Helen	1933–1938	Red dress. See HN 1508.
HN1573	Rhoda	1933–1949	Yellow-beige skirt. See HN 1574, 1688.
HN1574	Rhoda	1933–1938	Orange shawl, dark skirt. See HN 1573.
HN1575	Daisy	1933–1949	Blue dress. See HN 1961.

HN1576	Tildy	1933–1938	Red bodice, light skirt. See HN 1859.
HN1577	Suzette	1933–1949	Blue dress, red underskirt. See HN 1487.
HN1578	Hinged Parasol, The	1933–1949	Blue-dotted skirt. See HN 1579.
HN1579	Hinged Parasol, The	1933–1949	Red dress, purple ruffles. See HN 1578.
HN1580	Rosebud	1933–1938	Pink dress. See HN 1581.
HN1581	Rosebud	1933–1938	Light dress, flower sprays. See HN 1580.
HN1582	Marion	1933–1938	Pink skirt. See HN 1583.
HN1583	Marion	1933–1938	Blue skirt. See HN 1582.
HN1584	Willy-Won't He	1933–1949	Red jacket, blue hat. See HN 1561.
HN1585	Suzette	1933–1938	Green and yellow dress. See HN 1487.
HN1586	Camille	1933–1949	Red bodice and overskirt. See HN 1648, 1736.
HN1587	Fleurette	1933–1949	Red and white dress.
HN1588	Bride, The	1933–1938	White flowers. See HN 1600, 1762, 1841.
HN1589	Sweet and Twenty	1933–1949	Red-blue dress, green couch. See HN 1610.
HN1590–1597	Wall Masks		
HN1598	Clothilde	1933–1949	Cream dress, red cape. See HN 1599.
HN1599	Clothilde	1933–1949	Flowered dress, red and blue cape. See HN 1598.
HN1600	Bride, The	1933–1949	Yellow roses. See HN 1588.
HN1601–1603	Wall masks		
HN1604	Emir, The	1933–1949	Orange and green scarf. See HN 1605, 2095.
HN1605	Emir, The	1933–1949	Orange and purple scarf. See HN 1604.
HN1606	Falstaff	1933–1949	Green cloth with red circles. See HN 571.
HN1607	Cerise	1933–1949	
HN1608–1609	Wall masks		
HN1610	Sweet and Twenty	1933–1938	Red dress, yellow couch. See HN 1589.
HN1611–1614	Wall masks		
HN1615	Micawber, bookend		
HN1616	Tony Weller, bookend		
HN1617	Primroses	1934–1949	Red dress, gray shawl.
HN1618	Maisie	1934–1949	White dress. See HN 1619.
HN1619	Maisie	1934–1949	Pink dress. See HN 1618.

HN1620	Rosbell	1934–1938	Pink flowered shawl.
HN1621	Irene	1934–1951	Pale yellow dress. See HN 1697, 1952.
HN1622	Evelyn	1934–1949	Red bodice, red hat. See HN 1637.
HN1623	Mr. Pickwick, bookend		
HN1624			
HN1625	Sairey Gamp, bookend		
HN1626	Bonnie Lassie	1934–1953	Red plaid shawl.
HN1627	Curly Knob	1934–1949	Blue and red striped shawl.
HN1628	Margot	1934–1938	Blue bodice. See HN 1636, 1653.
HN1629	Grizel	1934–1938	Red multicolored bodice, light skirt.
HN1630	Wall mask		
HN1631	Sweet Anne	1934–1938	Pink and yellow flowered dress, blue trim. See HN 1318.
HN1632	A Gentlewoman	1934–1949	Lavender dress.
HN1633	Clemency	1934–1938	Lavender bodice. See HN 1634, 1643.
HN1634	Clemency	1934–1949	Cream dress, pink trim. See HN 1633.
HN1635	Marie	1934–1949	Pink flowered skirt. See HN 1370.
HN1636	Margot	1934–1938	Red bodice, yellow & pink skirt. See HN 1628.
HN1637	Evelyn	1934–1938	Light multicolored dress. See HN 1622.
HN1638	Ladybird	1934–1949	Pink costume. See HN 1640.
HN1639	Dainty May	1934–1949	Red dress, green underskirt. See HN 1656.
HN1640	Ladybird	1934–1938	Light blue costume. See HN 1638.
HN1641	Little Mother, The	1934–1949	Light skirt, green shawl. See HN 1399.
HN1642	Granny's Shawl	1934–1949	Blue cape. See HN 1647.
HN1643	Clemency	1934–1938	Green trim on dress, red top. See HN 1633.
HN1644	Herminia	1934–1938	White flower-print dress. See HN 1646, 1704.
HN1645	Aileen	1934–1938	Green dress. See HN 1664, 1803.
HN1646	Herminia	1934–1938	Red dress, white stripes. See HN 1644.
HN1647	Granny's Shawl	1934–1949	Red cape. See HN 1642.

HN1648 Camille	1934–1949	Light skirt, green bodice and hat. See HN 1586.
HN1649 Sweet and Twenty	1934–1949	Green shirt, orange couch. See HN 1298.
HN1650 Veronica	1934–1949	Green dress. See HN 1517.
HN1651 Charmian	1934–1938	Red bodice, green skirt. See HN 1568.
HN1652 Janet	1934–1949	Red bodice, pink flowered skirt. See HN 1537.
HN1653 Margot	1934–1938	White and red dress, red hat. See HN 1628.
HN1654 Rose	1934–1938	Green bodice, flowered skirt. See HN 1368.
HN1655 Marie	1934–1938	Pink bodice, flowered white skirt. See HN 1370.
HN1656 Dainty May	1934–1949	White flowered dress, purple hat. See HN 1639.
HN1657 Moor, The	1934–1949	Striped waistband, black cloak. See HN 33.
HN1658–1661 Wall masks		
HN1662 Delicia	1934–1938	Pale pink and purple dress. See HN 1663, 1681.
HN1663 Delicia	1935–1938	Purple, green and yellow flowered skirt. See HN 1662.
HN1664 Aileen	1934–1938	Pink skirt. See HN 1645.
HN1665 Miss Winsome	1934–1949	Pale lavender dress. See HN 1666.
HN1666 Miss Winsome	1934–1949	Green dress. See HN 1665.
HN1667 Blossom	1934–1949	Orange multicolored shawl.
HN1668 Sibell	1934$-1949	Red dress, green underskirt. See HN 1695, 1735.
HN1669 Anthea	1934–1938	Pink skirt, red jacket. See HN 1526.
HN1670 Gillian	1934–1949	Dark pink dress.
HN1671–1676 Wall masks		
HN1677 Tinkle Bell	1935–present	Pink dress.
HN1678 Dinky Doo	1934–present	Blue bodice, light skirt.
HN1679 Babie	1935–present	Green bodice, light skirt. See HN 1842.
HN1680 Tootles	1935–1975	Pink bodice.
HN1681 Delicia	1935–1938	Green and purple dress. See HN 1662.
HN1682 Teresa	1935–1949	Red dress. See HN 1683.

HN1683	Teresa	1935–1938	Light blue dress. See HN 1682.
HN1684	Lisette	1935–1938	Pink dress. Green trim. See HN 1523.
HN1685	Cynthia	1935–1949	Pink and green dress. See HN 1686.
HN1686	Cynthia	1935–1949	Blue and red dress. See HN 1685.
HN1687	Clarissa	1935–1949	Light blue dress, green shawl. See HN 1525.
HN1688	Rhoda	1935–1949	Orange dress, red shawl. See HN 1573.
HN1689	Calumet	1935–1949	Green costume, blue pot. See HN 1428.
HN1690	June	1935–1949	Green dress. See HN 1691, 1947, 2027.
HN1691	June	1935–1949	Pink shoes, light floral dress. See HN 1690.
HN1692	Sonia	1935–1949	Pink bodice, white skirt. See HN 1738.
HN1693	Virginia	1935–1949	Yellow dress. See HN 1694.
HN1694	Virginia	1935–1949	Green dress. See HN 1693.
HN1695	Sibell	1935–1949	Dark green dress, lilac trim. See HN 1668.
HN1696	Suzette	1935–1949	Green dress and hat. See HN 1487.
HN1697	Irene	1935–1949	Pink dress, green hat. See HN 1621.
HN1698	Phyllis	1935–1949	Green dress and hat. See HN 1420.
HN1699	Marietta	1935–1949	Green dress, red cape. See HN 1341.
HN1700	Gloria	1935–1938	Green dress, dark cloak. See HN 1488.
HN1701	Sweet Anne	1935–1938	Yellow and pink flowered dress, blue trim. See HN 1318.
HN1702	A Jester	1935–1949	Brown, purple, red costume. See HN 45.
HN1703	Charley's Aunt	1935–1938	White dress, no base.
HN1704	Herminia	1935–1938	Red dress, green purse. See HN 1644.
HN1705	Cobbler, The	1935–1949	Blue and red costume. See HN 1706.
HN1706	Cobbler, The	1935–1969	Green and blue striped shirt and hat with yellow. See HN 1705.

HN1707	Paisley Shawl	1935–1949	Purple shawl, green hat. See HN 1392.
HN1708	Bather, The	1935–1938	Black bathing suit added, green and red robe. See HN 597.
HN1709	Pantalettes	1935–1938	Red dress and hat. See HN 1362.
HN1710	Camilla	1935–1949	Pink dress. See HN 1711.
HN1711	Camilla	1935–1949	Green dress. See HN 1710.
HN1712	Daffy Down Dilly	1935–1975	Green dress and hat. See HN 1713.
HN1713	Daffy Down Dilly	1935–1949	White and red hat, green-purple dress. See HN 1712.
HN1714	Millicent	1935–1949	Pink shawl. See HN 1715, 1860.
HN1715	Millicent	1935–1949	Purple dress, flowered shawl. See HN 1714.
HN1716	Diana	1935–1949	Pink top, blue skirt. See HN 1717, 1986.
HN1717	Diana	1935–1949	Green dress, red hat. See HN 1716.
HN1718	Kate Hardcastle	1935–1949	Pink dress, green underskirt. See HN 1719, 1734, 1861, 1919, 2028.
HN1719	Kate Hardcastle	1935–1949	Green dress, pink underskirt. See HN 1718.
HN1720	Frangcon	1935–1949	Floral print dress. See HN 1721.
HN1721	Frangcon	1935–1949	Green dress. See HN 1720.
HN1722	Coming of Spring, The	1935–1949	Pink dress. See HN 1723.
HN1723	Coming of Spring, The	1935–1949	Light green dress. See HN 1722.
HN1724	Ruby	1935–1949	Pink and white dress. See HN 1725.
HN1725	Ruby	1935–1949	Blue and white dress. See HN 1724.
HN1726	Celia	1935–1949	Pink dress. See HN 1727.
HN1727	Celia	1935–1949	Green dress. See HN 1726.
HN1728	New Bonnet, The	1935–1949	Pink dress, green hat. See HN 1957.
HN1729	Vera	1935–1938	Pink blouse. See HN 1730.
HN1730	Vera	1935–1938	Green blouse. See HN 1729.
HN1731	Daydreams	1935–present	Pink bodice, light skirt. See HN 1732, 1944.
HN1732	Daydreams	1935–1949	Light blue dress, pink trim. See HN 1731.

HN1733	Wall Mask		
HN1734	Kate Hardcastle	1935–1949	White and green dress, pink flower. See HN 1718.
HN1735	Sibell	1935–1949	Blue and green dress. See HN 1668.
HN1736	Camille	1935–1949	Red and white dress. See HN 1586.
HN1737	Janet	1935–1949	Green and white dress. See HN 1537.
HN1738	Sonia	1935–1949	Green dress. See HN 1692.
HN1739	Paisley Shawl	1935–1949	Green-white dress, red-yellow and green shawl. See HN 1392.
HN1740	Gladys	1935–1949	Green blouse. See HN 1741.
HN1741	Gladys	1935–1938	Pink blouse. See HN 1740.
HN1742	Sir Walter Raleigh	1935–1949	Green cape. See HN 1751, 2015.
HN1743	Mirabel	1935–1949	Pale blue-green dress. See HN 1744.
HN1744	Mirabel	1935–1949	Pink dress. See HN 1743.
HN1745	Rustic Swain, The	1935–1949	Red suit. See HN 1746.
HN1746	Rustic Swain, The	1935–1949	Green suit. See HN 1745.
HN1747	Afternoon Tea	1935–present	Pink dress. See HN 1748.
HN1748	Afternoon Tea	1935–1949	Green dress. See HN 1747.
HN 1749	Pierrette	1936–1949	Pink and blue costume with playing cards. See HN 1391.
HN1750	Folly	1936–1949	Brown hat, white muff, earthenware. See HN 1335.
HN1751	Sir Walter Raleigh	1936–1949	Earthenware, purple-red mottled cape. See HN 1742.
HN1752	Regency	1936–1949	Purple and green costume.
HN1753	Eleanore	1936–1949	Blue bodice, green and pink skirt. See HN 1754.
HN1754	Eleanore	1936–1949	Orange dress, white bodice with flowers. See HN 1753.
HN1755	Court Shoemaker, The	1936–1949	Red Coat, lavender dress.
HN1756	Lizana	1936–1949	Pink dress, green cloak. See HN 1761.
HN1757	Romany Sue	1936–1949	Green dress, red shawl. See HN 1758.
HN1758	Romany Sue	1936–1949	Purple dress. See HN 1757.

HN1759	Orange Lady, The	1936–1975	Pink skirt. See HN 1953.
HN1760	4 o'Clock	1936–1949	Lavender dress.
HN1761	Lizana	1936–1938	Green dress, leopard cloak. See HN 1756.
HN1762	Bride, The	1936–1949	Cream dress. See HN 1588.
HN1763	Windflower	1936–1949	Red flowered dress. See HN 1764, 2029.
HN1764	Windflower	1949–1952	Blue flowered dress. See HN 1763.
HN1765	Chloe	1936–1950	White-blue dress. See HN 1470.
HN1766	Nana	1936–1949	Red dress. See HN 1767.
HN1767	Nana	1936–1949	Lilac dress. See HN 1766.
HN1768	Ivy	1936–1978	Pink hat, lavender dress. See HN 1769.
HN1769	Ivy	1936–1938	See HN 1768.
HN1770	Maureen	1936–1939	Red dress. See HN 1771.
HN1771	Maureen	1936–1949	Lilac dress. See HN 1770.
HN1772	Delight	1936–1967	Red dress. See HN1773.
HN1773	Delight	1936–1949	Green dress. See HN 1772.
HN1774	Spring (limited to 100)	1933–1939	Matt ivory finish. See HN 1827.
HN1775	Salome (limited to 100)	1933–1939	Matt ivory finish. See HN1828.
HN1776	West Wind (limited to 25)	1933–1939	Matt ivory finish. See HN 1826.
HN1777	Spirit of the Wind (limited to 50)	1933–1939	Matt ivory finish. See HN 1825.
HN1778	Beethoven (limited to 25)	1933–1939	Matt ivory.
HN1779	Bird		
HN1780	Lady of the Snows	1933–?	See HN 1830.
HN1781–1786	Wall masks		
HN1787–1790			
HN1791	Old Balloon Seller and Bulldog	1932–1938	On mahogany stand. See HN 1912.
HN1792	Henry VIII (limited to 200)	1933–1939	Ermine-trimmed cape.
HN1793	This Little Pig	1936–present	Red blanket. See HN 1794.
HN1794	This Little Pig	1936–1949	Purple and blue striped blanket. See HN 1793.
HN1795	M'Lady's Maid	1936–1949	Red dress. See HN 1822.
HN1796	Hazel	1936–1949	Green dress. See HN 1797.
HN1797	Hazel	1936–1949	Orange and green dress. See HN 1796.
HN1798	Lily	1936–1949	White shawl, pink dress. See HN 1799.

HN1799	Lily	1936–1949	Blue shawl, green dress. See HN 1798.
HN1800	St. George	1934–1950	See HN 385.
HN1801	An Old King	1937–1954	See HN 358.
HN1802	Estelle	1937–1949	Pink dress. See HN 1566.
HN1803	Aileen	1937–1949	Cream dress, blue shawl. See HN 1645.
HN1804	Granny	1937–1949	Gray dress. See HN 1832.
HN1805	To Bed	1937–1949	Green shirt and shorts. See HN 1806.
HN1806	To Bed	1937–1949	Light shirt and shorts. See HN 1805.
HN1807	Spring Flowers	1937–1959	Green skirt, gray-blue overskirt. See HN 1945.
HN1808	Cissie	1937–1951	Green dress. See HN 1809.
HN1809	Cissie	1937–present	Red dress. See HN 1808.
HN1810	Bo-Peep	1937–1949	Blue dress. See HN 1811.
HN1811	Bo-Peep	1937–present	Orange dress, green hat. See HN 1810.
HN1812	Forget-me-not	1937–1949	Pink dress, green ribbon. See HN 1813.
HN1813	Forget-me-not	1937–1949	Red dress, blue hat. See HN 1812.
HN1814	Squire, The	1937–1949	Earthenware. See HN 1409.
HN1815	Huntsman, The	1937–1949	Earthenware. See HN 1408.
HN1816–1817	Wall masks		
HN1818	Miranda	1937–1949	Red skirt. See HN 1819.
HN1819	Miranda	1937–1949	Green skirt. See HN 1818.
HN1820	Reflections	1937–1938	Red dress, lilac couch. See HN 1821, 1847, 1848.
HN1821	Reflections	1937–1938	Green dress, red couch. See HN1820.
HN1822	M'Lady's Maid	1937–1949	Multicolored dress. See HN 1795.
HN1823–1824	Wall masks		
HN1825	Spirit of the Wind	1937–1949	Green and white. See HN 1777.
HN1826	West Wind	1937–1949	Tinted finish. See HN 1776.
HN1827	Spring	1937–1949	Tinted finish. See HN1774.
HN1828	Salome	1937–1949	Tinted finish. See HN 1775.
HN1829	Bird		
HN1830	Lady of the Snows	1937–1949	Tinted finish. See HN 1780.
HN1831	Cloud, The	1937–1949	Ivory and gold.
HN1832	Granny	1937–1949	Yellow dress, red shawl. See HN 1804.

HN1833	Top o' the Hill	1937–1971	Green dress. See HN 1834.
HN1834	Top o' the Hill	1937–present	Red dress. See HN 1833.
HN1835	Verena	1938–1949	Rose and green dress. See HN 1854.
HN1836	Vanessa	1938–1949	Purple bodice, green skirt. See HN 1838.
HN1837	Mariquita	1938–1949	Red-lavender dress.
HN1838	Vanessa	1938–1949	Green bodice, red skirt. See HN 1836.
HN1839	Christine	1938–1949	Lilac dress, blue shawl. See HN 1840.
HN1840	Christine	1938–1949	Pink dress, blue shawl. See HN 1839.
HN1841	Bride, The	1938–1949	Blue dress. See HN 1588.
HN1842	Babie	1938–1949	Pink dress, green umbrella and hat. See HN 1679.
HN1843	Biddy-Penny-Farthing	1938–present	Cream skirt, gray shawl.
HN1844	Odds and Ends	1938–1949	Striped dress, yellow apron.
HN1845	Modena	1938–1949	Blue dress. See HN 1846.
HN1846	Modena	1938–1949	Red dress. See HN 1845.
HN1847	Reflections	1938–1949	Red dress, green couch. See HN 1820.
HN1848	Reflections	1938–1949	Green skirt. See HN 1820.
HN1849	Top o' the Hill	1938–1975	Orange dress, green and red scarf. See HN 1833.
HN1850	Antoinette	1938–1949	Red and white dress. See HN 1851.
HN1851	Antoinette	1938–1949	Blue and pink dress. See HN 1850.
HN1852	Mirror, The	1938–1949	Pink robe. See HN 1853.
HN1853	Mirror, The	1938–1949	Blue robe. See HN 1852
HN1854	Verena	1938–1949	Green dress. See HN 1835.
HN1855	Memories	1938–1949	Green bodice, red skirt. See HN 1856, 1857, 2030.
HN1856	Memories	1938–1949	White and blue dress, green book. See HN 1855.
HN1857	Memories	1938–1949	Red bodice, red and lilac skirt. See HN 1855.
HN1858	Dawn	1938–1949	Green drape.
HN1859	Tildy	1938–1949	See HN 1576.
HN1860	Millicent	1938–1949	See HN 1714.
HN1861	Kate Hardcastle	1938–1949	Red, blue, and green dress. See HN 1718.
HN1862	Jasmine	1938–1949	Floral jacket with lavender trim. See HN 1863, 1876.

HN1863	Jasmine	1938–1949	White dress, floral jacket with green trim. See HN 1862.
HN1864	Sweet and Fair	1938–1949	Blue shawl, pink dress. See HN 1865.
HN1865	Sweet and Fair	1938–1949	Green dress. See HN 1864.
HN1866	Wedding Morn	1938–1949	Cream dress. See HN 1867.
HN1867	Wedding Morn	1938–1949	Red dress. See HN 1866.
HN1868	Serena	1938–1949	Blue, red, pink dress.
HN1869	Dryad of the Pines	1938–1949	Ivory and gold.
HN1870	Little Lady Make Believe	1938–1949	Red cape.
HN1871	Annabella	1938–1949	Peach skirt, green bodice. See HN 1872, 1875.
HN1872	Annabelle	1938–1949	Green skirt. See HN 1871.
HN1873	Granny's Heritage	1938–1949	Red shawl. See HN 1874, 2031.
HN1874	Granny's Heritage	1938–1949	Blue shawl, green skirt. See HN 1873.
HN1875	Annabelle	1938–1949	Red dress. See HN 1871.
HN1876	Jasmine	1938–1949	Blue floral jacket, pink trim. See HN 1862.
HN1877	Jean	1938–1949	Pink dress, blue shawl. See HN 1878, 2032.
HN1878	Jean	1938–1949	Green dress, red shawl. See HN 1877.
HN1879	Bon Jour	1938–1949	Green dress. See HN 1888.
HN1880	Lambeth Walk, The	1938–1949	Blue dress. See HN 1881.
HN1881	Lambeth Walk, The	1938–1949	Pink dress, green hat. See HN 1880.
HN1882	Nell Gwynn	1938–1949	Blue skirt. See HN 1887.
HN1883	Prudence	1938–1949	Blue dress, See HN 1884.
HN1884	Prudence	1938–1949	Pink dress. See HN 1883.
HN1885	Nadine	1938–1949	Green dress. See HN 1886.
HN1886	Nadine	1938–1949	Orange dress, blue trim, purple ribbon. See HN 1885.
HN1887	Nell Gwynn	1938–1949	Orange skirt, green bodice. See HN 1882.
HN1888	Bon Jour	1938–1949	Red dress. See HN 1879.
HN1889	Goody Two Shoes	1938–1949	Green dress. See HN 1905, 2037.
HN1890	Lambing Time	1938–present	Light orange smock.
HN1891	Pecksniff	1938–1952	Color changes. See HN 553.
HN1892	Uriah Heep	1938–1952	Color changes. See HN 554.
HN1893	Fat Boy, The	1938–1952	Color changes. See HN 555.

HN1894	Mr. Pickwick	1938–1952	Color changes. See HN 556.
HN1895	Mr. Micawber	1938–1952	Color changes. See HN 557.
HN1896	Sairey Gamp	1938–1952	Color changes. See HN 558.
HN1897	Miss Fortune	1938–1949	Blue and white shawl, pink dress. See HN 1898.
HN1898	Miss Fortune	1938–1949	Green and yellow shawl, blue dress. See HN 1897.
HN1899	Midsummer Noon	1939–1949	Red dress. See HN 1900, 2033.
HN1900	Midsummer Noon	1949–1955	Blue dress. See HN 1899.
HN1901	Penelope	1939–1975	Red dress. See HN 1902.
HN1902	Penelope	1939–1949	Green petticoat, blue bodice and skirt. See HN 1901.
HN1903	Rhythm	1939–1949	Pink dress. See HN 1904.
HN1904	Rhythm	1939–1949	Pale green dress. See HN 1903.
HN1905	Goody Two Shoes	1939–1949	Pink skirt, red overdress. See HN 1889.
HN1906	Lydia	1939–1949	Orange-pink dress. See HN 1907, 1908.
HN1907	Lydia	1939–1949	Green dress. See HN 1906.
HN1908	Lydia	1939–present	Red dress. See HN 1906.
HN1909	Honey	1939–1949	Pink dress. See HN 1910, 1963.
HN1910	Honey	1939–1949	Green dress, blue jacket. See HN 1909.
HN1911	Autumn Breezes	1939–1976	Peach dress, green jacket. See HN 1913, 1934, 2147.
HN1912	Old Balloon Seller and Bulldog	1939–1949	See HN 1791.
HN1913	Autumn Breezes	1939–1971	Green dress, blue jacket. See HN 1911.
HN1914	Paisley Shawl	1939–1949	Yellow-green skirt and hat. See HN 1988.
HN1915	Veronica	1939–1949	Red and white dress, blue hat. Reduced size of HN 1517.
HN1916	Janet	1939–1949	Blue bodice, pink skirt. Reduced size of HN 1537, See HN 1964.
HN1917	Meryll	1939–1940	Red jacket, green skirt. See HN 1940.

HN1918	Sweet Suzy	1939–1949	Peach dress, green underskirt.
HN1919	Kate Hardcastle	1939–1949	Green dress, black base, red overskirt. See HN 1718.
HN1920	Windflower	1939–1949	Multicolored skirt. See HN 1939.
HN1921	Roseanna	1940–1949	Green dress. See HN 1926.
HN1922	Spring Morning	1940–1973	Green coat. See HN 1923.
HN1923	Spring Morning	1940–1949	Orange Coat. See HN 1922.
HN1924	Fiona	1940–1949	Pink skirt. See HN 1925, 1933.
HN1945	Fiona	1940–1949	Green skirt. See HN 1924.
HN1926	Roseanna	1940–1959	Red dress. See HN 1921.
HN1927	Awakening, The	1940–1949	
HN1928	Marguerite	1940–1959	Pink dress. See HN 1929, 1930, 1946.
HN1929	Marguerite	1940–1949	Pink to yellow trim on dress. See HN 1928.
HN1930	Marguerite	1940–1949	Blue dress with purple stripes. See HN 1928.
HN1931	Meriel	1940–1949	Pink dress. See HN 1932.
HN1932	Meriel	1940–1949	Green dress. See HN 1931.
HN1933	Fiona	1940–1949	Multicolored dress. See HN 1924.
HN1934	Autumn Breezes	1940–present	Red dress. See HN 1911.
HN1935	Sweeting	1940–1973	Pink dress. See HN 1938.
HN1936	Miss Muffet	1940–1967	Red coat. See HN 1937.
HN1937	Miss Muffet	1940–1952	Green coat. See HN 1936.
HN1938	Sweeting	1940–1949	Blue multicolored dress. See HN 1935.
HN1939	Windflower	1940–1949	Blue hat and gloves, pink skirt. See HN 1920.
HN1940	Toinette	1940–1949	Red dress. Renamed HN 1917.
HN1941	Peggy	1940–1949	Red dress, green trim. See HN 2038.
HN1942	Pyjams	1940–1949	Pink pajamas.
HN1943	Veronica	1940–1949	Blue hat, pink dress. See HN 1517.
HN1944	Daydreams	1940–1949	Red dress, blue hat. See HN 1731.
HN1945	Spring Flowers	1940–1949	Green skirt, pink overskirt. See HN 1807.
HN1946	Marguerite	1940–1949	Red dress, green hat. See HN 1928.

HN1947	June	1940–1949	Red-purple dress. See HN 1690.
HN1948	Lady Charmian	1940–1973	Green dress, red shawl. See HN 1949.
HN1949	Lady Charmian	1940–1975	Red dress, green shawl. See HN 1948.
HN1950	Claribel	1940–1949	Blue dress. See HN 1951.
HN1951	Claribel	1940–1949	Red dress. See HN 1950.
HN1952	Irene	1940–1950	Red-blue dress. See HN 1621.
HN1953	Orange Lady	1940–1975	Yellow dress, green shawl. See HN 1759.
HN1954	Balloon Man, The	1940–present	Dark jacket, green pants.
HN1955	Lavinia	1940–1978	Red dress.
HN1956	Chloe	1940–1949	Red skirt, green ribbon. See HN 1470.
HN1957	New Bonnet, The	1940–1949	Red dress, red flowers. See HN 1728.
HN1958	Lady April	1940–1959	Red dress. See HN 1965.
HN1959	Choice, The	1941–1949	Red dress, See HN 1960.
HN1960	Choice, The	1941–1949	Purple-pink dress. See HN 1959.
HN1961	Daisy	1941–1949	Pink dress. See HN 1575.
HN1962	Genevieve	1941–1975	Red dress.
HN1963	Honey	1941–1949	Red dress, blue hat, and shawl. See HN 1909.
HN1964	Janet	1941–1949	Pink dress. See HN 1916.
HN1965	Lady April	1941–1949	Green dress. See HN 1958.
HN1966	Orange Vendor	1941–1949	Earthenware. See HN 72.
HN1967	Lady Betty	1941–1951	Red dress.
HN1968	Madonna of the Square	1941–1949	Light green dress. See HN 10.
HN1969	Madonna of the Square	1941–1949	Lilac dress. See HN 10.
HN1970	Milady	1941–1949	Rust dress, black hat.
HN1971	Springtime	1941–1949	Peach dress, green hat.
HN1972	Regency Beau	1941–1949	Red suit, green cape.
HN1973	Corinthian, The	1941–1949	Beige trousers, black and red cape.
HN1974	Forty Winks	1945–1973	Dark dress, white apron.
HN1975	Shepherd, The	1945–1975	Orange smock.
HN1976	Easter Day	1945–1951	White dress, blue flowers. See HN 2039.
HN1977	Her Ladyship	1945–1959	Cream dress, red shawl.
HN1978	Bedtime	1945–present	White nightgown.
HN1979	Gollywog	1945–1959	White overalls. See HN 2040.
HN1980	Gwynneth	1945–1952	Red dress.
HN1981	Ermine Coat, The	1945–1967	Red dress undercoat.

HN1982	Sabbath Morn	1945–1959	Red dress, green-yellow shawl.
HN1983	Rosebud	1945–1952	Red shawl.
HN1984	Patchwork Quilt, The	1945–1959	Green dress.
HN1985	Darling	1946–present	White nightshirt.
HN1986	Diana	1946–1975	Red dress, purple hat ties. See HN 1716.
HN1987	Paisley Shawl	1946–1959	Cream dress, red shawl. See HN 1392.
HN1988	Paisley Shawl	1946–1975	Cream and yellow skirt, red hat. See HN 1914.
HN1989	Margaret	1947–1959	Red coat, green dress.
HN1990	Mary Jane	1947–1959	Pink dress.
HN1991	Market Day	1947–1955	Red flowered shawl, white apron.
HN1992	Christmas Morn	1947–present	Red dress.
HN1993	Griselda	1947–1953	Lilac dress, white floral underskirt.
HN1994	Karen	1947–1955	Red dress.
HN1995	Olivia	1947–1951	Red and green dress.
HN1996	Prue	1947–1955	Red dress, black bodice.
HN1997	Belle o' the Ball	1947–1978	Red dress, white underskirt.
HN1998	Collinette	1947–1949	Green robe. See HN 1999.
HN1999	Collinette	1947–1949	Red robe. See HN 1998.
HN2000	Jacqueline	1947–1951	Lilac dress. See HN 2001.
HN2001	Jacqueline	1947–1951	Rose dress. See HN 2000.
HN2002	Bess	1947–1969	Red cloak. See HN 2003.
HN2003	Bess	1947–1950	Purple cloak. See HN 2002.
HN2004	A 'Courting	1947–1953	Rose dress.
HN2005	Henrietta Maria	1948–1953	Cream mottled dress, red underskirt.
HN2006	Lady Anne Nevill, The	1948–1953	Purple dress, ermine trim.
HN2007	Mrs. Fitzherbert	1948–1953	Cream mottled dress, apricot bodice.
HN2008	Phillippa of Hainault	1948–1953	Blue dress, orange print.
HN2009	Eleanor of Provence	1948–1953	Purple dress, red print, red cape.
HN2010	Young Miss Nightingale, The		
		1948–1953	Green dress, red surcoat.
HN2011	Matilda	1948–1953	Purple dress, red print, red cape.
HN2012	Margaret of Anjou	1948–1953	Green dress.
HN2013	Angelina	1948–1951	Red dress.
HN2014	Jane	1948–1951	Red-rose dress.
HN2015	Sir Walter Raleigh	1948–1955	Orange costume, dark cloak. See HN 1742.

HN2016	A Jester	1949–present	Pink, purple and orange costume. See HN 45.
HN2017	Silks and Ribbons	1949–present	Green dress.
HN2018	Parson's Daughter, The	1949–1953	Patchwork skirt, purple hat and cloak. See HN 337.
HN2019	Minuet	1949–1971	White dress, floral print. See HN 2066.
HN2020	Deidre	1949–1955	Blue dress, red underskirt.
HN2021	Blithe Morning	1949–1971	Purple bodice, pastel skirt. See HN 2065.
HN2022	Janice	1949–1955	Green dress. See HN 2165.
HN2023	Joan	1949–1959	Glaze differences. See HN 1422.
HN2024	Darby	1949–1959	Glaze differences. See HN 1427.
HN2025	Gossips, The	1949–1967	Glaze differences. See HN 1426.
HN2026	Suzette	1949–1959	Glaze differences. See HN 1487.
HN2027	June	1949–1952	Glaze differences. See HN 1690.
HN2028	Kate Hardcastle	1949–1952	Glaze differences. See HN 1718.
HN2029	Windflower	1949–1952	As HN 1763, larger.
HN2030	Memories	1949–1959	Green and red dress. See HN 1855.
HN2031	Granny's Heritage	1949–1969	Green skirt, light multicolored shawl. See HN 1873.
HN2032	Jean	1949–1959	Green dress, red cloak. See HN 1877
HN2033	Midsummer Noon	1949–1955	Color change. See HN 1899.
HN2034	Madonna of the Square	1949–1951	Light green-blue costume. See HN 10.
HN2035	Pearly Boy	1949–1959	Red jacket.
HN2036	Pearly Girl	1949–1959	Red jacket.
HN2037	Goody Two Shoes	1949–present	Red dress. See HN 1889.
HN2038	Peggy	1949–1978	Red dress, green trim. See HN 1941.
HN2039	Easter Day	1949–1969	Multicolored dress, green hat. See HN 1976.
HN2040	Gollywog	1949–1959	Blue overalls, green hat. See HN 1979.
HN2041	Broken Lance, The	1949–1975	White horse, blue blanket.
HN2042	Owd Willum	1949–1973	Brown jacket.
HN2043	Poacher, The	1949–1959	Dark gray jacket.

HN2044	Mary Mary	1949–1973	Pink dress.
HN2045	She Loves Me Not	1949–1962	Blue shorts and shirt.
HN2046	He Loves Me	1949–1962	Pink dress.
HN2047	Once Upon a Time	1949–1955	Pink dotted dress.
HN2048	Mary Had a Little Lamb	1949–present	Lilac dress.
HN2049	Curly Locks	1949–1953	Pink flowered dress.
HN2050	Wee Willie Winkie	1949–1953	Blue nightshirt.
HN2051	St. George	1950–present	White horse and costume.
HN2052	Grandma	1950–1959	Red multicolored shawl.
HN2053	Gaffer, The	1950–1959	Dark jacket, yellow plaid scarf.
HN2054	Falstaff	1950–present	Red jacket, brown belt and boots.
HN2055	Leisure Hour, The	1950–1965	Mottled green and peach dress.
HN2056	Susan	1950–1959	Purple dress.
HN2057	Jersey Milkmaid, The	1950–1959	Red bodice, blue skirt. See HN2057.
HN2057A	Milkmaid, The	1975–present	Incorrectly numbered 2100 at first. Green dress, white hat. Renamed version of Jersey Milkmaid, above.
HN2058	Hermione	1950–1952	Purple overdress.
HN2059	Bedtime Story, The	1950–present	Rose dress (mother).
HN2060	Jack	1950–1971	Green jacket.
HN2061	Jill	1950–1971	Red dress.
HN2062	Little Boy Blue	1950–1973	Blue smock.
HN2063	Little Jack Horner	1950–1953	Red jacket.
HN2064	My Pretty Maid	1950–1954	Green dress.
HN2065	Blithe Morning	1950–1973	Red dress. See HN 2021.
HN2066	Minuet	1950–1955	Red dress. See HN 2019.
HN2067	St. George	1950–1978	Purple, red, and orange blanket. See HN 385.
HN2068	Calumet	1950–1953	Glaze differences. See HN 1428.
HN2069	Farmer's Wife	1951–1955	Red jacket, green skirt.
HN2070	Bridget	1951–1973	Peach shawl, green skirt.
HN2071	Bernice	1951–1953	Pink dress.
HN2072	Rocking Horse, The	1951–1953	White horse, blue suit.
HN2073	Vivienne	1951–1967	Red dress.
HN2074	Marianne	1951–1953	Red-rose dress.
HN2075	French Peasant	1951–1955	Gray-green jacket, peach skirt.
HN2076	Promenade	1951–1953	Blue overdress, peach skirt.
HN2077	Rowena	1951–1955	Red overdress, green skirt.

HN2078	Elfreda	1951–1955	Red overdress, blue skirt.
HN2079	Damaris	1951–1952	Green dress, purple cape.
HN2080	Jack Point	1952–present	Red tights, red and purple costume. See HN 2080.
HN2081	Princess Badoura	1952–present	Large, multicolored figure. Pink dress.
HN2082	Moor, The	1952–present	Red costume, dark cloak. See HN 33.
HN2083	N.I.A.		
HN2084	King Charles I	1952–present	Tan base. See HN 404.
HN2085	Spring	1952–1959	Lavender dress.
HN2086	Summer	1952–1959	Rose dress.
HN2087	Autumn	1952–1959	Red dress.
HN2088	Winter	1952–1959	Green and red cape.
HN2089	Judith	1952–1959	Rose dress, lilac bodice.
HN2090	Midinette	1952–1965	Blue dress.
HN2091	Rosemary	1952–1959	Red dress, blue shawl.
HN2092	Sweet Maid	1952–1955	Pale lavender dress.
HN2093	Georgiana	1952–1955	Rust overdress, blue skirt.
HN2094	Uncle Ned	1952–1965	Brown jacket.
HN2095	Ibrahim	1952–1955	Earthenware. Renamed. See HN 1604.
HN2096	Fat Boy, The	1952–1967	Blue jacket, yellow scarf.
HN2097	Mr. Micawber	1952–1967	Black jacket, beige trousers.
HN2098	Pecksniff	1952–1967	Black jacket, brown trousers.
HN2099	Mr. Pickwick	1952–1967	Black jacket, beige trousers.
HN2100	Sairey Gamp	1952–1967	White dress, green cape.
HN2101	Uriah Heep	1952–1967	Black jacket, green trousers.
HN2102	Pied Piper	1953–1976	Brown cloak, gray hat and boots. See HN 1215.
HN2103	Mask Seller	1953–present	Green coat, black hat. See HN 1361.
HN2104	Abdullah	1953–1962	Yellow chair, orange turban. See HN 1410.
HN2105	Bluebeard	1953–present	Dark cloak, orange and green costume. See HN 1528.
HN2106	Linda	1953–1976	Red cloak.
HN2107	Valerie	1953–present	Red overdress, pink skirt.
HN2108	Baby Bunting	1953–1959	Brown and white bunny suit.
HN2109	Wendy	1953–present	White dress.
HN2110	Christmas Time	1953–1967	Red dress.
HN2111	Betsy	1953–1959	Lilac dress.

HN2112	Carolyn	1953–1965	White floral print dress.
HN2113	Maytime	1953–1967	Rose-pink dress.
HN2114	Sleepyhead	1953–1955	White dress, orange mottled chair.
HN2115	Coppelia	1953–1959	Blue and red tutu.
HN2116	Ballerina	1953–1973	White costume, red shoes.
HN2117	Skater, The	1953–1971	Red and white dress.
HN2118	Good King Wenceslas	1953–1976	Peach robe, brown cloak.
HN2119	Town Crier	1953–1976	Orange jacket, green weskit.
HN2122	Yeoman of the Guard	1954–1959	Minor glaze differences. See HN 688.
HN2123–2127	Not issued		
HN2128	River Boy	1962–1975	Blue trousers, white shirt.
HN2129–2131	Not issued		
HN2132	Suitor, The	1962–1971	Blue-gray overskirt, brown jacket.
HN2133	Faraway	1958–1962	White dress, blue trim.
HN2134	An Old King	1954–present	Red shirt, green and purple robe. See HN 358.
HN2135	Gay Morning	1954–1967	Pale peach dress.
HN2136	Delphine	1954–1967	Blue overdress, pink skirt.
HN2137	Lilac Time	1954–1969	Red dress.
HN2138	La Sylphide	1956–1965	White costume.
HN2139	Giselle	1954–1969	Blue dress.
HN2140	Giselle, Forest Glade	1954–1965	White dress.
HN2141	Choir Boy	1954–1975	Red and white robe.
HN2142	Rag Doll	1954–present	Blue dress, white apron.
HN2143	Friar Tuck	1954–1965	Brown robe.
HN2144	Jovial Monk, The	1954–1967	Brown robe.
HN2145	Wardrobe Mistress	1954–1967	White dress.
HN2146	Tinsmith, The	1962–1967	Brown shirt, black vest.
HN2147	Autumn Breezes	1955–1971	White dress, black jacket. See HN 1911.
HN2148	Bridesmaid, The	1955–1959	Cream dress.
HN2149	Love Letter	1958–1976	Pink and white dress, blue dress.
HN2150	Willy Won't He	1955–1959	Glaze differences. See HN 1561.
HN2151	Mother's Help	1962–1969	Black dress, white apron.
HN2152	Adrienne	1964–1976	Rose red dress. See HN 2304
HN2153	One That Got Away, The	1955–1959	Brown slicker.
HN2154	A Child from Williamsburg	1964–present	Blue dress.
HN2155	Not issued		
HN2156	Polka, The	1955–1969	Pale pink dress.
HN2157	A Gypsy Dance	1955–1957	Purple and white dress.

HN2158	Alice	1960–present	Pale green dress.
HN2159	Fortune Teller	1955–1967	Orange dress, green shawl.
HN2160	Apple Maid, The	1957–1962	Green blouse, black skirt.
HN2161	Hornpipe, The	1955–1962	Blue jacket, blue and white striped trousers.
HN2162	Foaming Quart, The	1955–present	Orange and brown costume.
HN2163	In the Stocks	1955–1959	Rust jacket.
HN2164	Not issued		
HN2165	Janice	1955–1965	Dark overdress. See HN 2022.
HN2166	Bride, The	1956–1976	Pale pink dress.
HN2167	Home Again	1956–present	Orange-red dress.
HN2168	Esmeralda	1956–1959	Cream dress, red shawl.
HN2169	Dimity	1956–1959	White skirt, green bodice.
HN2170	Invitation	1956–1975	Pink dress.
HN2171	Fiddler, The	1956–1962	Green and cream striped jacket.
HN2172	Jolly Sailor	1956–1965	Blue and white striped shirt.
HN2173	Organ Grinder, The	1956–1965	Green jacket.
HN2174	Tailor, The	1956–1959	Orange vest.
HN2175	Beggar, The	1956–1962	Black coat, orange sash.
HN2176	Not issued		
HN2177	My Teddy	1962–1967	Pale green dress.
HN2178	Enchantment	1957–present	Green dress.
HN2179	Noelle	1957–1967	Red, Ermine-trimmed coat.
HN2180	Not issued		
HN2181	Summer's Day	1957–1962	White dress.
HN2182	Not issued		
HN2183	Boy from Williamsburg	1969–present	Purple jacket, red vest.
HN2184	Sunday Morning	1963–1969	Rose-red dress.
HN2185	Columbine	1957–1969	Pale pink dress.
HN2186	Harlequin	1957–1969	Pale blue costume.
HN2187–2190	Not issued		
HN2191	Sea Sprite	1958–1962	Pink dress.
HN2192	Wood Nymph	1958–1962	Blue-green dress
HN2193	Fair Lady	1963–present	Green dress. See HN 2832, 2835.
HN2194–2195	Not issued		
HN2196	Bridesmaid, The	1960–1976	White dress, pink trim.
HN2197–2201	Not issued		
HN2202	Melody	1957–1962	Green top, beige skirt.
HN2203	Teenager	1957–1962	Red shawl, white skirt.
HN2204	Long John Silver	1957–1965	Dark uniform.
HN2205	Master Sweep	1957–1962	Green shirt.
HN2206	Sunday Best	1979–present	Yellow dress.
HN2207	Stayed at Home	1958–1969	Green dress.

HN2208	Silversmith of Williamsburg	1960–present	Green Jerkin.
HN2209	Hostess of Williamsburg	1960–present	Pink dress.
HN2210	Debutante	1963–1967	Pale blue dress.
HN2211	Fair Maiden	1967–present	Green dress.
HN2212	Rendezvous	1962–1971	Red to pink dress.
HN2213	Not issued		
HN2214	Bunny	1960–1975	Blue-green dress.
HN2215	Sweet April	1965–1967	Pink dress.
HN2216	Pirouette	1959–1967	White dress.
HN2217	Old King Cole	1963–1967	Ermine-lined robe.
HN2218	Cookie	1958–1975	Pink dress.
HN2219	Not issued		
HN2220	Winsome	1960–present	Red dress.
HN2221	Nanny	1958–present	Blue dress.
HN2222	Camellia	1960–1971	Pink dress.
HN2223	Schoolmarm	1958–present	Gray dress, brown shawl.
HN2224	Not issued		
HN2225	Make Believe	1962–present	White dress.
HN2226	Cellist, The	1960–1967	Black suit.
HN2227	Gentleman from Williamsburg	1960–present	Green jacket.
HN2228	Lady from Williamsburg	1960–present	Green dress.
HN2229	Southern Belle	1958–present	Red and cream dress.
HN2230	A Gypsy Dance	1959–1971	Purple and white dress.
HN2231	Sweet Sixteen	1958–1965	White blouse, pale blue skirt.
HN2232	Not issued		
HN2233	Royal Governor's Cook	1960–present	Black dress, white apron.
HN2234	Michelle	1967–present	Green dress.
HN2235	Dancing Years	1965–1971	Lilac to peach dress.
HN2236	Affection	1962–present	Brown-purple dress.
HN2237	Celeste	1959–1971	Green dress.
HN2238	My Pet	1962–1975	White blouse, blue skirt.
HN2239	Wigmaker of Williamsburg	1960–present	Beige jerkin.
HN2240	Blacksmith of Williamsburg	1960–present	White skirt, brown hat.
HN2241	Not issued		
HN2242	First Steps	1959–1965	Blue dress.
HN2243	Treasure Island	1962–1975	Blue shorts, beige skirt.
HN2244	Newsboy	1959–1965	Dark jacket, plaid hat.
HN2245	Basket Weaver, The	1959–1962	Green dress.
HN2246	Cradle Song	1959–1962	Green dress.
HN2247	Omar Khayyam	1965–present	Red turban, brown and black costume.
HN2248	Tall Story	1968–1975	Green sweater and trousers.
HN2249	Favourite, The	1960–present	Blue dress.
HN2250	Toymaker, The	1959–1973	Green shirt, brown trousers.

HN2251	Masquerade	1960–1965	Blue-green overskirt. See HN 2259.
HN2252	Not issued		
HN2253	Puppetmaker, The	1962–1973	Green vest, brown trousers.
HN2254	Shore Leave	1965–1978	Dark uniform.
HN2255	Teatime	1972–present	Red dress.
HN2256	Twilight	1971–1976	Dark green dress.
HN2257	Sea Harvest	1969–1976	Blue jacket.
HN2258	A Good Catch	1966–present	Dark green suit.
HN2259	Masquerade	1960–1965	Red dress. See HN 2251.
HN2260	Captain, The	1965–present	Black, white, and gold uniform.
HN2261	Marriage of Art and Industry (limited to 12)	1958	Bronze color.
HN2262	Lights Out	1965–1969	Yellow polka-dot top.
HN2263	Seashore	1961–1965	Red shorts.
HN2264	Elegance	1961–present	Beige and green dress.
HN2265	Not issued		
HN2266	Ballad Seller	1968–1973	Pink dress.
HN2267	Rhapsody	1961–1973	Green dress.
HN2268	Daphne	1963–1975	Pink dress.
HN2269	Leading Lady	1965–1976	Lavender overdress.
HN2270	Pillow Fight	1965–1959	Pink nightgown.
HN2271	Melanie	1965–present	Blue dress.
HN2272	Repose	1972–1978	Pink dress.
HN2273	Denise	1964–1971	Red dress.
HN2274	Golden Days	1964–1973	White dress.
HN2275	Sandra	1969–present	Apricot dress.
HN2276	Heart to Heart	1961–1971	Lavender dress. White and green dress.
HN2277–2278	Not issued		
HN2279	Clockmaker, The	1961–1975	Dark green shirt.
HN2280	Mayor, The	1963–1971	Red cape.
HN2281	Professor, The	1965–present	Rust suit, dark robe.
HN2282	Coachman, The	1963–1971	Purple coat.
HN2283	Dreamweaver	1972–1976	Blue shirt.
HN2284	Craftsman, The	1961–1965	Blue shirt.
HN2285–2286	Not issued		
HN2287	Symphony	1961–1965	Brown top, yellow-green skirt.
HN2288–2303	Not issued		
HN2304	Adrienne	1964–present	Blue dress. See HN 2152.
HN2305	Not issued		
HN2306	Reverie	1964–present	Peach dress.
HN2307	Coralie	1964–present	Yellow dress.
HN2308	Picnic	1965–present	Yellow dress.
HN2309	Buttercup	1964–present	Pale yellow dress, green bodice.

HN2310	Lisa	1969–present Violet and white dress.
HN2311	Lorna	1965–present Green dress, apricot shawl.
HN2312	Soiree	1967–present Green overskirt.
HN2313	Not issued	
HN2314	Old Mother Hubbard	1964–1975 Green dress, polka dot apron.
HN2315	Last Waltz	1967–present Apricot dress.
HN2316	Not issued	
HN2317	Lobster Man, The	1964–present Blue sweater.
HN2318	Grace	1966–present Green dress.
HN2319	Bachelor, The	1964–1975 Black vest, beige trousers.
HN2320	Tuppence a Bag	1968–present Green dress, blue shawl.
HN2321	Family Album	1966–1973 Green skirt, green and black striped shawl.
HN2322	Cup of Tea, The	1964–present Black dress, gray sweater.
HN2323	Not issued	
HN2324	Matador and Bull	1964–present Black and gold costume.
HN2325	Master, The	1967–present Gray-green jacket.
HN2326	Antoinette	1967–1978 White dress.
HN2327	Katrina	1965–1969 Red dress.
HN2328	Not issued	
HN2329	Lynne	1971–present Olive green dress.
HN2330	Meditation	1971–present Peach and white dress.
HN2331	Cello (limited to 750)	1970–1978 Yellow dress.
HN2332–2333	Not issued	
HN2334	Fragrance	1966–present Blue dress.
HN2335	Hilary	1967–present Blue dress.
HN2336	Alison	1966–present Blue overdress.
HN2337	Loretta	1966–present Rose-red dress, yellow shawl.
HN2338	Penny	1968–present Green overdress.
HN2339	My Love	1969–present White dress, gold trim.
HN2340	Belle	1968–present Green dress.
HN2341	Cherie	1966–present Blue-gray dress.
HN2342	Not issued	
HN2343	Premiere	1969–1978 White dress, green cape.
HN2344	Not issued	
HN2345	Clarissa	1968–present Olive green dress.
HN2346	Not issued	
HN2347	Nina	1969–1976 Blue dress.
HN2348	Geraldine	1972–1976 Brown dress.
HN2349	Flora	1966–1973 Brown dress, white apron.
HN2350–2351	Not issued	
HN2352	A Stitch in Time	1966–present Purple dress, apricot shawl.
HN2353–2355	Not issued	
HN2356	Ascot	1968–present Gray green dress.
HN2357–2358	Not issued	

HN2359	Detective, The	1977–present	Brown coat.
HN2360	Not issued		
HN2361	Laird, The	1969–present	Green and white plaid kilt, brown jacket.
HN2362	Wayfarer, The	1970–1976	Green jacket, gray trousers.
HN2363–2367	Not issued		
HN2368	Fleur	1968–present	Green dress.
HN2369–2374	Not issued		
HN2375	Viking, The	1973–1976	Blue and brown costume.
HN2376	Indian Brave (limited to 500)	1967–1978	Black and white horse, multicolored costume.
HN2377	Not issued		
HN2378	Simone	1971–present	Olive green dress.
HN2379	Ninette	1971–present	Yellow dress.
HN2380	Sweet Dreams	1971–present	Cream chair, greentrim, multicolored clothes.
HN2381	Kirsty	1971–present	Apricot dress.
HN2382	Secret Thoughts	1971–present	Green dress.
HN2383–2384	Not issued		
HN2385	Debbie	1969–present	Blue overdress.
HN2386–2392	Not issued		
HN2393	Rosalind	1970–1975	Blue dress.
HN2394–2395	Not issued		
HN2396	Wistful	1979–present	Red overdress, white skirt.
HN2397	Not issued		
HN2398	Alexandra	1970–1976	Olive green dress, yellow cape.
HN2399–2416	Not issued		
HN2417	Boatman, The	1971–present	Yellow slicker.
HN2418–2420	Not issued		
HN2421	Charlotte	1972–present	Rose dress.
HN2422	Francine	1972–present	Green dress.
HN2423–2425	Not issued		
HN2426	Tranquility (black)	1978–present	See HN 2469.
HN2427	Virginals (limited to 750)	1971–1978	Green overdress.
HN2428	Palio, The (limited to 500)	1971	Brown horse, Multicolored costume.
HN2429	Elyse	1972–present	Blue dress.
HN2430	Romance	1972–present	Apricot dress.
HN2431	Lute (limited to 750)	1972–1978	Blue and white dress.
HN2432	Violin (limited to 750)	1972–1978	Brown overdress.
HN2433	Peace	1978–present	Black. See HN2470.
HN2434–2435	Not issued		
HN2436	Scottish Highland Dancer (limited to 750)	1978–present	Red plaid dress.
HN2437–2438	Not issued		

HN2439	Phillipine Dancer (limited to 750)	1978–present	Pale blue-green dress.
HN2440–2441	Not issued		
HN2442	Sailors Holiday	1972–1978	Apricot jacket.
HN2443	Judge, The	1972–present	Red robe.
HN2444	Bon Appetit	1972–1976	Gray coat.
HN2445	Parisian	1972–1975	Blue shirt.
HN2446	Thanksgiving	1972–1976	Blue overalls.
HN2447–2454	Not issued		
HN2455	Seafarer, The	1972–1976	Beige sweater.
HN2456–2460	Not issued		
HN2461	Janine	1971–present	Green overdress.
HN2462	Not issued		
HN2463	Olga	1972–1975	Green overdress.
HN2464–2468	Not issued		
HN2469	Tranquility	1978–present	White. See HN2426.
HN2470	Peace	1978–present	White. See HN2433.
HN2471	Victoria	1973–present	Pink dress.
HN2472	Not issued		
HN2473	At Ease	1973–1978	Yellow dress.
HN2474	Not issued		
HN2475	Vanity	1973–present	Deep pink dress.
HN2476–2481	Not issued		
HN2482	Harp (limited to 750)	1973–1978	Brown overdress.
HN2483	Flute (limited to 750)	1973–1978	Red overdress.
HN2484	Past Glory	1973–1978	Red uniform.
HN2485	Lunchtime	1973–present	Beige coat.
HN2486	Not issued		
HN2487	Beachcomber	1973–1976	Purple shirt.
HN2488–2491	Not issued		
HN2492	Huntsman, The	1974–1978	Gray-green jacket.
HN2493	Not issued		
HN2494	Old Meg	1974–1976	Blue dress, purple shawl.
HN2495–2498	Not issued		
HN2499	Helmsman	1974–present	Cream coat.
HN2500–2501	Animals and birds		
HN2502	Queen Elizabeth II (limited to 750)	1973–1978	Pale blue dress.
HN2503–2519	Animals and birds		
HN2520	Farmer's Boy, The	1938–1960	
HN2521–2541	Animals and birds		
HN2542	Boudoir	1974–1978	White dress.
HN2543	Eliza	1974–1978	Rust dress.
HN2544	A la Mode	1974–1978	Olive green dress.
HN2545	Carmen	1974–1978	White blouse, blue skirt.
HN2546	Buddies	1973–1976	Blue skirt.
HN2547–2553	Birds		
HN2554	Masque	1973–present	Dark blue cape.

HN2555–2670 Animals and birds
HN2671 Good Morning   1974–1976   Apricot dress, white
                                                                                     apron.
HN2672–2676 Not issued
HN2677 Taking Things Easy   1975–present Blue jacket.
HN2678 Not issued
HN2679 Drummer Boy   1976–present Red uniform.
HN2680–2682 Not issued
HN2683 Stop Press   1977–present Brown jacket.
HN2684–2693 Not issued
HN2694 Fiona   1974–present Red and white dress.
HN2695–2698 Not issued
HN2699 Cymbals (limited to 750)   1974–1978   Green overdress.
HN2700 Chitarrone (limited to 750)   1974–1978   Blue overdress.
HN2701–2703 Not issued
HN2704 Pensive Moments   1975–present Blue dress.
HN2705 Julia   1975–present Deep apricot dress.
HN2706–2708 Not issued
HN2709 Regal Lady   1975–present Blue overdress.
HN2710–2711 Not issued
HN2712 Mantilla   1974–1978   Red dress, blacklace
                                                                                     mantilla.
HN2713–2715 Not issued
HN2716 Cavalier   1976–present Dark costume, apricot
                                                                                     cape.
HN2717 Private, 2nd South Carolina
            Regiment (limited to 350)   1975–present Blue, red, beige uniform.
HN2718 Lady Pamela   1974–present Pink dress.
HN2719 Laurianne   1974–1978   Dark blue overdress.
HN2720 Family   1978–present White. See HN 2721.
HN2721 Family   1978–present Black. See HN 2720.
HN2722 Veneta   1974–present Olive green overdress.
HN2723 Grand Manner   1975–present Pale bluedress.
HN2724 Clarinda   1975–present Bluedress.
HN2725–2730 Not issued
HN2731 Thanks Doc   1975–present White coat.
HN2732–2733 Not issued
HN2734 Sweet Seventeen   1975–present White dress.
HN2735 Young Love   1975–present White dress, brown jacket.
HN2736–2751 Not issued
HN2752 Major, 3rd New Jersey
            Regiment, 1776 (limited to
            350)   1975–present Pale blue uniform.
HN2753 Not issued
HN2754 Private, 3rd North Carolina
            Regiment (limited to 350)   1976–present Beige buckskin uniform.
HN2755 Captain, 2nd New York
            Regiment, 1775 (limited to
            350)   1976–present Brown and blue uniform.

HN2756–2758	Not issued	
HN2760	Private, Massachusetts Regiment, 1778 (limited to 350)	1977–present White uniform.
HN2761	Private, Delaware Regiment, 1776 (limited to 350)	1977–present Blue, white, red uniform.
HN2762	Lovers	1978–present White. See HN 2763.
HN2763	Lovers	1978–present Black. See HN 2762.
HN2764–2778	Not issued	
HN2779	Private, 1st Georgia Regiment, 1777 (limited to 350)	1975–present Olive green uniform.
HN2780	Corporal, 1st New Hampshire Regiment, 1778 (limited to 350)	1975–present Gray-green and red uniform.
HN2781–2787	Not issued	
HN2788	Marjorie	1980–present White skirt, blue top.
HN2789	Kate	1978–present White dress.
HN2790	Not issued	
2791	Elaine	1980–present Blue dress.
HN2792	Christine	1978–present Blue flowered overdress.
HN2793	Clare	1980–present Pale blue print dress, yellow shawl.
HN2794	Not issued	
HN2795	French Horn (limited to 750)	1976–1978 Purple overdress.
HN2796	Hurdy Gurdy (limited to 750)	1975–1978 Blue overdress.
HN2797	Viola d'Amore (limited to 750)	1976–1978 Pale blue flowered overdress.
HN2798	Dulcimer (limited to 750)	1975–1978 Pink overdress.
HN2799	Ruth	1976–present Olive green dress.
HN2800	Carrie	1976–present Blue coat.
HN2801	Lori	1976–present White dress.
HN2802	Anna	1976–present Purple dress, white apron.
HN2803	First Dance	1977–present White dress.
HN2804	Not issued	
HN2805	Rebecca	1980–present
HN2806	Not issued	
HN2807	Stephanie	1977–present Dark yellow dress.
HN2808–2809	Not issued	
HN2810	Solitude	1977–present White dress, multicolored flowers.
HN2811–2813	Not issued	
HN2814	Eventide	1977–present Pale blue dress.

HN2815	Sergeant, 6th Maryland Regiment, 1777 (limited to 350)	1976–present White uniform, green and red trim.
HN2816	Votes for Women	1978–present Rust coat.
HN2817–2823	Not issued	
HN2824	Harmony	1978–present Gray dress.
HN2825–2829	Not issued	
HN2830	Indian Temple Dancer (limited to 750)	1977–present Yellow sari.
HN2831	Spanish Flamenco Dancer (limited to 750)	1977–present Red and white dress.
HN2832	Fair Lady	1977–present Red dress. See HN 2193.
HN2833	Sophie	1977–present Pink dress, white apron.
HN2834	Emma	1977–present Pink dress, white apron.
HN2835	Fair Lady	1977–present Orange dress. See HN 2193.
HN2836	Not issued	
HN2837	Awakening	1980–present Black. See HN2875.
HN2838	Sympathy	1980–present Black. See HN 2876.
HN2839	Nicola	1978–present Lavender dress, yellow flowers.
HN2840	Not issued	
HN2841	Mother and Daughter	1980–present White. See HN 2843.
HN2842	Innocence	1979–present Red dress.
HN2843	Mother and Daughter (black)	1980–present Black. See HN2841.
HN2844	Sergeant, Virginia 1st Regiment Continental Light Dragoons, 1779 (limited to 350)	1978–present Brown horse, brown and green uniform.
HN2845	Private, Connecticut Regiment 1777 (limited to 350)	1978–present Brown and beige uniform.
HN2846	Private, Pennsylvania Rifle Battalion 1776 (limited to 350)	1978–present Gray buckskin.
HN2847–2850	Not issued	
HN2851	Christmas Parcels	1978–present Dark green dress.
HN2852–2854	Not issued	
HN2855	Embroidering	1980–present
HN2856	St. George	1978–present White horse, gray armor.
HN2857	Not issued	
HN2858	Doctor, The	1979–present Blue suit, black jacket.
HN2859–2860	Not issued	
HN2861	George Washington at Prayer (limited to 750)	1977 Blue and beige uniform, red-lined cape.

HN2862	First Waltz	1979–present Red dress, blue pattern.
HN2863	Not issued	
HN2864	Tom	1978–present Cream shirt, blue trousers.
HN2865	Tess	1978–present Green dress.
HN2866–2870	Not issued	
HN2871	Beat You To It	1980–present White dress, yellow sleeves.
HN2872	Young Master, The	1980–present Blue pants, burgundy jacket.
HN2873	Bride	1980–present White dress.
HN2874	Bridesmaid	1980–present White dress.
HN2875	Awakening	1980–present White. See HN 2837.
HN2876	Sympathy	1980–present White. See HN 2838.
HN2877	Wizard	1979–present Blue cloak.
HN2878–2879	Not issued	
HN2880	Paula	1980–present Yellow-green dress, dark green trim.
HN2881–2889	Not issued	
HN2890	Clown	1979–present Blue pants, tan jacket.
HN2891	Not issued	
HN2892	Chief	1979–present Burnt orange costume.
HN2893–2897	Not issued	
HN2898	Ko-Ko	1980–present Yellow kimono, black and green design, blue jacket.
HN2899	Yum-Yum	1980–present Green kimono, yellow triangles.
HN2900–2906	Not issued	
HN2907	Piper	1980–present Blue plaid kilt, white shirt.
HN2908–2910	Not issued	
HN2911	Gandalf	1980–present Blue cloak.
HN2912	Frodo	1980–present Navy blue shorts and vest.
HN2913	Gollum	1980–present Green.
HN2914	Bilbo	1980–present Brown shorts, beige vest.
HN2915	Galadriel	1980–present Ivory dress.
HN2916	Aragorn	1980–present Tan costume.

CHARACTER JUGS

Anne Boleyn   1974–present
L – D6644

Apothecary   1961–present
L – D6567
M – D6581
S – D6574

Aramis   1955–present
L – D6441
M – D6508
S – D6454

'Ard of Earing **L – D6588** **M – D6594** **S – D6591**	**1963–1967**	
'Arriet **L – D6208** **M – D6250** **S – D6236** **T – D6256**	**1946–1960**	**Color change in 1951.**
'Arry **L – D6207** **M – D6249** **S – D6235** **T – D6255**	**1946–1960**	**Color change in 1951.**
Athos **L – D6439** **M – D6509** **S – D6452**	**1955–present**	
Auld Mac	**1937–present**	**Titled "Owd Mac" between 1938 and 1945.**
L – D5823 **M – D6253** **S – D5824** **T – D6257**	**1946–present** **1946–1960**	
Bacchus **L – D6499** **M – D6521** **S – D6505**	**1958–present**	
Baseball Player		**Experimental**
Beefeater	**1946–present**	**Royal cypher GR (George Rex) on the handle was changed in 1953 to ER (Elizabeth Regina).**
L – D6206 **M – D 6251** **S – D 6233**		
Blacksmith **L – D6571** **M – D6585** **S – D6578**	**1961–present**	
Bootmaker **L – D6572** **M – D6586** **S – D6579**	**1961–present**	
Buffalo Bill		**Experimental**

Captain Ahab   1958–present
L – D6500
M – D6522
S – D6506

Cap'n Cuttle   1937–1949   Original size was 4½ inches; in 1949 it
                                    was scaled down.

Special Size D5842
S – D5842   1947–1960

Captain Henry Morgan   1957–present
L – D6467
M – D6510   1959–present
S – D6469

Captain Hook   1964–1970
L – D6597
M – D6605
S – D6601

Cardinal
L – D5614   1935–1960
M – D6129   1939–1960
S – D6033   1938–1960
T – D6258   1946–1960

Catherine Howard   1977–present
L – D6645

Catherine of Aragon   1974–present
L – D6643

Cavalier
L – D6114   1939–1960   In 1950 color was changed, the collar
S – D6173   1940–1960   was altered, and his goatee was
                                    removed.

Clown (red hair)   1936–1942
L – D5610

Clown (white hair)   1950–1955
L – D6322

**Dick Turpin (gun
   handle)**
L – D5485   1934–1960
M – D6128   1934–1960
S – D5618   1935–1960

**Dick Turpin (horse
   handle and masked)**   1959–present
L – D6528
M – D6542
S – D6535

Dick Whittington   1952–1960
L – D6375

Don Quixote **L – D6455** **M – D6511** **S – D6460**	1956–present	
Drake **L – D6115** **S – D6174**	1939–1960	**Color was changed in 1950, and an earlier version shows him without a hat and with a pair of earrings.**
Falconer **L – D6533** **M – D6547** **S – D6540**	1959–present	
Falstaff **L – D6287** **M – D6519** **S – D6385**	1949–present 1959–present	
Farmer John **L – D5788** **S – D5789**	1937–1960	
Fat Boy **Special Size D5840** **M – D6139** **T – D6142** **S – D5840**	 1937–1949 1939–1960 1939–1960 1947–1960	**Original size was 4½ inches; in 1949 it was scaled down.**
Field Marshall Smuts **L – D6198**	1945–1948	
Fortune Teller **L – D6497** **M – D6523** **S – D6503**	 1958–1967 1960–1967 1958–1967	
Friar Tuck **L – D6321**	1950–1960	
Gaoler **L – D6570** **M – D6584** **S – D6577**	1961–present	
Gardener **L – D6630** **M – D6638** **S – D6634**	1972–present	
Gladiator **L – D6550** **M – D6556** **S – D6553**	1960–1967	

Golfer L – D6623	1970–present	
Gondolier L – D6589 M – D6595 S – D6592	1963–1969	
Gone Away L – D6531 M – D6545 S – D6538	1960–present	
Granny L – D5521 M – D6520 S – D6384	1934–present 1959–present 1952–present	In 1952 version was changed from toothless to one front tooth.
Guardsman L – D6568 M – D6582 S – D6575	1961–present	
Gulliver L – D6560 M – D6566 S – D6563	1961–1967	
Gunsmith L – D6573 M – D6587 S – D6580	1962–present	
Henry VIII L – D6642 M – D6648 S – D6647	1974–present 1979–present 1979–present	
Issac Walton L – D6404	1953–present	
Jane Seymour L – D6646	1979–present	
Jarge L – D6288 S – D6295	1949–1960	
Jester S – D5556	1935–1960	
Jockey L – D6625	1970–1975	

John Barleycorn

L – D5327	1933–1960	Early versions show different handle.
M – D6041	1938–1960	In 1978 a reissue of limited editions
S – D5735	1936–1960	was made.

John Peel

L – D5612	1935–1960
M – D6130	1939–1960
S – D5731	1936–1960
T – D6259	1946–1960

Johnny Appleseed 1952–1968
L – D6372

Lawyer

L – D6498	1958–present
M – D6524	1960–present
S – D6504	1958–present

Lobster Man 1967–present
L – D6617
S – D6620

Long John Silver

L – D6335	1951–present
M – D6512	1960–present
S – D6386	1951–present

Lord Nelson 1957–1968
L – D6336

Lumberjack 1966–present
L – D6610
S – D6613

McCallum 1930s Kingsware

Mad Hatter 1964–present
L – D6598
M – D6606
S – D6602

Maori Experimental

Mephistopheles 1936–1948
L – D5757
S – D5758

Merlin 1959–present
L – D6529
M – D6543
S – D6536

Mikado
L – D6501 1958–1968

M – D6525   1960–1968
S – D6507   1958–1968

Mine Host
L – D6468   1957–present
M – D6513   1960–present
S – D6470   1957–present

Monty   1945–present   **Color was changed in 1954.**
L – D6202

Mr. Micawber
Special Size D5843   1937–1949   **Original size was 4½ inches; in 1949 it**
M – D6138   1939–1960   **was scaled down.**
S – D5843   1947–1960
T – D6143   1939–1960

Mr. Pickwick
Special Size D5839   1939–1949   **Original size was 4½ inches; in 1949 it**
L – D6060   1939–1960   **was scaled down.**
M – D6254   1939–1960
S – D5839   1947–1960
T – D6260   1947–1960

Neptune   1960–present
L – D6548
M – D6555
S – D6552

Night Watchman   1961–present
L – D6559
M – D6583
S – D6576

North American Indian   1966–present
L – D6611
S – D6614

Old Charley
L – D5420   1933–present
M – D6046   1938–present
S – D5527   1933–present
T – D6144   1939–1960

Old King Cole   1938–1960   **Earlier versions show yellow crown.**
L – D6036
S – D6037

Old Salt   1960–present
L – D6551
S – D6554

Paddy
L – D5753   1936–1960

M – D6042   1938–1960
S – D5768   1936–1960
T – D6145   1939–1960

Parson Brown   1934–1960
L – D5486
S – D5529

Pied Piper
L – D6403   1953–present
M – D6514   1959–present
S – D6462   1956–present

Poacher
L – D6429   1954–present
M – D6515   1959–present
S – D6464   1956–present

Porthos
L – D6440   1955–present
M – D6516   1959–present
S – D6453   1955–present

Punch and Judy Man   1963–1968
L – D6590
M – D6596
S – D6593

Regency Beau   1961-1967
L – D6559
M – D6565
S – D6562

Rip Van Winkle
L – D6438   1954–present
M – D6517   1959–present
S – D6463   1956–present

Robin Hood (plain
   handle)   1946–1960
L – D6205
M – D6252
S – D6234

Robin Hood (bow
   handle)   1959–present
L – D6527
M – D6541
S – D6534

Robinson Crusoe   1959–present
L – D6532
M – D6546
S – D6539

St. George
L – D6618
S – D6621   **1967–1975**

Sairey Gamp
L – D5451	**1934–present**
M – D6045	**1938–present**
S – D5528	**1934–present**
T – D6146	**1939–1960**

Samuel Johnson   **1949–1960**
L – D6289
S – D6296

Sam Weller
Special Size D5841	**1939–1949**
L – D6064	**1939–1960**
M – D6140	**1939–1960**
S – D5841	**1947–1960**
T – D6147	**1939–1960**

Sancho Panza
L – D6456	**1956–present**
M – D6518	**1959–present**
S – D6461	**1956–present**

Scaramouche   **1961–1967**
L – D6558
M – D6564
S – D6561

Sergeant Buz Fuz
Special Size D5838	**1937–1949**	**Original size was 4½inches; in 1949 it**
S – D5838	**1947–1960**	**was scaled down.**

Simon the Cellarer   **1934–1960**
L – D5504
S – D5616   **1935–1960**

Simple Simon   **1952–1960**
L – D6374

Sir Winston Churchill   **1940–1941**
L – D6170

Sleuth   **1972–present**
L – D6631
M – D6639
S – D6635

Smuggler   **1967–present**
L – D6616
S – D6619

Toby Philpots   **1936–1969**
L – D5736
M – D6043   **1938–1969**
S – D5737

Tom O'Shanter   **1972–present**
L – D6632
M – D6640
S – D6636

Tony Weller   **1935–1960**
L – D5531
M – D6044   **1938–1960**
S – D5530

Touchstone   **1935–1960**
L – D5613

Town Crier   **1959–1973**
L – D6530
M – D6544
S – D6537

Trapper   **1966–present**
L – D6609
S – D6612

Ugly Duchess   **1964–1973**
L – D6599
M – D6607
S – D6603

Uncle Tom Cobbleigh   **1951–1960**
L – D6337

Veteran Motorist   **1972–present**
L – D6633
M – D6641
S – D6637

Vicar of Bray   **1935–1960**
L – D5615

Viking   **1958–1975**
L – D6496
M – D6526   **1959–1975**
S – D6502

Walrus and Carpenter   **1964–present**
L – D6600
M – D6608
S – D6604

Yachtsman   **1970–present**
L – D6622

SERIES WARES

*Indicates this series is not included in this price list.

Information about the series wares is still incomplete. We have been receiving reports about different pieces from all parts of the world. To help in the collecting and to be able to continue our research of the series wares we are including a list of reported pieces, series designs, dates, and so forth.

We know that there are some errors and omissions in our list, but it is a start. We always welcome all comments, and if you can add anything to our list, please let us hear from you. Write to Kovel, c/o Crown Publishers, Inc., One Park Avenue, New York, New York 10016. If it is possible, please include a photograph or a photocopy of any patterns or marks.

Alice in Wonderland is a child's set. Titles and scene on plate. Known pieces: cup and saucer, mush and milk set (bowl, milk pitcher, and plate), plate, and tumbler. Known patterns: "Alice and the Catepillar," "Alice and the Duchess," "Doormouse," "King," "Mad Hatter," and "Mock Turtle."

* *All Black Cricketeers* depicts black children playing cricket. Made about 1915. Known pieces: nursery set (plate, mug, and bowl), tumbler, and vases. Pictured in 1915 Doulton Burslem catalog.

* *Arabian Knights.* Known pieces: pitcher, 8-inch and 10½-inch plates. Known pattern: "Arrival of the Unknown Princess."

Babes in Woods. Flow blue transfer and black painted decoration. Marked with Royal Doulton mark in either green or brown. Some pieces have gold handles. Known pieces: bowl, cup, 10-inch jardinere, 5-inch and 9-inch pitchers, 7½ by 9½-inch plaque, several sizes of plates, 11 by 13-inch platter, sauce bowl, 5 ¾-inch and 6½-inch saucers, soup bowl, vases, and vegetable bowl. Probably a full dinner set with serving pieces.

Bayeux Tapestry. First made in earthenware in 1906. Known pieces: 8½- inch bowl, candlestick, creamer and sugar, 6-inch and 7-inch pitchers, 10½-inch plate, and tobacco jar.

Bobby Burns. A piece dated 1926 is known. Known pieces: 8-inch and 9½-inch bowls, mug, and 6½-inch, 10½-inch, and 12-inch plates.

Bunnykins was designed by Barbara Vernon, a nun from a Sussex convent.

Canterbury Pilgrims. Known pieces: cup and saucer, milk pitcher, pin tray, 7½-inch and 8-inch pitchers, 10½-inch plate, and 3-inch vase. Another set has been seen in pastel colors with a different border.

* *Cathedrals.* Name appeared in early articles about series ware. Not positively identified. Made in 1920s. Probable pieces: 11½-inch bowl, "Tintern Abbey"; 5-inch pitcher, "Croyden Church"; 10½-inch plate, "Salisbury Cathedral"; and 11½-inch plate, "Tintern Abbey."

Cavaliers. Known pieces: ice cream tray, 8-inch plate, tankard, and tobacco jar.

Character Plates. Newly released series first made in 1979. Each plate pictures a figurine.

Coaching Days. Known pieces: full dinner and luncheon sets and many other pieces, such as: hair receiver, milk and mush set, punch bowl, and tobacco jar.

Coaching Days in Old England. Known pieces: pitcher and plate. Known characters depicted on plate: The Coachman, Old Bob Ye Guard, Old Jarvie, and William Ye Driver.

* *Countryside.* Name used by several dealers. May or may not be an actual series. Plates depict a scenic landscape.

David Teniers Flemish Paintings. Made about 1910. Known pieces: pitcher and plates. Known patterns: "Five Senses," "Meeting of the Civic Guards," "The Village Fete," "The Prodigal Son," and "Topers."

Desert Scenes. Known pieces: full dinner and luncheon sets and many other pieces, such as: ashtray, bowl, nappy, pitcher, plate, spittoon, sugar, and vase.

Dickens Ware.

Don Quixote. Known pieces: 9-inch pitcher, 7½-inch triangular pitcher, and 10-inch and 10½-inch plates.

Dutch. Made in either earthenware or bone china. Known pieces: beaker, cookie jar, 5½-inch pitcher, teapot, tobacco jar, toothpick, 5-inch and 7-inch vases.

* *Dutch Interior Scenes* is possibly a series based on David Teniers paintings. We have seen a tan plate, black design, with a mark on the back of a ribbon and a man's portrait. The ribbon says, "Sketches from Teniers."

Eglinton Tournament. Known pieces: creamer, 7-inch jug, 5½-inch pitcher, 9½-inch and 10-inch plates, and teapot.

Egyptian Tour. Known piece: 10-inch plate.

English Old Proverbs. Known pieces: plates. Known patterns: "Count Not Your Chickens," "Fine Feathers Make Fine Birds," and "Handsome Is That Handsome Does."

English Old Scenes. Known pieces: 8½-inch bowl, 7-inch pitcher, 13-inch plaque, 10-inch and 12-inch plates, square salad plate, and 6½-inch vase.

Fairy Tales. Known pieces: cup, mug, pitchers, plates, and tobacco jar. Known stories: "Gulliver," "Pied Piper," and "Rip Van Winkle."

Falconry. Known piece: plate.

Famous Ships. Known pieces: creamer, 5½-inch pitcher, and 10-inch plate. Known ships: *The Acorn, The Hydra, HMS Victory,* and *The Revenge.*

*Flower Sellers. Ladies sitting and selling flowers on a cobblestone street. May be recent name used by dealer, not by Doulton. Known piece: ashtray.

Fox-Hunting. Some pieces are marked, "Geo. Moreland pinxit 1784." George Moreland was an English painter of hunting scenes. Known pieces: beaker, 4-inch butter dish, creamer and sugar, mug, 10-inch plate, punch set, 6-inch salad plate, soup and under plate, and tumbler. Probably a full dinner set was made.

Gaffers. Known pieces: 9½ by 2-inch bowl, creamer and sugar, cup and saucer, 6-inch milk jug, 4½-inch, 5½-inch, 6½-inch, 9-inch, and 10½-inch plates, and a three-piece tea set. Known patterns: "All the Way from Zummerset" and "Zunday Zmocks." Probably made a full dinner set.

Gallant Fishers. Known pieces: 5-inch jug, plate, and 12-inch tray. Known patterns: "And When the Timerous Trout," "Of Recreation There Is None So Free as Fishing Alone," and "The Gallant Fishers Life It Is the Best."

*Galleon has Doulton Burslem mark and a special mark. Series made about 1924. Pictures sailing ships and has a seashell border. Known piece: 7-inch pitcher.

Gibson Girl plates were ordered and distributed by George F. Bassett & Co. of New York in 1901. Another set of twelve 9-inch plates pictures the head of the Gibson Girl in blue; these were *not* made by Royal Doulton. The 10½-inch plates were marked with the Royal Doulton lion and crown trademark. Known patterns: "A Message from the Outside World," "A Quiet Dinner with Dr. Bottles and He Reads Miss Babbles' Book," "And Here Winning New Friends," "Day after Arriving at Journey's End," "Failing to Find Rest and Quiet in the Country She Decided to Return Home," "Miss Babbles Brings a Copy of the Morning Paper with a Scurrilous Article," "Miss Babbles, the Authoress, Calls and Reads Aloud," "Mr. Waddles Arrives Late and Finds Her Cards Filled," "Mrs. Diggs Is Alarmed for the Safety of Child," "She Becomes a Trained Nurse," "She Contemplates the Cloister," "She Decides to Die in Spite of Dr. Bottles," "She Finds Some Consolation in Her Mirror," "She Goes into Colors," "She Goes to the Fancy Dress Ball as Juliet" "She Is Disturbed by a Vision," "She Is the Subject of More Hostile Criticism," "She Looks for Relief among the Old Ones," "She Longs for Seclusion," "Some Think She Has Remained in Retirement Too Long," "They All Go Fishing," "They All Go Skating," and "They Take a Morning Run."

Golfing. Known pieces: 6½-inch and 9¼-inch bowls, 6-inch mug, 5¼-inch pitcher, 10½-inch plate, and tobacco jar. Known patterns: "Every Dog Has His Day, Every Man His Hour," "He Hath a Good Judgement Who Reliath Not Wholly on His Own," "He That Always Complains Is Never Pitied," and "Nothing Venture, Nothing Win."

Gondoliers. Known pieces: creamer and sugar, 8-inch pitcher, 8½-inch plate, and vase.

Historical Britain. Translucent china. Known pieces: lighter, pin tray, and plate. Known patterns: "Anne Hathaway's Cottage, Shottery, North Stratford-On-Avon," "Clovelly, North Devon," "The Houses of Parliament, London," "The Tower of London," and "Tudor Mansion, Little Moreton Hall, Cheshire."

Historic Characters. Known patterns: "Forbisher" and "Sir Walter Raleigh." The same ship border appears on a plate called "Battle of Trafalgar."

Historic England. Known pieces: 9¼-inch bowl, 14-inch charger, 13-inch plaque, 10-inch plate, 5¼ by 6½-inch platter, and teapot. Known patterns: "Dr. Johnson at Cheshire Cheese," "Dr. Johnson at Temple Bar," "Dick Turpin at Sootham Bar," "Henry the VIII at Hampton Court," "Queen Elizabeth at Kenilworth Castle," and "Sir Frances Drake at Plymouth Hoe."

Isaac Walton. Known pieces: 6 by 5½-inch biscuit barrel, 8-inch bowl, 7-inch candle holder, 5-inch, 6-inch, 7-inch, and 10-inch pitchers, 9½-inch and 10-inch plates, trivet, 5¼-inch tumbler, and 10-inch and 13-inch vases. Known patterns: "Behold the Fisherman," "But Yet Though while I Fish," "I Care Not I to Fish in Seas, Fresh Rivers Best My Mind Do Please," "My Hand Alone My Work Can Do So I Can Fish and Study Too," "O the Gallant Fishers Life It Is the Best as Any," "Of Recreation There Is None So Free as Fishing Is Alone," "Perch or Pike Roach or Dace We Do Chase," and "Where in a Brook with a Hook or a Lake Fish We Take."

Jackdaw of Rheims. Made of bone china or earthenware. Known pieces: 10-inch bowl, 8½-inch square bowl, creamer, cup and saucer, humidor, 4-inch platter, sugar, tea tile, 5⅜-inch, 6-inch, 8½-inch, and 8¾-inch vases. Known patterns: "And Off That Terrible Curse He Took," "He Solemnly Cursed That Rascally Thief," "So They Canonized Him by the Name of Jim Crow," "The Cardinal Drew Off Each Plum Colored Shoe," and "The Cardinal Lord Archbishop at Rheims."

*Jessopeak Pressgang series was made from 1906 to 1914. Known patterns: "The Men Being Pressganged (forced into service on ships)," "The Sailors Working," and "The Tavern Celebration."

King Arthur's Knights. Known piece: 10-inch plate. Known pattern: "Lancelot."

May Day Children. Known pieces: mush and milk three-piece set or breakfast set (bowl, milk pitcher, and plate) and 10½-inch plate.

Monks. humorous series. Known piece: 11½-inch vase.

Monks green and tan series. Known pieces: 5½-inch mug, mustard pot, and 6½-inch and 10-inch plates.

Monks blue and tan series. Known pieces: 7½-inch and 10-inch plates and 6-inch vase.

Motor series. Known pieces: 12 by 16-inch bowl, cuspidor, 5-inch, 6½-inch, and 7¼-inch pitchers, 14½-inch pitcher and mug set (chocolate set), 9-inch, 10-inch, and 14-inch plates, soup plate, tobacco pot, 9¼-inch vase, and a report of a large platter that was broken. Known patterns: "After the Run," "A Horse! A Horse!" "A Nerve Tonic," "Blood Money," "Deaf," "Itch Yer On Governor," "Room for One," and "The New and the Old." Also scenes without titles. Although it appears a dinner set was made, there has been no creamer and sugar seen by a man who has collected this pattern for 25 years.

Munchkins. Plate seen with 1885–1902 mark. Known pieces: 9-inch bowl, 6-inch and 10¼-inch and 6-inch vase.

Night Watchman. Possibly made in 1902. Known pieces: 8-inch bowl, creamer and sugar,

7-inch, 8-inch, and 8½-inch jugs, 10-inch plate, tankard, and two-piece washstand. Known pattern: "What of the Night."

Nursery Rhymes. Designed by Savage Cooper. Known pieces: 5-inch and 6-inch bowls, box, cup and saucer, mug, pitcher, 6-inch, 7-inch, and 8-inch plates, and 2½-inch vase.

Old English Inns. Known pieces: 8-inch, 10-inch, 10½-inch and 11½-inch bowls, and 5 by 8-inch tray. Known patterns: "The Boar's Head, Breton," "Crab Inn," "Leather Bottle," and "The Talbot, Chaddesley Corbett."

Old Sea Dogs. Known pieces: pitcher and 7½-inch vase. Known patterns: "Jack's the Lad for Work" and "They All Love Jack."

Polar Bear. Known pieces: creamer, sugar, and syrup.

Proverbs. Known pieces: 10-inch plates. Known patterns: "A Bird in the Hand Is Worth Two in the Bush/Nothing Venture Nothing Have" and "Happy Is the Wooing That's No Longer in the Doing/Marry in Haste Repent at Leisure."

Queen Elizabeth at Old Moreton Hall. Known pieces: 6½ by 8-inch bowl, creamer, 4-inch and 5-inch pitchers, 6½-inch, 8-inch, 10-inch, and 10½-inch plates, 17 by 8-inch platter, soup bowl, sugar, tankard, and tea set.

Reynard the Fox. Known pieces: coffee set (coffee pot, creamer and sugar, demitasse cups, and covered hot-milk pitcher).

Rustic England. Known pieces: 10-inch plate and square plate. Known pattern: "Thatcher Cottage."

*Sailing Vessels. Known pieces: 12-inch bowl, 13-inch charger, creamer, planter, 8-inch, 8½-inch, 10-inch, and 10½-inch plates, and vase. Known patterns: "Sailing Ships" and "Whale Boats with Sails."

Sayings Wares. Known pieces: 10-inch and 10½-inch plates, teapot, and 4-inch vase. Known patterns: "A Good Cup of Tea/The Cup That Cheers," "A Merry Heart," "Bread at Pleasure," and "Heart's Content." Some pieces have no sayings.

Shakespeare Characters in pastel. Known pieces: hair receiver, hat-pin holder, full luncheon and dinner set, and vase. Known characters depicted on wares: "Anne Page," "Falstaff," "Hamlet," "Juliet," "Katharine," "Ophelia," "Orlando," "Portia," "Romeo," "Rosalind," "Shylock," and "Cardinal Wolsey."

Shakespere Characters on cobblestone street. Known pieces: 10-inch plates. Known characters depicted on wares: "Falstaff" and "Sir Andrew Aguecheek."

Shakespeare in flow blue. Known piece: 10-inch plate. Known pattern: "As You Like It."

Shakespeare Plays. 1907 cream-colored plate, *Midsummer Night's Dream.* Known pieces: 2-inch, 4¼-inch, 5-inch, and 7-inch pitchers, 9½-inch, 10-inch, 10½-inch, and 14-inch plates, salt and pepper, 5¾-inch jug, teapot, and tea tile. Known plays depicted on wares: *Hamlet, Henry VI, MacBeth, Merchant of Venice, Merry Wives of Windsor, Midsummer Night's Dream, Much Ado about Nothing, Romeo and Juliet,* and *Twelfth Night.*

*Shakespeare's Country. Described as a set of twelve 10¼-inch plates titled on reverse.

Sir Roger de Coverley. Known pieces: seven-piece berry set, creamer, demitasse set, feeding dish, 2-inch jug, 4-inch pitcher, 10-inch and 10½-inch plates, teapot, and 7½-inch vase. Known patterns: "Ballroom Scene," "Horse Grooming," "Man and Woman in House," and "The Widow."

Under the Greenwood Tree. Known pieces: ashtray, berry set, 6-inch and 6½-inch bowls, 12½-inch bread plate, 15-inch charger, chocolate pot, cigarette box, 3¾-inch creamer, cup, 9-inch two-handled cup, dresser tray, 8-inch mug, 4½-inch, 6-inch, and 6¾-inch pitchers, pin tray, plaque, 7-inch, 8¾-inch, and 10-inch plates, teapot, tea tile, toothpick holder, 6 by 7¾-inch tray, and 8½-inch vase. Probably full dinner and luncheon sets were made. Known patterns: "Alan-a-Dale," "Friar Tuck Joins Robin Hood," "Friar Tuck," "Life in Sherwood Forest," "Robin Hood and Little John," "Robin Hood and Maid Marion," "Robin Hood Fights with Friar Tuck," "Robin Hood Friend of the Poor," "Robin Hood Kneeling before King Arthur," "Robin Hood Slays Guy Gisborne," and "Will Scarlett."

* Viking Ships. Reported humidor and a 7½-inch jug with blue decoration. No other information.

Welsh Ladies. Known pieces: 9¾-inch berry bowl, 3-inch round bowl with silver top, 6½-inch square candlestick, creamer and sugar, cup and saucer, 2-inch and 4½-inch jugs, match holder, 5¼-inch and 6-inch milk jugs, 1¾-inch, 2-inch, 2½-inch, and 8¾-inch pitchers, 3¾-inch, 5-inch, 9-inch, and 10¾-inch plates, tea tile, toothpick holder, and 2½-inch, 2¾-inch, 3-inch, 3½-inch, 4¼-inch, 4½-inch, 5¾-inch, and 8¾-inch vases. Probably a full dinner set was made.

DICKENS WARE KNOWN PIECES

Ash Bowl
Ash Pot
Ashtray
Asparagus Dish
Biscuit Barrel
Biscuit Jar
Bowl (various sizes)
Brandy Keg
Bread Plate
Bulb Bowl
Butter Pat
Candlestick
Candy Dish
Coffeepot
Compote
Covered Box
Covered Jar
Creamer

Cream Soup Bowl
Cup and Saucer (coffee, tea, and demitasse)
Fruit Bowl
Hair Receiver
Hat-Pin Stand
Hot Plate
Humidor
Jardiniere
Match Stand
Milk Jug
Mug
Mustard Pot
Oatmeal Saucer
Oval Platter
Oval Vegetable Dish
Pitcher
Plate (round and square, various sizes)
Porridge Plate
Salad Bowl
Soap Dish
Sugar Bowl
Sugar Shaker
Tankard
Tea Caddy
Teapot
Tobacco Jar
Toothbrush Holder
Toothpick
Tray (round, square, and rectangular)
Trivet
Tumbler
Tureen
Vase (various sizes and shapes)
Wall Plaque
Wash Set

DICKENS WARE KNOWN PATTERNS

Alfred Jingle (*Pickwick Papers*)
Artful Dodger (*Oliver Twist*)
Bardell, Mrs. (*Pickwick Papers*)
Barkis (*David Copperfield*)
Barnaby Rudge (*Barnaby Rudge*)
Bill Sykes (*Oliver Twist*)
Bumble, Mr. (*Oliver Twist*)
Buz Fuz, Sgt. (*Pickwick Papers*)
Cap'n Cuttle (*Dombey and Son*)

Chandband, Rev. (*Bleak House*)
David Copperfield (*David Copperfield*)
Dick Sullivan
Dick Swiveller (*Old Curiosity Shop*)
Dodson, Mr. (*Pickwick Papers*)
Fagin (*Oliver Twist*)
Fat Boy (*Pickwick Papers*)
Little Nell (*Old Curiosity Shop*)
Mark Tapley (*Martin Chuzzlewit*)

Micawber, Mr. (*David Copperfield*)
Old Charley
Old Peggotty (*David Copperfield*)
Oliver (*Oliver Twist*)
Pecksniff, Mr. (*Martin Chuzzlewit*)
Pickwick, Mr. (*Pickwick Papers*)
Poor Jo (*Bleak House*)
Sairey Gamp (*Martin Chuzzlewit*)
Sam Weller (*Pickwick Papers*)

Scrooge (*Christmas Carol*)
Sidney Carton (*Tale of Two Cities*)
Squeers, Mr. (*Nicholas Nickleby*)
Stiggins (*Pickwick Papers*)
Toby Philpot
Tom Pinch (*Pickwick Papers*)
Tony Weller (*Pickwick Papers*)
Trotty Veck (*The Chimes*)
Uriah Heep (*David Copperfield*)

"HEAD" RACK PLATES

	D Number
Admiral	6278
Bobby Burns	6344
Bookworm	—
Cobbler	6302
Dickens	6306
Doctor	6281
Drake	—
Falconer	6279
Hunting Man	6282
Jester	6277
Mayor	6283
Parson	6280
Shakespeare	6303
Squire	6284
Town Crier	—

SCENIC PLATES

	D Number
Aborigines with Hunting Weapons	6421
African Elephants	6481
Australian Aborigine	6422
Balmoral Castle	—
Bow Falls (Canada)	6471
Bow Valley (Canada)	6475
Castle	6308
Edinburgh Castle	—
Giraffes	6482
Koala Bears	6424
Lake Louise and Victoria Glacier (Canada)	6474
Lion	6359
Lioness	6360

Loch Lomond	—
Maori Girls	6305
Maritime Provinces (Canada)	6493
Montmorency Falls (Canada)	6472
Mother Kangaroo with Joey	6423
Mount Egmont (Canada)	6436
Murray River Gums (Canada)	6425
New Guinea Native	6437
Niagara Falls (Canada)	6475
Queen's View, Loch Tummel	—
Timber Wagon	6307
Vermilion Lake and Mount Rundle (Canada)	6473
Waterbuck	6484
Young Kookaburras	6426
Zulu Girl at Water Hole	6363
Zulu Warrior	6364

Some pieces of series wares have been reported to us and for various reasons have presented problems as yet unsolved. The following list is included so that you may help sort out the series wares for future editions of this book. If you have any of these plates or know anything about these wares, please let us know. A photocopy or a photograph of the piece and the mark would help.

Mottos Found on Plates

"Old Woman Wither so High"
"When I last saw him he was a venerable Old Man"
"Come Landlord fill the flowing"
"Now I have my sheep"
"Everybody bid me good-morrow"
"The pleasure of doing good"
"As the wind slows down set your sails"

Motto Found on Pitcher

"Doc Berry"

Possible Series Designs Found on Plates. (Some of these may be dinnerware patterns.)

Old man and the sea, plate.
The complete angler, clock of old St. Dunstan's Church, plate.
Harvest scene and castle, plate.
Lambs in meadow and castle, plate.
Castle and large tree, marked on back "Cawder Castle," plate.
Castle and pastoral scene, plate.
Heads of dogs based on drawings by Cecil Aldin, plate.
Ivanhoe scenes, plate.
Head of Indian, titled "Hiawatha," tepee border, plate.
Egyptian figures, titled "Egyptian Pottery," plate.

Yellow with black silhouette of horses and tree, plate.

Scene with house, brown road, red roof, green tree, numbered D2647, plate.

Blue and white, marked, "The Geo M Bowman Co/Sole Importers/Cleveland." Front pictures buildings in Washington. The U.S. Capitol and the Congressional Library are known, plate.

Brown sailing ships, blue sky and water, black border, black handle, numbered D2872, pitcher.

Pewter-colored border, design of trees in dull gray, green, and red, two different designs are known, plates.

Sepia decoration with pictures and an inscription, "Sir George Summers "Wrecked on the Island 1609," border of town views, plate.

Seascape, marked "Home Waters," numbered D6434, oval dish.

Roman processional, Doulton Burslem mark, plate.

TOBY JUGS, COMPLETE LIST

D. Numbers

Best Is Not Too Good	6107	4½ in.	1939–1960	
Cap'n Cuttle	6266	4½ in.	1948–1960	
Charrington Toby	—	9¼ in.	1954	Two were made: Toby Ales and One Toby Leads to Another.
Cliff Cornell	—	5½ 9 in.	1956	
Double XX	6088	6½ in.	1939–1969	
Falstaff	6063	5¼ in.	1939–present	
Falstaff	6062	8½ in.	1939–present	
Fat Boy	6264	4½ in.	1948–1960	
George Robey	—	10½ in.	1910	
Happy John	6070	5½ in.	1939–present	
Happy John	6031	9 in.	1939–present	
Hoare	—		1930s	
Honest Measure	6108	4½ in.	1939–present	
Huntsman	6320	7½ in.	1950–present	
Jolly Toby	6109	6½ in.	1939–present	
Mr. Micawber	6262	4½ in.	1948–1960	
Mr. Pickwick	6261	4½ in.	1948–1960	
Old Charley	6069	5½ in.	1939–1960	
Old Charley	6030	8¾ in.	1939–1960	
Sairey Gamp	6263	4½ in.	1948–1960	
Sam Weller	6265	4½ in.	1948–1960	
Sir Winston Churchill	6175	4 in.	1941–present	
Sir Winston Churchill	6172	5½ in.	1941–present	
Sir Winston Churchill	6172	9 in.	1941–present	
Squire	6319	6 in.	1950–1969	

MISCELLANEOUS ANIMALS

HN 100 Fox (red Coat)
HN 101 Hare (red Coat)
HN 102 Hare (white coat)
HN 107 Hare
HN 108 Hare
HN 117 Foxes
HN 126 Hare
HN 130 Hare
HN 138 Squirrel
HN 142 Hare
HN 147 Fox
HN 151 Hare
HN 179 Foxes
HN 193 Tortoise
HN 207 Mouse**
HN 209 Hares
HN 217 Hares
HN 218 Hares
HN 219 Hares
HN 226 Mouse**
HN 228 Mouse**
HN 237 Mouse with Babies**
HN 273 Hare
HN 276 Hare
HN 803 Hare
HN 859 Tortoise
HN 866 Fox

*miniature
**character
***char-mini

HN 905 Frog
HN 920 Foxes
HN 922 Hare**
HN 925 Foxes
HN 926 Foxes*
HN 963 Fox
HN 969 Hares
HN 978 Fox
HN 979 Hare
HN 984 Hare
HN 985 Hare
HN 994 Fox
HN1009 Hare and Babies
HN1071 Hare
HN1096 Fox with Goose**
HN1102 Fox with Goose**
HN1130 Fox
HN2502 Deer
HN2503 Deer
HN2504 Lamb
HN2505 Lamb
HN2527 Fox
HN2592 Hare**
HN2593 Hare**
HN2594 Hare, 1¾ in.**
HN2595 Lamb**
HN2596 Lamb**
HN2597 Lamb**
HN2598 Lamb**
HN2599 Lamb**
HN2642 Squirrel
HN6448 Huntsman Fox, 4½ in.

PARTIAL LIST OF ROUGE FLAMBÉ ANIMALS

Name	Number	Size
Ape	52	2½ in.
Cat	9	4¾ in.
Drake	137	6 in.
Duck	112	1½ in.
Duck	395	2½ in.
Elephant	489	6½ in.
Elephant	489A	5½ in.

Elephant	489B	
Fox	14	4 in.
Fox	29	
Fox	29A	
Fox	29B	1 in.
Fox	102	9¼ in.
Guinea Fowl	69	3 in.
Hare	119	
Hare	656	3¼ in.
Hare	656A	1¾ in.
Hare	1157	2¾ in.
Leaping Salmon	666	
Mallard	654	4 in.
Pekinese		
Penguin	84	6 in.
Penguin	239	
Penguin	585	8¾ in.
Penguin	1287	
Pigs	61	
Polar Bear		
Rabbit	113	1½ in.
Tiger	111	
Tiger	809	6 in.

BIBLIOGRAPHY

Catalogs by Doulton and Company, Inc.

Character and Toby Jugs by Royal Doulton (1950s)
Character and Toby Jugs by Royal Doulton (c. 1954)
Character and Toby Jugs by Royal Doulton (1973)
Royal Doulton Character and Toby Jugs (1978)
Royal Doulton Character and Toby Jugs (1979)
Royal Doulton Figurine Booklets, 1 through 16.

Pamphlets

Champions by Royal Doulton (c. 1945)
Character Jugs by Royal Doulton (c. 1945)
Character Jugs by Royal Doulton (c. 1950)
Figurines by Royal Doulton (c. 1950)
Giftware Price List (1979)
Giftware Price List (1979)
Haute Ensemble (1974)
Lady Musicians (1970)
Nursery Rhymes and Lines (c. 1948)
Period Figures in English History (c. 1948)

Royal Doulton (1971)
Royal Doulton Figures Supplement to Figurine Booklet No. 1 (c. 1950)

Some of the above catalog and pamphlet reprints can be obtained by writing to:
Antiqua 4, P.O. Box 371, La Mesa, Calif. 92041
Arthur H. Mills, P.O. Box 8742, Detroit, Mich. 48224
Frank Daniell, 50 Parkwood Blvd., Mansfield, Ohio 44906
J & S Antique Products, P.O. Box 4883, Chattanooga, Tenn. 37405

Books

Dennis, Richard, *Doulton Character Jugs,* London: Malvern Press, 1976.
Eyles, Desmond, and Dennis, Richard. *Royal Doulton Figures Produced at Burslem c.1890–1978.* Stoke-on Trent, Eng.: Royal Doulton Tableware Limited, 1978.
Eyles, Desmond. *The Doulton Lambeth Wares.* London: Hutchinson & Co., 1975.
———. *Royal Doulton Character and Toby Jugs.* Stoke-on-Trent, Eng.: Royal Doulton Tableware Limited, 1979.
———. *Royal Doulton 1815–1965: The Rise and Expansion of the Royal Doulton Potteries.* London: Hutchinson & Co., 1965.
———. *Royal Doulton Figures Produced at Burslem.* Royal Doulton Tableware, 1978.
Hadley's Antiques. *Royal Doulton Figurines Price Guide.* Magnolia Springs, Ala.: 1975.
Lynch, Rebecca, and Lynch, Robert. *A Price Guide to Royal Doulton Figurines.* East Hartford, Conn.: 1978.
———. *Supplement to First Edition of "A Price Guide to Royal Doulton Figurines."* East Hartford, Conn.: 1979.
McClinton, Katharine Morrison. *Royal Doulton Figurines and Character Jugs.* Des Moines: Wallace-Homestead, 1978.
Mills, Arthur H., *Royal Doulton Figurines Old and New.* Detroit: 1975.
Royal Doulton Figures. Royal Doulton Tableware, published annually.
Weiss, Princess, and Weiss, Barry. *A Price Guide to the Royal Doulton Discontinued Character Jugs.* New York: Lawton-York Corp., 1977.
Wempe, Wanda Bowman. *Character Jugs.* Champlin, Minn.: The Trinket Box, 1976.
———. *Royal Doulton Figurines.* Champlin, Minn.: The Trinket Box, 1976.
Yeager, Mary Lou. *The Price Guide to the Complete Royal Doulton Figurine Collection.* New York: Harmony Press, 1978.

Newsletter

Hillis, Jeffrey. *The Newsletter.* Crestline, Ohio: The Post House, 1975.